COLERIDGE

SELECTED POEMS

RICHARD HOLMES

PENGUIN BOOKS

PENGUIN BOOKS

Published by the Penguin Group
Penguin Books Ltd, 27 Wrights Lane, London W8 5TZ, England
Penguin Books USA Inc., 375 Hudson Street, New York, New York 10014, USA
Penguin Books Australia Ltd, Ringwood, Victoria, Australia
Penguin Books Canada Ltd, 10 Alcorn Avenue, Toronto, Ontario, Canada M4V 3B2
Penguin Books (NZ) Ltd, 182–190 Wairau Road, Auckland 10, New Zealand

Penguin Books Ltd, Registered Offices: Harmondsworth, Middlesex, England

First published by HarperCollins Publishers 1996
Published in Penguin Books 1996
1 3 5 7 9 10 8 6 4 2

The moral right of the editor has been asserted

Printed in England by Clays Ltd, St Ives plc

PENGUIN POETRY LIBRARY

SAMUEL TAYLOR COLERIDGE

Samuel Taylor Coleridge was born in 1772 at Ottery St Mary, Devon, the youngest son of a clergyman. A precocious reader and talker as a child, he was educated at Christ's Hospital School, London, where he began his friendship with Charles Lamb and wrote his early sonnets, and Jesus College, Cambridge. In 1794 he met Robert Southey and together they planned Pantisocracy, an ideal community to be founded in America, but the project collapsed after a quarrel. Coleridge's sonnets were published in the *Morning Chronicle*, and in 1795 he wrote 'The Eolian Harp' for Sara Fricker, whom he married in the same year, although the marriage was an unhappy one. He first met Dorothy and William Wordsworth in 1797 and a close association developed between them. Coleridge wrote his famous 'Kubla Khan' in the same year, followed in 1798 by 'Frost at Midnight'. In 1799 he and Wordsworth published the *Lyrical Ballads*, which marked a conscious break with eighteenth-century tradition and included one of Coleridge's greatest poems, 'The Rime of the Ancient Mariner'. During a visit to the Wordsworths in 1799 he met Sara Hutchinson, who became his lifelong love and the subject of his Asra poems. In the following year Coleridge and his family settled at Greta Hall, Keswick, where he completed the second part of 'Christabel', begun in 1798, but also became addicted to opium. In 1804 he separated from his wife and spent the following years in the Mediterranean or London, returning in 1808 to live with the Wordsworths in Grasmere. In 1809 he established *The Friend*, a political, literary and philosophical weekly journal, which he published regularly over the next year. After a disagreement with Wordsworth in 1810 Coleridge left the Lake District for ever, centring his life thereafter in London, where he gave his *Shakespeare Lectures*. He presented his literary and philosophical theories in the two-volume *Biographia Literaria*, published in 1817, and collected his poems in *Sibylline Leaves*. In an attempt to control his opium addiction, he entered the household and care of Dr James Gillman at Highgate in 1816. Here he was to remain for the last eighteen years of his life, writing a number of late confessional poems and prose works, including *Aids to Reflection*, published in 1825. Coleridge died in 1834, having overseen a final edition of his Poetical Works.

Poet, philosopher, ... one of the seminal figures of his ... ... ts did not seem to come with labour and effort; but as if borne on the gusts of genius, and as if the wings of his imagination lifted him from off his feet', and Wordsworth called him 'the only wonderful man I ever knew'.

Richard Holmes is the author of *Coleridge: Early Visions*, which won the 1989 Whitbread Book of the Year Prize. His other books include *Shelley: The Pursuit*, which won the 1974 Somerset Maugham Award; *Footsteps*, hailed by Michael Holroyd as 'a modern masterpiece'; and *Dr Johnson & Mr Savage*, which won the 1993 James Tait Black Memorial Prize. He has presented biographical works of Mary Wollstonecraft, William Godwin and Rudyard Kipling for Penguin Classics and a highly praised critical study of Coleridge for Oxford Past Masters. Richard Holmes is a Fellow of the Royal Society of Literature and in 1992 was made an OBE.

CONTENTS

LIST OF POEMS   vii
INTRODUCTION   xi
THE POET'S CHRONOLOGY   xxi
NOTE ON THE TEXT   xxxi
SELECT BIBLIOGRAPHY   xxxiii

I   Sonnets   1
II   Conversation Poems   29
III   Ballads   63
IV   Hill Walking Poems   133
V   Asra Poems   157
VI   Confessional Poems   193
VII   Visionary Fragments   223
VIII Political, Ideological and Topical   261
      Poems

NOTES   295
INDEX OF TITLES AND FIRST LINES   353

LIST OF POEMS

I · SONNETS

1. To the Autumnal Moon 7
2. Life 8
3. On Receiving an Account that his Only Sister's Death was Inevitable 9
4. On Quitting School for College 10
5. To the River Otter 11
6. To the Author of *The Robbers* 12
7. To the Rev. W. L. Bowles 13
8. Pantisocracy 14
9. Pity 15
10. On Receiving a Letter Informing me of the Birth of a Son 16
11. Composed on a Journey Homeward 17
12. To a Friend who Asked, How I Felt 18
13. On a Ruined House in a Romantic Country 19
14. To Asra 20
15. Lady, to Death we're Doomed . . . 21
16. Farewell to Love 22
17. Fancy in Nubibus 23
18. To Nature 24
19. Work Without Hope 25
20. Duty Surviving Self-Love 26
21. To the Young Artist 27

II · CONVERSATION POEMS

22. To a Friend (Charles Lamb) 35
23. The Eolian Harp 36
24. Reflections on Having Left a Place of Retirement 38
25. To the Rev. George Coleridge 40
26. This Lime-Tree Bower My Prison 43
27. Frost at Midnight 46

28.	Fears in Solitude	49
29.	The Nightingale	56
30.	To William Wordsworth	59

III · BALLADS

31.	The Three Graves	69
32.	The Rime of the Ancient Mariner	81
33.	Christabel	101
34.	The Ballad of the Dark Ladié	121
35.	Love	123
36.	Alice Du Clos	127

IV · HILL WALKING POEMS

37.	Lines Composed while Climbing the Left Ascent of Brockley Coomb, Somersetshire, May 1795	139
38.	To a Young Friend on his Proposing to Domesticate with the Author	140
39.	Lines Written in the Album at Elbingerode, in the Hartz Forest	143
40.	A Thought Suggested by a View of Saddleback in Cumberland	145
41.	Inscription for a Fountain on a Heath	146
42.	A Stranger Minstrel	147
43.	Hymn before Sun-Rise, in the Vale of Chamouni	149
44.	The Picture, or The Lover's Resolution	152

V · ASRA POEMS

45.	The Keepsake	163
46.	The Language of Birds	165
47.	A Day-Dream: My Eyes Make Pictures	166
48.	The Day-Dream: If Thou Wert Here	168
49.	A Letter to Sara Hutchinson	169
50.	Dejection: An Ode	179
51.	Separation	184
52.	Phantom	185
53.	O Sara! Never Rashly Let Me Go	186
54.	Ad Vilmum Axiologum	187
55.	You Mould My Hopes	188
56.	An Angel Visitant	189
57.	Recollections of Love	190
58.	Constancy to an Ideal Object	192

VI · CONFESSIONAL POEMS

59. An Ode to the Rain   199
60. The Pains of Sleep   202
61. To Two Sisters   204
62. A Tombless Epitaph   206
63. The Pang More Sharp Than All   208
64. Hope and Time   210
65. The Suicide's Argument   211
66. The Visionary Hope   212
67. Human Life   213
68. Limbo   214
69. Youth and Age   215
70. The Garden of Boccaccio   217
71. Phantom or Fact   220
72. Love's Apparition and Evanishment   221
73. Epitaph   222

VII · VISIONARY FRAGMENTS

74. Kubla Khan   229
75. The Wanderings of Cain   232
76. The Mad Monk   239
77. The Blossoming of the Solitary Date-Tree   241
78. A Sunset   244
79. A Dark Sky   245
80. The Tropic Tree   246
81. Psyche   247
82. The Sea Mew   248
83. The Yellow Hammer   249
84. On Donne's Poetry   250
85. The Knight's Tomb   251
86. Four Metrical Experiments   252
87. Song from *Remorse*   254
88. Song from *Zapolya*   255
89. Ars Poetica   256
90. Aria Spontanea   257
91. The World That Spidery Witch   258
92. The Netherlands   260

VIII · POLITICAL, IDEOLOGICAL AND TOPICAL POEMS

93. An Ode on the Destruction of the Bastille   265
94. To a Young Ass   267
95. The Present State of Society (Extract from "Religious Musings")   269
96. Invisible Powers (Extract from "The Destiny of Nations")   273
97. Fire, Famine, and Slaughter   277
98. France: An Ode   280
99. The Devil's Thoughts   284
100. A Character   287
101. The Delinquent Travellers   290

INTRODUCTION

COLERIDGE IS A GREAT and daring poet. His presence is felt echoing through the English language by anyone who has heard the magical names of "Kubla Khan" or "Christabel" or "The Ancient Mariner". But he is also an unknown poet, much of whose work has been neglected for many years, and whose range and skill has never been properly appreciated. "The Poet", he once said, "is the man made to solve the riddle of the Universe."

The aim of this new selection of one hundred and one poems is to transform Coleridge's reputation, and find him a new generation of readers. What did the older generation think of him? From T. S. Eliot to Ted Hughes, he has been considered as a man "briefly visited" by the Muse in a period of dazzling intensity, quickly obliterated by the darkness of drugs, metaphysics and obsessive theological speculation. He was thought of as the author of "a handful of golden poems" (the influential phrase comes from his hostile biographer E. K. Chambers) which were produced in a few inspired months between 1797 and 1798, when Coleridge was intimate with William and Dorothy Wordsworth.

It was held that much of his best poetry was fragmented or unfinished. The critic I. A. Richards even went so far as to say that Coleridge wrote "no completed poem to match his fragments". It was generally considered that his inspiration died at the age of thirty in 1802, after he had written "Dejection: An Ode". Coleridge, in other words, was a sort of poetic star-shell or firework, who lit up the sky for one brilliant bursting moment, and then dropped back to earth, burnt out and blackened into prose, conservatism and apologetic piety.

This selection sets out to prove otherwise. It offers a new way into the intellectual scope, the beauty and the fine workmanship of Coleridge's poetry over his whole lifetime. Darkness, disaster, drugs and metaphysics certainly feature a great deal in his work (see "Limbo", No. 68, dated 1811–15). The possibilities of visionary and religious experience are a recurrent, and often agonizing, concern (see "A Dark Sky", No. 79, dated 1807). The question of creative inspiration – its sources, its loss and its recovery – is a major preoccupation in a quite modern way (see "The Blossoming of the Solitary Date-Tree", No. 77, dated 1805). But these are part of a larger effort of artistic experiment, and psychological exploration, which Coleridge sustained over more than forty years.

He began writing poetry in 1789 at the age of sixteen, and continued to the year before his death. Though he did many other kinds of literary work – as a journalist, travel-writer, naturalist, dramatist, critic, public lecturer, philosopher and theologian – it is the poetry that gives us the continuing story of his imaginative life, at its deepest symbolic level. His letters (six volumes of them), and even his remarkable Notebooks, do not go further than the poetry (see "Human Life", No. 67, dated 1814–15).

*   *   *

The Chronology will show that Coleridge lived in many places during his working life – the West Country, Germany, the Lake District, the southern Mediterranean, Leicestershire, Wiltshire, London and Highgate – and these wanderings in search of a spiritual home are also reflected continuously in his poems. Coleridge is a master of imaginary or dream topography, but these vistas are often inspired by his physical journeys, especially in the unsettled years between 1794 and 1816. During all these years he was very rarely at one address for more than eighteen months at a time. The exterior landscapes of his travels are gradually converted into the interior heartlands of his poetry (see "Constancy to an Ideal Object", No. 58, dated 1825).

Coleridge's restlessness, which he eventually defined as his own "Inquiring Spirit", was a measure of the times in which he lived. From the fall of the Bastille in 1789, through the twenty-year upheaval of the Napoleonic Wars, to the industrial agitation leading up to the Great Reform Bill of 1832, Coleridge lived through what Tom Paine called "the times that try men's souls", and what modern cultural historians call the Romantic revolution.

Fundamental questions were being asked about the scope of individual liberty, the meaning of political democracy, and the impact of science on religious beliefs. The complexities of human psychology (a favourite Coleridge word), the discoveries of the early explorers and anthropologists, and the symbolic patterning of folklore, dreams and mythology, were suggesting new depths to the human spirit and the Kantian notion of our "subjective" perceptions of time and space. All these touched on the poetry that Coleridge wrote, from the early years when his verse is still a scrapbook of his student reading and speculations (see "Invisible Powers", No. 96, dating from 1795). It is impossible to appreciate a great sequence like the Conversation Poems (see Nos. 22–30, which date between 1794 and 1807) without seeing the breadth of this intellectual engagement with the world around him.

Coleridge believed that the poet, "described in ideal perfection, brings the whole soul of man into activity" (see chapter 14 of his *Biographia Literaria*, dated 1817). He also thought that the poet should be a "metaphysician": one who uses language to explore the nature of existence, the experience of being alive and conscious in a mysterious universe:

> A great Poet must be, implicitè if not explicitè, a profound Metaphysician. He may not have it in logical coherence, in his Brain & Tongue; but he must have it by *Tact*: for all sounds, & forms of human nature he must have the *ear* of a wild Arab listening in the silent Desert, the *eye* of a North American Indian tracing the footsteps of an Enemy upon the Leaves that strew the Forest; the *touch* of a Blind Man feeling the face of a darling Child.
>
> (*Letters*, 13 July 1802)

From these beliefs, which transcend a merely "magical" approach to poetry, arose the fundamentally autobiographical and philosophical drive of his imagination. Even his highly stylized ballads are powered by this sense of daring enquiry into spiritual and psychological truths which everyone can recognize in themselves (see "The Three Graves", No. 31, with its preface, dated 1809).

Coleridge used poetry to ask the most profound questions he could conceive:

> The Poet is not only the man who is made to solve the riddle of the Universe, but he is also the man who feels where it is not solved and which continually awakens his feelings . . . What is old and worn out, not in itself, but from the dimness of the intellectual eye brought on by worldly passions, he makes new: he pours upon it the dew that glistens, and blows round us the breeze which cooled us in childhood.
>
> (*Lecture on Poetry*, 12 December 1811)

What is our place in the natural universe? What are the sources of human love and hope? What are the origins of evil, guilt, cruelty and depression? Can we learn anything from the extremes of suffering and disaster? Can we depend, in any sense at all, upon a visionary or religious view of the world? And what is the meaning, if any, of the creative faculty: the gift which produces the consolations of poetry and art itself, in a troubled existence of change, grief, and decay? These are the great, recurrent themes of Coleridge's one hundred and one poems in this selection.

*   *   *

In order to reveal them fully, a basic shift in the way of approaching Coleridge's work is put forward. This selection abandons the principle of simple chronological ordering, which has been traditionally used since the *Poetical Works* of 1834. Instead, for the first time, it reorganizes Coleridge's poetry within eight thematic sections. Each section is provided with a short explanatory preface, and every poem has a full critical note at the back of the book. The order of composition is retained within the sections, as far as it is known.

The editor's prefaces and notes can of course be ignored; or they can be read through consecutively as a single, continuous essay on Coleridge's poetic development. What counts is the new and startling coherence that emerges in the sequence of poems, giving an entirely fresh and enlarged sense of Coleridge's creative powers. The transforming effect of this will be immediately clear from the new layout of the Contents page.

Coleridge himself once argued against thematic selection. "After all you can say, I still think the chronological order the best for arranging a poet's work. All your divisions are in particular instances inadequate, and they destroy the interest which arises from watching the progress, maturity, and even the decay of genius." (*Table Talk*, 1823.) This is a strong argument; and characteristic of Coleridge's interest in the psychology of the creative process.

Yet in practice, Coleridge also used thematic divisions in his own collections, and they are peculiarly appropriate to his otherwise bewildering versatility. His edition of *Sibylline Leaves* in 1817 contained five separate sections: (1) Political Events, (2) Love Poems, (3) Meditative Poems, (4) Odes, (5) Epigrams, Moralities, and Things without a Name, together with an early grouping of the Ballads.

The present selection is an extension of these generic categories into eight sections. Broadly speaking, the early Meditative Poems become the full Conversation sequence; the Ballads are extended to everything Coleridge wrote in this narrative form; the Love Poems become the mysterious Asra sequence; the Odes expand into the revealing Confessional group; and the Political Events become an ideological survey of Coleridge's ideas, with an unexpected emphasis on comedy. The grouping of Sonnets, Hill Walking Poems, and Visionary Fragments are essentially new.

All are based on the same principle of thematically developed sequences, retaining the chronological order of composition within each section. So the natural parabola of "progress, maturity and even decay" (which Coleridge regarded as so important) is never lost. Moreover, as explained in the Prefaces, each section reflects a new phase in his biography as a poet, over forty years.

This should help the general reader explore Coleridge's wonderful energy and range of output; as well as the student who is assigned some particular aspect of his craftsmanship, such as the intimate, blank-verse conversation line; or the magical imagery of the ballads; or shifts in ideological rhetoric in the public poems. It is hoped that certain sections – the emotional intensity of the Asra Poems, the physical immediacy of the Hill Walking Poems – will be something of a revelation even to Coleridge scholars.

Most important of all, the thematic principle of selection should produce virtually a new Coleridge for the contemporary reader. In the first place, his whole work is given a strong and immediate autobiographical quality, with the beautiful group of Conversation Poems lying at its centre. Next, the weight of Coleridge's output is moved away from the juvenilia, and thrown towards the moving, but far less familiar, work of the middle years such as the Asra Poems and Confessional Poems. Finally, Coleridge's sustained and conscious interest in the experimental and psychological aspects of his craft, is revealed in the Ballads and Visionary Fragments as the work of many years.

Altogether this shift of emphasis radically alters the idea of Coleridge's creative "peak" lying isolated in a few, inspired, golden months in his mid-twenties in the Quantock hills. Coleridge may have written, or at least begun, many of his best-known pieces at this time; though several of them were worked on for long periods afterwards. "The Rime of the Ancient Mariner" did not reach its final form until 1817; "Christabel" took nearly three years to reach Part II in autumn 1800; "The Eolian Harp" and several of the other

Conversation Poems received significant additions over more than a decade; and even "Kubla Khan" was probably being altered as late as 1816.

Coleridge's Notebooks really suggest that he had several, recurrent bursts of intense poetic activity during his lifetime: in 1797–8 in the Quantocks; in 1801–2 in the Lake District; in 1804–5 in the Mediterranean; in 1807–11 in London; when he first moved to Highgate in 1816–17, and again after 1825. The shape of his creative career is less of a single peak, and more of a jagged mountain range (though with many chasms and landslides, to be sure).

More than fifty of the poems in this selection date from 1802 onwards (the year in which his inspiration was supposed to have been extinguished forever). So more than half were begun between the ages of 30 and 60, and this significantly alters our profile of Coleridge's poetic development and maturity. If the later poems tend to be shorter, they are also denser in texture and allusion. Yet there are still long, sustained poems after 1820, such as "Alice Du Clos" (No. 36), "The Garden of Boccaccio" (No. 70) and "The Delinquent Travellers" (No. 101). This last is representative of a mass of comic and occasional verse which is still being disinterred from Coleridge's later letters, notebooks and inscriptions. From 1827 a number of editors of rival anthologies – the annual *Bijou*, *Amulet*, and *Literary Souvenir* – were pressing him for new and unpublished work, and the demand produced an Indian summer of inspiration.

When urged by an old friend, Lady Beaumont, in 1828 to rekindle his "spirit of imagination", Coleridge characteristically denied that he could "resume Poetry" at so late a date. But in the very act of denying it, he gave one of his most moving and suggestive descriptions of that inspiration at work:

> Is the power extinct? No! No! As in a still Summer Noon, when the lulled Air at irregular intervals wakes up with a startled *Hush-st*, that seems to re-demand the silence which it breaks, or heaves a long profound Sigh in its Sleep, and an Aeolian Harp has been left in the chink of the not quite shut Casement – even so – how often! – scarce a week of my Life shuffles by, that does not at some moment feel the spur of the old genial impulse – even so do there fall on my inward Ear swells, and broken snatches of sweet Melody, reminding me that I still have that within me which is both Harp and Breeze.
>
> (*Letters*, 17 March 1828)

So if the youthful, inspired Coleridge is still very much present and never quite lost; the darker, more subtle and meditative Coleridge of the mature years makes a formidable and disturbing appearance, in a way that I hope will be challenging to many readers. The familiar author of "Kubla Khan" (No. 74) is also the strange author of "Limbo" (No. 68), and "Phantom or Fact" (No. 71) and "The World That Spidery Witch" (No. 91).

The thematic sections are also intended to place Coleridge's familiar major poems in a larger and more revealing critical context, which may again help the student to read them freshly. The Sonnets, with their rapid stylistic development, influenced later Victorian writers such as Christina Rossetti to find an intimate domestic and religious voice. The Ballads form a consistent, brilliantly crafted experiment into various aspects of folklore and fairytale, which created a revolution in Romantic archetypes of disaster and possession, pushed to extremes of psychic violence and disruption. Coleridge's interest in symbolic, transcendental and non-rational experiences, often with strong sexual and occult undertones from the Gothic tradition, opened up a powerful line of narrative poetry through Keats and Robert Browning. By contrast, the tender, low-key meditative style of the Conversation Poems, with their quiet English radiance of sacred pastoral, established a characteristic voice that continued through Tennyson, Hardy and Edward Thomas.

The Hill Walking Poems show how Coleridge's poetry grew almost physically out of his striding, observant movement through wild landscapes and uplands. The remarkable love poems dedicated to Sara Hutchinson (Wordsworth's sister-in-law, and Coleridge's muse-figure for more than a decade after 1799) are brought together in the new sequence of the Asra Poems. Their mixture of obsessive sensual imagery, and intense philosophic speculation, provides a revealing new context for that great, pivotal Romantic poem – about depression and imagination – "Dejection: An Ode" (No. 50). Similarly, the baffling genius of "Kubla Khan" (No. 74) takes on an even greater resonance when it is read as just one of a whole sequence of Visionary Fragments which Coleridge worked on and discarded over many years, including the haunting, isolated images of "A Sunset" (No. 78), "The Tropic Tree" (No. 80), and "Psyche" (No. 81).

*　　*　　*

A great deal of Coleridge's poetry is experimental, in the sense that it pushes the limits of conventional eighteenth-century forms. The Odes of Thomas Gray and William Collins (which he read at Cambridge), the blank verse meditations of William Cowper, the introspective sonnets of William Bowles, the descriptive landscapes of James Thomson, the lurid Border Ballads collected by Bishop Percy, all these are absorbed and then transformed into something new and distinctive. Coleridge's correspondence with Charles Lamb in 1794–6, his discussions with Wordsworth in 1797–8 (later continued as formal criticism in the *Biographia Literaria*) and his brilliant series of six long literary letters to the translator William Sotheby in the summer of 1802, record this process of creating a new Romantic theory of poetry and the imagination.

The key propositions of this new Poetics are threefold: passionate expression, intensity of subjective conception, and organic unity of thought and feeling. Writing to Sotheby in 1802, he remarked how even an emotional eighteenth-century poet like Bowles (only ten years his senior) seemed to lack the intensity and intellectual risk he was looking for:

> Bowles has indeed the *sensibility* of a poet; but he has not the *passion* of a great Poet. His latter writings all want *native* Passion – Milton here and there supplies him with an appearance of it – but he has no native Passion, because he is not a Thinker – and has probably weakened his Intellect by the haunting Fear of becoming extravagant.
>
> (*Letters*, 10 September 1802)

For Coleridge, extravagance or intellectual daring was essential to poetry. To solve the riddle of the Universe, it was necessary to take risks. All his images of the poet–metaphysician as wild Arab, or American Indian, or Blind man (which can also be found throughout the poetry) are symbols of praeternatural sensitivity and daring. The poet is a metaphysical hunter, a mariner on the high seas of existence, an enquiring spirit in the remotest hills (see the preface to the Hill Walking Poems).

As so often in Coleridge, this most serious and subtle conception of the poet's task can also be found in a memorable and self-mocking joke. Quite late in life he recalled the difference between himself and Robert Southey as writers:

Southey once said to me; You are nosing every Nettle along the Hedge, while the Greyhound (meaning himself, I presume) wants only to get sight of the Hare, and flash – straight as a line! he has it in his mouth! Even so, I replied, might a Cannibal say to an Anatomist, who has watched him dissecting a body. But the fact is – I do not care two pence for the Hare; but I value most highly the excellencies of scent, patience, discrimination, free Activity; and find a Hare in every Nettle I make myself acquainted with.

(British Library, Egerton MS. 2801 f.126)

Yet for all its originality, Coleridge's poetry also reflects a distinct and beautiful literary tradition. It is deeply English, bucolic, and tenderly observant, with a strong idealizing, religious or neo-Platonic strain. His characteristic imagery is drawn from sun, moon, and stars; rivers, lakes and seas; woods, wild animals, and birds; gardens, villages, and harbours. One can never forget that his father (who died when Coleridge was only nine) was a country parson. It is recognizably the same world as that of Constable, Turner, and Samuel Palmer. Even its more exotic elements are drawn from sources deep within the popular late eighteenth-century culture: Gothic romance, folk ballads, travellers tales, scientific lectures, church hymns, and of course the Bible.

What Coleridge did as a poet was to make this familiar world seem suddenly strange and perilous; and, as we can now see, distinctively modern. The metaphysical daring of his poetry called everything into question. Beneath the material surface always lay a spiritual mystery, waiting to be recognized. In middle age, during the worst period of his opium addiction (as revealed by the Confessional Poems), when he was thought to be long-finished as a poet, Coleridge wrote this in his Notebook:

I would compare the human Soul to a Ship's Crew cast on an unknown Island (a fair Simile: for these questions could not suggest themselves unless the mind had previously felt convictions, that the present World was not its whole destiny and abiding Country). What would be their first business? Surely, to enquire what the Island was? in what Latitude? what ships visited that Island? when & whither they went? ... The moment, when the Soul begins to be sufficiently self-conscious, to ask concerning itself, & its relations, is the first moment of its *intellectual* arrival in the World. Its *Being* – enigmatic as it must seem – is posterior to its

Existence. Suppose the shipwrecked man stunned, & for many
weeks in a state of Idiotcy or utter loss of Thought & Memory.
And then gradually awakened . . .

(*Notebooks*, 1809)

For Coleridge, poetry was this continual awakening into the mystery
of the world that surrounds us all.

THE POET'S CHRONOLOGY

(The numbers in brackets refer to poems in this collection.)

1772   Born 21 October, the youngest and favourite child of the
        Reverend John Coleridge, vicar and headmaster at Ottery
        St Mary, a small market town on the river Otter in Devon.
        His eight elder brothers subsequently became soldiers,
        doctors or clergymen; he himself was destined for the church.

1778   Coleridge remembers long talks with his father about the
        moon and stars. Already a precocious reader, dreamer and
        talker.

1780   Intense rivalry with his elder brother Frank, and arguments
        with his mother. Runs away one night after a quarrel to the
        river Otter. Period of childhood fevers and nightmares.

1781   Sudden death of his father, after Frank had been sent away
        to India as a soldier.

1782   Sent away by widowed mother as "charity boy" to Christ's
        Hospital School, London. Rarely returns home, except for
        summer visits, over next decade. Refers to himself as
        "orphan".

1789   Early sonnets (Nos. 1–2), and poems in the Christ's Hospital
        "Book of Gold". "An Ode on the Destruction of the Bastille"
        (No. 93). Friendship with Charles Lamb. Reads poetry of
        William Bowles (No. 7).

1791   Exhibitioner to Jesus College, Cambridge. Death of his
        beloved sister Anne, commemorated in Sonnets (Nos. 3–4.)

1792   Wins Browne Poetry Medal, with "Ode on the Slave Trade"
        in Greek. Works hard, reads widely.

1793   Fails to win Browne Poetry Medal, with "Ode on
        Astronomy" in Greek. Political activity, drinking, debts,
        unrequited love. First published poem in the *Morning
        Chronicle*. *December*:-runs away to London, enlists in 15th
        Light Dragoons.

1794   Coleridge nurses a fellow dragoon with smallpox quarantined
        in Henley Pest House. *April*: discharged from Dragoons as
        "insane", returns to Cambridge. *June*: meets Southey at

Oxford, plans Pantisocracy, writes topical sonnets (Nos. 6–9), begins "Religious Musings" (No. 95). "To a Young Ass" (No. 94). *December*: twelve sonnets published in the *Morning Chronicle*. Abandons Cambridge degree.

1795   Settles in Bristol with Southey, gives Political Lectures, begins "The Destiny of Nations" (No. 96). First Conversation Poems written "To a Friend (Charles Lamb)" (No. 22) and "The Eolian Harp" (No. 23) to Sara Fricker, whom Coleridge marries on 4 October. Quarrels with Southey, abandons Pantisocracy.

1796   Publishes ten issues of his radical Christian newspaper the *Watchman* in Bristol (see No. 24). *April*: first book published *Poems on Various Subjects*. *September*: first child, Hartley, born (see Nos. 10–12). "To the River Otter" (No. 5) completed. Evidence of opium-taking from letters.

1797   January: Settles in cottage at Nether Stowey, at foot of Quantock hills, North Somerset, near Tom Poole (see No. 25). Completes play *Osorio*, and publishes enlarged second edition of *Poems*. *June*: brings William and Dorothy Wordsworth to Alfoxden, and writes "This Lime-Tree Bower My Prison" (No. 26). *October*: "Kubla Khan" (No. 74). *November*: begins "The Rime of the Ancient Mariner" (No. 32).

1798   *February*: "Frost at Midnight" (No. 27). Begins "Christabel Part I" (No. 33). £150 annuity from Wedgwood brothers. *April*: "Fears in Solitude" (No. 28), and "France: An Ode" (No. 98). Collaborates with Wordsworth on *Lyrical Ballads*. *September*: to Germany for a nine-month period of academic study.

1799   *February*: enrols at University of Gottingen. Learns of death of second child, Berkeley. Climbs the Brocken in the Hartz mountains (see No. 39). *July*: returns to England. "The Devil's Thoughts" (No. 99). *November*: first visit to the Lake District, meets "Asra" (see No. 45), and writes ballad "Love" (No. 35).

1800   In London, writing political journalism for the *Morning Post* and translating Schiller's *Wallenstein*. *July*: settles at Greta Hall, Keswick in Lake District near the Wordsworths at Grasmere. *October*: completes "Christabel Part II" (No. 33) which Wordsworth rejects for second edition of the *Lyrical Ballads*. Long and often solitary hill walking expeditions (see Nos. 40–42).

1801	Bedridden until the spring, studies Kant and Schelling. Now begins heavy opium-taking which will become serious drug-addiction over next fifteen years (see No. 60). *July*: visits Asra at Durham and Scarborough, and writes "Day-Dream" poems (Nos. 47–8). *November*: marital discord, goes to London to write political journalism again.
1802	Returns to Greta Hall. *April*: "A Letter to Sara Hutchinson" (No. 49) written and then edited as "Dejection: An Ode" (No. 50). Letters to William Sotheby on the metaphysical nature of poetry and inspiration. *August*: solo fell-climbing expedition over Buttermere and Scafell. "Hymn before Sun-Rise" (No. 43). Spends winter with Wedgwoods in Wales.
1803	Writes will, takes out life insurance, dreams of Mediterranean escape, returns to Greta Hall. *June*: third edition of *Poems*. More political journalism. *August*: Highland walking tour, partly to break opium addiction. "Pains of Sleep" (No. 60). Southey moves into Greta Hall. Christmas at Grasmere.
1804	*April*: sails to Mediterranean in wartime convoy. Visits Sicily, settles in Malta as Private Secretary to the Governor, Sir Alexander Ball. Beautiful Notebook entries on his travels, recollections of Asra, and fragmentary poems including "Phantom" (No. 52) and "A Sunset" (No. 78).
1805	*January*: appointed Acting Public Secretary at Valletta. Spends summer at Governor's Palace at San Antonio, where he writes "The Blossoming of the Solitary Date-Tree" (No. 77) and probably begins "Constancy to an Ideal Object" (No. 58). Opium addiction increases. *September*: leaves for Sicily, Naples and Rome.
1806	Visits galleries in Rome and Florence. Mixes with German expatriate intellectuals (including Tieck and Von Humboldt), and befriends American painter Washington Allston. *June*: flees French invasion and sails for England from Livorno, nearly dying on voyage. Determines to separate from his wife, and start new career in London, lecturing on Art and Literature. In fact settles with the Wordsworths and Asra at Coleorton, Leicestershire.
1807	*January*: listens to Wordsworth's *Prelude* (dedicated to Coleridge) and writes "To William Wordsworth" (No. 30), "The Tropic Tree" (No. 80), and Asra fragments (Nos. 53–6). *June*: stays with Poole at Stowey in further attempt to break opium addiction, and meets De Quincey.

"Recollections of Love" (No. 57). *November*: moves back to London to plan lectures. "To Two Sisters" (No. 61) dedicated to Mary Morgan and Charlotte Brent.

1808   *January*: begins first Lecture Series, "Poetry and the Principles of Taste", at the Royal Institution, with central concept of the dynamic Imagination. *July*: reviews Clarkson's *History of the Abolition of the Slave Trade* for the *Edinburgh Review*. Plans to publish a newspaper, *The Friend*, in London. *September*: moves to Allan Bank, near Grasmere, with Wordsworths and Asra. November: issues prospectus for *The Friend* to be published from Penrith.

1809   *June*: after many delays begins *The Friend*, a journal of political, philosophical and literary essays, with Asra as his amanuensis. It runs regularly for twenty-eight weekly issues, publishing "The Three Graves" (No. 31) and "A Tombless Epitaph" (No. 62).

1810   *March*: Asra leaves abruptly for Wales; last issue of *The Friend*. *May*: Coleridge leaves Allan Bank and returns to his wife at Greta Hall, Keswick. *October*: moves back to London to lecture and seek opium cure. The chance remark of a mutual friend, Basil Montagu, brings into the open Coleridge's quarrel with Wordsworth (see Nos. 54 and 80). Long confessional entries in the Notebooks.

1811   *January*: settles with the Morgans and Charlotte Brent in Hammersmith. Heavy drinking and opium-taking; journalism for the *Courier*. Friendship with Henry Crabb Robinson of *The Times*. The start of several Confessional Poems, "The Pang More Sharp Than All" (No. 63), "Hope and Time" (No. 64), "The Suicide's Argument" (No. 65) belongs to this period. *November*: second Lecture Series, "On Shakespeare, Milton and Modern Poetry", at the Philosophical Society (which Byron and Rogers attend).

1812   Moves with Morgans to Berners Street, Soho. *May*: third Lecture Series, "On Shakespeare and the Drama" at Willis's Rooms in fashionable Mayfair. Begins to rewrite his play *Osorio* (1797) as *Remorse* (see No. 87). "Psyche" (No. 81) and "The Visionary Hope" (No. 66) at about this period. *November*: fourth Lectures Series, at the Surrey Institution.

1813   *January*: *Remorse* runs successfully at Drury Lane for twenty nights, text is published in three editions, earns £400. Dines out, meets Madame De Staël, plunges deeper into opium. *August*: John Morgan bankrupt and flees to Ireland. *October*:

Coleridge moves to Bristol and Bath, gives fifth and sixth Lectures Series, and supports Mary and Charlotte Brent in lodgings at Ashley, near Bath. *December*: opium crisis at the Greyhound Inn, Bath, brings Coleridge close to death.

1814   Taken in by his old Unitarian friend Josiah Wade, at Bristol, and treated for six months for addiction and suicidal depression. *June*: during slow recovery meets Washington Allston again, who paints his sombre portrait (National Gallery); friendship with Dr Joseph Brabant; many confessional letters, poems and fragments, including "Human Life" (No. 67). Essays on Kantian aesthetics ("On the Principles of Genial Criticism") for *Felix Farley's Bristol Journal*. *December*: settles with re-united Morgan family at Calne in Wiltshire. Plans collected edition of his poems and essays.

1815   Preface to his poems expands into an Autobiography. *May*: correspondence with Wordsworth about "The Excursion". Autobiography now expands again into two-volume *Biographia Literaria*, largely complete by September. The marginal glosses to "The Rime of the Ancient Mariner" (No. 32) written at about this period, as the *Sibylline Leaves* (collected poems) is prepared. Correspondence with Byron about publication of his works; writes celebrated Preface to "Kubla Khan" (No. 74). *December*: *Zapolya*, a Christmas play with songs (see No. 88).

1816   Grant from Literary Fund, and £100 gift from Byron. *March*: moves back to London with the Morgans to publish his works. *April*: further opium crisis, settles with the young surgeon James Gillman and his wife Ann at Highgate, London (see "Limbo" No. 68 and "The Garden of Boccaccio" No. 70). *May*: *Christabel, Kubla Khan and the Pains of Sleep*, published by Murray through Byron's influence. *December*: *The Statesman's Manual*, a political sermon, with important Appendix on symbolical language. Hazlitt's bitter attacks begin in the liberal press (see No. 100).

1817   Coleridge finds new London publisher, Rest Fenner, who brings out the accumulated body of his work. *March*: *Second Lay Sermon*; *July*: *Biographia Literaria* (with accounts of his early poetry and collaboration with Wordsworth in Chapters 4, 10, and 14); *August*: *Sibylline Leaves* (with early groupings of the Ballads, Conversation and Confessional Poems); *November*: *Zapolya*. Meets J. H. Green (future president of the

Royal College of Surgeons) who will replace Morgan as his amanuensis. "The Poet in the Clouds" (No. 17).

1818   *January*: new series of Lectures "On European Literature" at the Philosophical Society; meets his first Highgate "disciple" Thomas Allsop. Introduced to William Blake's poetry by the Swedenborgian C. A. Tulk, MP. *April*: two pamphlets in support of Peel's Child Labour Bill (limiting child labour hours in factories). *November*: three-volume edition of *The Friend* (with essays on language and the nature of logic, vision and inspiration). *December*: second Lecture Series "On the History of Philosophy". T. L. Peacock caricatures Coleridge as Mr Flosky, the incomprehensible metaphysician, in *Nightmare Abbey* (alongside Shelley and Byron).

1819   *March*: publisher Fenner goes bankrupt and reneges on all Coleridge's royalties, amounting to about £1,000, leaving him penniless. Financial support comes from Gillman, Green and Allsop. *April*: meets John Keats in Millfield Lane, Highgate, and talks of nightingales. Contributes to *Blackwood's Magazine*. Hartley appointed Fellow at Oriel College, Oxford.

1820   *March*: renewed plans for his *Opus Maximum* with J. H. Green, to be the philosophical "harvesting of my Life's labour". Begins a series of confessional and autobiographical letters to Allsop, who starts recording Coleridge's table talk. *May*: Hartley dismissed from Oriel Fellowship for eccentricity and drunkenness; Coleridge tries unsuccessfully to retrieve the situation with passionate letters and interviews defending his son (really himself). "To Nature" (No. 18).

1821   Dictating first part of *Opus Maximum* to Green, which will become a separate treatise on Logic. Letters to Allsop discussing philosophical view of love and marriage. *September*: articles on "Witchcraft", "Faery Land" etc. for *Blackwoods Magazine*. Hartley in London, looking for literary work with Coleridge's help, but continually "vanishing" on drinking bouts.

1822   *February*: advertises (in the *Courier*) weekly philosophy classes at Highgate, as extensions of his talks with Allsop: two hours' dictation from the *Opus Maximum*, followed by an hour's discussion, for young men in their twenties (ideally post-graduates training for the Law, Medicine, or Church). These continue over next five years. The MS. of the *Logic* completed (but not published till 1990). *October*: celebrates fiftieth birthday sea-bathing at Ramsgate. Hartley returns to the Lakes, supposedly to teach.

1823   *January*: Coleridge's daughter Sara and nephew H. N. Coleridge meet at Highgate and fall secretly in love. H. N. Coleridge begins recording Coleridge's *Table Talk*. *April*: "Parnassus" dinner-party hosted by Monkhouse, at which "half the Poetry of England constellated": Coleridge, Wordsworth, Tom Moore, Samuel Rogers, Charles Lamb. *July*: working on a Life of Archbishop Leighton (the seventeenth-century Scottish divine) whose moral "aphorisms" Coleridge has used in philosophy classes and which will become *Aids to Reflection*. *September*: "Youth and Age" (No. 69). *December*: moves with Gillmans to 3 The Grove, Highgate, with new study and attic bedroom overlooking Hampstead Heath.

1824   *March*: elected Fellow of the Royal Society of Literature, with an annuity of 100 guineas. *April*: brief estrangement from the Gillmans over his secret opium supplies from the Highgate chemist, T. H. Dunn. As part of reconciliation, "Thursday evenings" are established at Highgate when Coleridge's visitors and disciples can call without invitation for several hours of Coleridge's poetry recitations and "*One*versation". *June*: Thomas Carlyle's visit upon which he later based his satiric portrait of Coleridge as the mystic "Sage of Highgate".

1825   Hazlitt's critical assessment of "Mr Coleridge" and his wasted genius appears in *The Spirit of the Age*, deeply wounding Coleridge. *February*: writes his great sonnet "Work Without Hope" (No. 19) as part of a long poem to Ann Gillman, "The World That Spidery Witch" (No. 91). *May*: delivers lecture "On the Prometheus of Aeschylus" to Royal Society of Literature. Publication of *Aids to Reflection in the Formation of A Manly Character*, with Coleridge's meditations on the process of spiritual self-discovery, and an important concluding chapter on the nature of "mystical" or "poetical" experience, and the validity of "inspired" language in a scientific world.

1826   Still reacting to Hazlitt's attacks, writes "Duty Surviving Self-Love" (No. 20) and the comic apologia "A Character" (No. 100). Long letters to his nephew Edward Coleridge (a master at Eton), on the concepts of Evolution and Individuation, the "Ascent of Powers", and the metaphysics of "Hope". (These ideas were clearly intended as part of the unfinished *Opus Maximum*, to which the *Aids* was now seen as another prelude, like the *Logic*.) Probably visited William Blake at Fountain Court this or previous winter.

1827   *Spring*: during a period of illness and depression writes "The Garden of Boccaccio" (No. 70) to Ann Gillman. Growing interest in his unpublished poetry is encouraged by his nephew H. N. Coleridge, who continues with *Table Talk* at Highgate. (Coleridge has agreed to the marriage of Sara and H. N. C., who will become the most important Victorian editors of both his poetry and prose.) Begins his last ballad "Alice Du Clos" (No. 36) at this time.

1828   *March*: secretly writes that his poetic power is "not extinct". *June*: embarks on six-week tour, with Wordsworth and his daughter Dora, down the Rhine through Germany and Holland. Coleridge's Notebook sketches include "The Netherlands" (No. 92), and the comic "The Delinquent Travellers" (No. 101). *July*: *Poetical Works* published by Thomas Pickering in three volumes. Green is appointed Professor of Anatomy, and made Coleridge's chief literary executor. Editors of annual anthologies (*Friendship's Garland*, the *Amulet*, the *Literary Souvenir*) compete for Coleridge's poems.

1829   Progressive heart-failure begins to weaken Coleridge. *May*: second edition of *Poetical Works*. The famous Paris bookseller Galignani brings out a popular, but unauthorized, collection, *Poetical Works of Coleridge, Keats and Shelley*, which identifies Coleridge with the younger Romantic generation. *July*: Coleridge passes on a bequest of £50 to Hartley, who is adrift in the Lake District, writing sonnets. *December*: *On the Constitution of Church and State*, containing the concept of an independent "clerisy" or intelligentsia (including poets) who will shape and unify the national "culture" outside established political or religious institutions.

1830   Coleridge's health continues to decline, and he writes few letters, but H. N. C.'s *Table Talk* is recorded almost daily. Second editions of *Church and State* and *Aids to Reflection*. Coleridge has bequeathed the unfinished MS. of *Opus Maximum* to J. H. Green (which will eventually be published as volume 15 of the *Collected Coleridge*). "Phantom or Fact" (No. 71). Visits from the young philosopher John Stuart Mill, and John Sterling from Cambridge, continue to expand

Coleridge's influence among youthful intellectuals. Death of Hazlitt, and last meeting with Wordsworth.

1831   Coleridge shows lively interest in Parliamentary Reform, though now an invalid confined to his rooms at Highgate. Significant American editions of *The Friend* and *Aids to Reflection* appear (edited by Professor Marsh of Vermont University), and Coleridge's poetry and prose is widely read by the New England Transcendentalists, Ralph Waldo Emerson and Edgar Allan Poe. Coleridge writes a short appreciation of Shelley's beliefs and genius.

1832   Coleridge's health temporarily improves as opium doses are increased. Talks for five hours at granddaughter's christening, and begins work on third revised edition of *Poetical Works* with H. N. C.

1833   Hartley's first *Poems* appear, dedicated to his father in a touching sonnet which refers to "Frost at Midnight" (No. 27). Coleridge makes a final visit to Cambridge for the British Association conference. Continues work on revised edition with H. N. C.; writes "To the Young Artist" (No. 21), "Love's Apparition and Evanishment" (No. 72) and "Epitaph" (No. 73), his last poems.

1834   *March*: publication of revised third edition of *Poetical Works*, the standard text (Coleridge refers to "my poetical publisher, Mr Pickle-Herring"). *May*: last visit to Highgate by Asra. The Gillmans, H. N. Coleridge and J. H. Green are in constant attendance at Coleridge's bedside. *5 July*: Coleridge makes last painful journey to his bedroom window to gaze over "the glorious landscape" of Hampstead Heath. Gillman begins opium injections. *24 July*: Coleridge writes a note requesting a legacy for his faithful maidservant, and tells Green that he knows he is dying but his mind is still clear: "I could even be witty". *25 July*: Coleridge slips into a coma and dies just after sunrise. Buried at Highgate Churchyard. H. N. C. writes a major re-assessment of Coleridge's poetry which is published in the *Quarterly Review*.

NOTE ON THE TEXT

I BEGAN COMPILING this selection of Coleridge's poetry over ten years ago, as I was working on his biography. It was purely for my own use, and took early shape as a treasured collection of notes and photocopies in a scarlet binder, which went with me to the Quantocks and the Hartz mountains, to Etna and to Highgate. As it grew more battered, it grew more interesting. It was my private, travelling edition of what I loved best and what intrigued me most about Coleridge's haunting work. As I added to it progressively, with annotations and cross-references, it began to shape itself in the way I have described in the introduction. It also became an instrument of research, a way of looking at the deep patterns of creativity which ran through Coleridge's troubled and restless life. I hope it has retained something of both these original impulses: personal affection and scholarly enquiry.

The primary aim of this edition is to present Coleridge afresh for the reader, through a new clarity of text, selection and commentary. The considerable textual difficulties behind many of the poems, like the problem of plagiarism or "adaptation", are clearly indicated in the Notes but not exaggerated. The discovery of a growing number of Coleridge's manuscript versions and later alterations has brought a notion of "textual instability" to many of his poems, particularly given Coleridge's life-long habit of revision. (See Jack Stillinger, *Coleridge and Textual Instability: The Multiple Versions of the Major Poems*, OUP, 1994.) Nevertheless the two-volume *Poetical Works* edited by E. H. Coleridge (Oxford, 1912) which is based on the *Poetical Works* of 1834 (the last overseen by Coleridge himself in his lifetime) remains a sound basis for the general reader and student. This is the primary text used here.

However, as indicated in my notes, I have also consulted Coleridge's very important earlier edition, *Sibylline Leaves* (1817); the great Victorian edition by J. D. Campbell (1893); and Professor John Beer's scholarly Everyman edition (1974). Many points have been clarified by reference to *The Letters of Samuel Taylor Coleridge*, edited by E. L. Griggs, 6 volumes, Oxford; and of course the great *Notebooks of Samuel Taylor Coleridge*, edited by Kathleen Coburn, four double volumes, Routledge (1957–90). The editorial work of Professor Heather Jackson has also been an inspiration.

For permission to quote from copyright materials thanks are due to the Oxford University Press, Princeton University Press, and Routledge. For the use of specific versions of manuscript sources thanks are due to Cornell University Press for No. 49; Routledge for No. 53; Everyman for the Latin translation to No. 54, and for No. 64; Princeton University Press for the marginal gloss to No. 33 (Note). Grateful acknowledgment is also due to Mrs Joan M. Coleridge, of East Wittering, West Sussex, for general permission to quote from manuscripts to which she holds copyright. Any reader wishing to pursue Coleridge's poems in greater textual depth should certainly consult volume 16 of the Bollingen Series Collected Coleridge edition, *Poetical Works*, edited by J. C. C. Mays, Routledge and Princeton, due in 1997.

A SELECT BIBLIOGRAPHY
OF THE MAIN EDITIONS OF
COLERIDGE'S POEMS

Poems on Various Subjects, by S.T. Coleridge, Late of Jesus College, Cambridge. J. Robinsons, London, and J. Cottle, Bristol. 1796.

[An Anthology of Sonnets] Untitled, by S.T. Coleridge and others. Privately printed, Bristol, 1796.

Poems, by S.T. Coleridge, second edition, to which are now added Poems by Charles Lamb, and Charles Lloyd. J. Cottle, Bristol, and J. Robinsons, London, 1797.

Fears in Solitude. To which are added, France, an Ode; and Frost at Midnight, by S.T. Coleridge. J. Johnson, in St Paul's Churchyard, London, 1798.

Lyrical Ballads, [by W. Wordsworth and S.T. Coleridge,] anonymous, J. Cottle, Bristol, 1798. Second edition, London, 1800.

Poems, by S.T. Coleridge, third edition. T.N. Longman and O. Rees, Paternoster Row, London, 1803.

Christabel; Kubla Khan, A Vision; The Pains of Sleep, by S.T. Coleridge Esq. John Murray, Albemarle Street, London, 1816. Second edition, 1816. Third edition, 1816.

Sibylline Leaves: A Collection of Poems, by S.T. Coleridge Esq. Rest Fenner, 23 Paternoster Row, London, 1817.

The Poetical Works of S.T. Coleridge, 3 vols. William Pickering, London, 1828. Second edition, 1829.

The Poetical Works of Coleridge, Shelley, and Keats, 1 vol. A. and W. Galignani, 18 rue Vivienne, Paris, 1829.

The Poetical Works of S.T. Coleridge, 3 vols. William Pickering, London, 1834. Reprinted 1835, 1840, 1844, 1847, 1848.

Literary Remains of S.T. Coleridge, edited by H.N. Coleridge. London, 1836.

The Poems of Samuel Taylor Coleridge, edited by Derwent and Sara Coleridge. Edward Moxon, Dover Street, London, 1852. Reprinted 1863, 1870.

The Poetical Works of Samuel Taylor Coleridge, edited with a biographical introduction by James Dykes Campbell. Macmillan and Co., London. and New York, 1893.

The Complete Poetical Works of Samuel Taylor Coleridge, edited with
textual and bibliographical notes by Ernest Hartley Coleridge,
2 vols., Oxford University Press, 1912. Reprinted in one volume,
Oxford University Press paperback, 1969.

Samuel Taylor Coleridge: Poems, selected and edited by John Beer.
Everyman Library, J.M. Dent, London, 1963. New edition, 1974.

Coleridge: Poems, selected and edited by Heather Jackson. Oxford
Poetry Library, 1994.

Coleridge: Poetical Works, edited by J.C.C. Mays. The Collected
Coleridge, volume 16, Bollingen Series, Routledge and Kegan Paul,
and Princeton University Press, due in 1997.

I

SONNETS

Sonnets

NO ONE NOW THINKS of Coleridge as a "sonneteer". The form seems too decorous, too limited and much too tidy for him. Yet Coleridge wrote sonnets at crucial moments throughout his life: when he went to school in London (No. 1); when he invented Pantisocracy at University (No. 8); when he got married and had his first child in Bristol (No. 12); when he fell in love again in the Lake District (No. 14); when he went abroad to Malta (No. 15); when he despaired of his writing (No. 19); and when he felt better about it (No. 17); and when he was slowly dying at Highgate (No. 21).

This section is made up of a chronological selection of twenty-one sonnets – less than half Coleridge's total output – written across the entire arc of his career, between the ages of sixteen ("To the Autumn Moon") and sixty-one ("To the Young Artist"). Part of its interest lies in the sort of miniature, snapshot history it provides of Coleridge's life over these forty-five years, with its extreme variations in mood, situation and outlook. There are a few great poems here – No. 5, No. 12, No. 19 perhaps – but all of them are revealing: funny, tragic, brilliant or absurd, just like their protean author.

The sonnets also show the broad development of Coleridge's literary style, seen through the magnifying glass of one particular and extremely demanding form. As a young man he learned a great deal from his contemporary William Bowles (see No. 4), and later from the seventeenth-century religious poet George Herbert (see No. 19). The early poems tend to be fulsome and derivative, the middle ones clear and highly original, the later ones denser and much more difficult to absorb. In general, there is a sense of Coleridge's language becoming quieter, and more personal. His voice gets steadily closer to us and more confidential.

The old, baroque Miltonic conventions of eighteenth-century

3

poetic diction – double-epithets, exclamations, personifications, decorative periphrasis (see No. 6) – slowly drop away. They are replaced by a plainer, but often more openly emotional style (see No. 14) which can be disturbingly bitter (see No. 20). The picture is further complicated by sonnets based on translations, adaptations, and one startling parody of the language of contemporary "Sensibility" in the form of a sonnet–nursery rhyme (No. 13).

Coleridge was not greatly interested in the mere technicalities of sonnets. This was simply a matter of adapting the rhyme schemes of the Petrarchean, Shakespearean or Miltonic forms; and of varying the iambic pentameter line to carry speech rhythms (see "The Poet in the Clouds", No. 17). "Respecting the Metre of a Sonnet, the Writer should consult his own convenience. – Rhymes, many or few, or no rhymes at all – whatever the chastity of his ear may prefer, whatever the rapid expression of his feeling will permit." (Preface, *Poems*, 1796).

But he was fascinated by the challenge of the sonnet's brevity and finality. He wondered what sort of subjects, and what kind of emotional materials, such a compact and definitively "closed" form could contain. The idea of the sonnet as a small, sculpted, elegant shape, which its materials must fit snugly and exactly, is the very opposite of the "open", irregular and unfinished form which Coleridge often used so spectacularly elsewhere (see VII Visionary Fragments).

Traditionally, the sonnet lent itself to love poetry, but Coleridge rarely used it in this way (though see Nos. 14–16). It also lent itself to sequences, and public occasions: Coleridge first made his name as a young poet with a sequence of twelve "Sonnets to Eminent Characters" (radical writers, politicians and scientists, as well as an actress) published in the *Morning Post* for winter 1794 (see Nos. 6–7).

But when in 1796 he privately published a critical anthology of sonnets, he wrote a preface suggesting that the true purpose of the form was to develop a single, inward line of emotion which was inspired by Nature – "a development of some lonely feeling deduced from, and associated with, the scenery of Nature." His definition of the sonnet depended, paradoxically, on the subject-matter rather than the form. "Poems, in which no lonely feeling is developed, are not Sonnets because the Author has chosen to write them in fourteen lines; they should rather be entitled Odes, or Songs, or Inscriptions."

It is remarkable how many of Coleridge's best sonnets conform to this psychological definition of their structure. A moment of intense isolation or self-awareness is progressively resolved by the revelation of some common law or experience in Nature. A mood of romantic solipsism (grief, anxiety, longing) is released into a more general or familiar pattern of feeling, a sense of shared human destiny. As he wrote in the 1796 Preface: "They create a sweet and indissoluble union between the intellectual and the material world. Easily remembered from their briefness, and interesting alike to the eye and the affections . . . they domesticate with the heart, and become, as it were, a part of our identity."

Coleridge's technical mastery, never lost, shows most in his ability to produce sonnets of wildly different moods, without ever losing his own voice. But the sonnet is not, finally, his ideal form because it placed him under restraints, made him self-conscious, and tempted him to fall back on pastiche. Yet he left his distinct mark on it: no other poet could have written "To the River Otter" (No. 5), or "To a Friend Who Asked, How I felt When the Nurse First Presented my Infant to Me" (No. 12), or "Work Without Hope" (No. 19).

With Wordsworth, Coleridge was responsible for a powerful recovery of interest in the possibilities of the sonnet (as with seventeenth-century poetry as a whole, especially in the work of George Herbert, Edmund Spenser, and Fulke Greville – all notable sonnet-writers). He helped to liberate it from the weight of Shakespeare and Milton, and make it feel more intimate and modern. His influence shows in the great Victorian revival of sonnet writing which followed: by his own son, Hartley Coleridge, by Elizabeth Barrett Browning, Christina Rossetti, and George Meredith.

To the Autumnal Moon

Mild Splendour of the various-vested Night!
    Mother of wildly-working visions! hail!
I watch thy gliding, while with watery light
    Thy weak eye glimmers through a fleecy veil;
And when thou lovest thy pale orb to shroud   5
    Behind the gather'd blackness lost on high;
And when thou dartest from the wind-rent cloud
    Thy placid lightning o'er the awaken'd sky.

Ah such is Hope! as changeful and as fair!
    Now dimly peering on the wistful sight;   10
Now hid behind the dragon-wing'd Despair:
    But soon emerging in her radiant might
She o'er the sorrow-clouded breast of Care
    Sails, like a meteor kindling in its flight.

Life

As late I journey'd o'er the extensive plain
   Where native Otter sports his scanty stream,
Musing in torpid woe a Sister's pain,
   The glorious prospect woke me from the dream.

At every step it widen'd to my sight –   5
   Wood, Meadow, verdant Hill, and dreary Steep,
Following in quick succession of delight, –
   Till all – at once – did my eye ravish'd sweep!

May this (I cried) my course through Life portray!
New scenes of Wisdom may each step display,   10
   And Knowledge open as my days advance!
Till what time Death shall pour the undarken'd ray,
   My eye shall dart thro' infinite expanse,
And thought suspended lie in Rapture's blissful trance.

On Receiving an Account that his Only Sister's Death was Inevitable

The tear which mourn'd a brother's fate scarce dry –
Pain after pain, and woe succeeding woe –
Is my heart destin'd for another blow?
O my sweet sister! and must thou too die?
Ah! how has Disappointment pour'd the tear   5
O'er infant Hope destroy'd by early frost!
How are ye gone, whom most my soul held dear!
Scarce had I lov'd you ere I mourn'd you lost;
Say, is this hollow eye, this heartless pain,
Fated to rove thro' Life's wide cheerless plain –   10
Nor father, brother, sister meet its ken –
My woes, my joys unshared! Ah! long ere then
On me thy icy dart, stern Death, be prov'd; –
Better to die, than live and not be lov'd!

On Quitting School for College

Farewell parental scenes! a sad farewell!
To you my grateful heart still fondly clings,
Tho' fluttering round on Fancy's burnish'd wings
Her tales of future Joy Hope loves to tell.
Adieu, adieu! ye much-lov'd cloisters pale!   5
Ah! would those happy days return again,
When 'neath your arches, free from every stain,
I heard of guilt and wonder'd at the tale!
Dear haunts! where oft my simple lays I sang,
Listening meanwhile the echoings of my feet,   10
Lingering I quit you, with as great a pang,
As when erewhile, my weeping childhood, torn
By early sorrow from my native seat,
Mingled its tears with hers – my widow'd Parent lorn.

To the River Otter

Dear native Brook! wild Streamlet of the West!
   How many various-fated years have past,
   What happy and what mournful hours, since last
I skimm'd the smooth thin stone along thy breast,
Numbering its light leaps! yet so deep imprest   5
Sink the sweet scenes of childhood, that mine eyes
   I never shut amid the sunny ray,
But straight with all their tints thy waters rise,
   Thy crossing plank, thy marge with willows grey,
And bedded sand that vein'd with various dyes   10
   Gleam'd through thy bright transparence! On my way,
    Visions of Childhood! oft have ye beguil'd
Lone manhood's cares, yet waking fondest sighs:
   Ah! that once more I were a careless Child!

To the Author of *The Robbers*

Schiller! that hour I would have wish'd to die,
If thro' the shuddering midnight I had sent
From the dark dungeon of the Tower time-rent
That fearful voice, a famish'd Father's cry –
Lest in some after moment aught more mean   5
Might stamp me mortal! A triumphant shout
Black Horror scream'd, and all her *goblin* rout
Diminish'd shrunk from the more withering scene!
Ah! Bard tremendous in sublimity!
Could I behold thee in thy loftier mood   10
Wandering at eve with finely-frenzied eye
Beneath some vast old tempest-swinging wood!
Awhile with mute awe gazing I would brood:
Then weep aloud in a wild ecstasy!

To the Rev. W. L. Bowles

My heart has thank'd thee, BOWLES! for those soft strains,
  That, on the still air floating, tremblingly
Wak'd in me Fancy, Love, and Sympathy!
For hence, not callous to a Brother's pains

Thro' Youth's gay prime and thornless paths I went;   5
And, when the *darker* day of life began,
And I did roam, a thought-bewilder'd man!
Thy kindred Lays an healing solace lent,

Each lonely pang with dreamy joys combin'd,
  And stole from vain REGRET her scorpion stings;   10
  While shadowy PLEASURE, with mysterious wings,
Brooded the wavy and tumultuous mind,

Like that great Spirit, who with plastic sweep
Mov'd on the darkness of the formless Deep!

Pantisocracy

No more my visionary soul shall dwell
On joys that were; no more endure to weigh
The shame and anguish of the evil day,
Wisely forgetful! O'er the ocean swell
Sublime of Hope, I seek the cottag'd dell   5
Where Virtue calm with careless step may stray,
And dancing to the moonlight roundelay,
The wizard Passions weave an holy spell.
Eyes that have ach'd with Sorrow! Ye shall weep
Tears of doubt-mingled joy, like theirs who start   10
From Precipices of distemper'd sleep,
On which the fierce-eyed Fiends their revels keep,
And see the rising Sun, and feel it dart
New rays of pleasance trembling to the heart.

Pity

Sweet Mercy! how my very heart has bled
   To see thee, poor Old Man! and thy grey hairs
   Hoar with the snowy blast: while no one cares
To clothe thy shrivell'd limbs and palsied head.
My Father! throw away this tatter'd vest   5
   That mocks thy shivering! take my garment – use
   A young man's arm! I'll melt these frozen dews
That hang from thy white beard and numb thy breast.
My Sara too shall tend thee, like a child:
   And thou shalt talk, in our fireside's recess,   10
   Of purple Pride, that scowls on Wretchedness –
He did not so, the Galilaean mild,
   Who met the Lazars turn'd from rich men's doors
   And call'd them Friends, and heal'd their noisome sores!

On Receiving a Letter Informing me of the Birth of a Son

When they did greet me father, sudden awe
  Weigh'd down my spirit: I retired and knelt
  Seeking the throne of grace, but inly felt
  No heavenly visitation upwards draw
  My feeble mind, nor cheering ray impart.   5
    Ah me! before the Eternal Sire I brought
    Th' unquiet silence of confuséd thought
  And shapeless feelings: my o'erwhelméd heart
  Trembled, and vacant tears stream'd down my face.
  And now once more, O Lord! to thee I bend,   10
    Lover of souls! and groan for future grace,
  That ere my babe youth's perilous maze have trod,
    Thy overshadowing Spirit may descend,
    And he be born again, a child of God.

Composed on a Journey Homeward; the Author having received Intelligence of the Birth of a Son, Sept. 20, 1796

Oft o'er my brain does that strange fancy roll
   Which makes the present (while the flash doth last)
   Seem a mere semblance of some unknown past,
Mixed with such feelings, as perplex the soul
Self-questioned in her sleep; and some have said   5
   We liv'd, ere yet this robe of flesh we wore.
   O my sweet baby! when I reach my door,
If heavy looks should tell me thou art dead,
(As sometimes, through excess of hope, I fear)
I think that I should struggle to believe   10
   Thou wert a spirit, to this nether sphere
Sentenc'd for some more venial crime to grieve;
Did'st scream, then spring to meet Heaven's quick reprieve,
   While we wept idly o'er thy little bier!

To a Friend who Asked,
How I Felt When the Nurse First
Presented my Infant to me

Charles! my slow heart was only sad, when first
   I scann'd that face of feeble infancy:
For dimly on my thoughtful spirit burst
   All I had been, and all my child might be!
But when I saw it on its mother's arm,   5
   And hanging at her bosom (she the while
   Bent o'er its features with a tearful smile)
Then I was thrill'd and melted, and most warm
Impress'd a father's kiss: and all beguil'd
   Of dark remembrance and presageful fear,   10
   I seem'd to see an angel-form appear –
'Twas even thine, belovéd woman mild!
   So for the mother's sake the child was dear,
And dearer was the mother for the child.

On a Ruined House in
a Romantic Country

And this reft house is that the which he built,
Lamented Jack! And here his malt he pil'd,
Cautious in vain! These rats that squeak so wild,
Squeak, not unconscious of their father's guilt.
Did ye not see her gleaming thro' the glade?   5
Belike, 'twas she, the maiden all forlorn.
What though she milk no cow with crumpled horn,
Yet *aye* she haunts the dale where *erst* she stray'd;
And *aye* beside her stalks her amorous knight!
Still on his thighs their wonted brogues are worn,   10
And thro' those brogues, still tatter'd and betorn,
His hindward charms gleam an unearthly white;
As when thro' broken clouds at night's high noon
Peeps in fair fragments forth the full-orb'd harvest-moon!

To Asra

Are there two things, of all which men possess
That are so like each other and so near,
As mutual Love seems like to Happiness?
Dear Asra, woman beyond utterance dear!
This Love which ever welling at my heart,   5
Now in its living fount doth heave and fall,
Now overflowing pours thro' every part
Of all my frame, and fills and changes all,
Like vernal waters springing up through snow,
This Love that seeming great beyond the power   10
Of growth, yet seemeth ever more to grow,
Could I transmute the whole to one rich Dower
Of Happy Life, and give it all to Thee,
Thy lot, methinks, were Heaven, thy age, Eternity!

Lady, to Death we're Doom'd . . .

TRANSLATED FROM MARINO

Lady, to Death we're doom'd, our crime the same!
Thou, that in me thou kindled'st such fierce heat;
I, that my heart did of a Sun so sweet
The rays concentre to so hot a flame.
I, fascinated by an Adder's eye –   5
Deaf as an Adder thou to all my pain;
Thou obstinate in Scorn, in Passion I –
I lov'd too much, too much didst thou disdain.
Hear then our doom in Hell as just as stern,
Our sentence equal as our crimes conspire –   10
Who living bask'd at Beauty's earthly fire,
In living flames eternal these must burn –
Hell for us both fit places too supplies –
In my heart *thou* wilt burn, I *roast* before thine eyes.

Farewell to Love

Farewell, sweet Love! yet blame you not my truth;
  More fondly ne'er did mother eye her child
Than I your form: *yours* were my hopes of youth,
  And as *you* shaped my thoughts I sighed or smiled.

While most were wooing wealth, or gaily swerving   5
  To pleasure's secret haunts, and some apart
Stood strong in pride, self-conscious of deserving,
  To you I gave my whole weak wishing heart.

And when I met the maid that realised
  Your fair creations, and had won her kindness,   10
Say, but for her if aught on earth I prized!
  Your dreams alone I dreamt, and caught your blindness.

O grief! – but farewell, Love! I will go play me
With thoughts that please me less, and less betray me.

Fancy in Nubibus

OR THE POET IN THE CLOUDS

O! It is pleasant, with a heart at ease,
　　Just after sunset, or by moonlight skies,
To make the shifting clouds be what you please,
　　Or let the easily persuaded eyes
Own each quaint likeness issuing from the mould　　　　5
　　Of a friend's fancy; or with head bent low
And cheek aslant see rivers flow of gold
　　'Twixt crimson banks; and then, a traveller, go
From mount to mount through Cloudland, gorgeous land!
　　Or list'ning to the tide, with closéd sight,　　　　10
Be that blind bard, who on the Chian strand
　　By those deep sounds possessed with inward light,
Beheld the Iliad and the Odyssee
　　Rise to the swelling of the voiceful sea.

To Nature

It may indeed be phantasy, when I
    Essay to draw from all created things
    Deep, heartfelt, inward joy that closely clings;
And trace in leaves and flowers that round me lie
Lessons of love and earnest piety.   5
    So let it be; and if the wide world rings
    In mock of this belief, it brings
Nor fear, nor grief, nor vain perplexity.
So will I build my altar in the fields,
    And the blue sky my fretted dome shall be,   10
And the sweet fragrance that the wild flower yields
    Shall be the incense I will yield to Thee,
Thee only God! and thou shalt not despise
Even me, the priest of this poor sacrifice.

Work Without Hope

All Nature seems at work. Slugs leave their lair –
The bees are stirring – birds are on the wing –
And Winter slumbering in the open air,
Wears on his smiling face a dream of Spring!
And I the while, the sole unbusy thing,   5
Nor honey make, nor pair, nor build, nor sing.

   Yet well I ken the banks where amaranths blow,
Have traced the fount whence streams of nectar flow.
Bloom, O ye amaranths! bloom for whom ye may,
For me ye bloom not! Glide, rich streams, away!   10
With lips unbrightened, wreathless brow, I stroll:
And would you learn the spells that drowse my soul?
Work without Hope draws nectar in a sieve,
And Hope without an object cannot live.

Duty Surviving Self-Love

Unchanged within, to see all changed without,
Is a blank lot and hard to bear, no doubt.
Yet why at others' wanings should'st thou fret?
Then only might'st thou feel a just regret,
Hadst thou withheld thy love or hid thy light   5
In selfish forethought of neglect and slight.
O wiselier then, from feeble yearnings freed,
While, and on whom, thou may'st – shine on! nor heed
Whether the object by reflected light
Return thy radiance or absorb it quite: 10
And though thou notest from thy safe recess
Old Friends burn dim, like lamps in noisome air,
Love them for what they are; nor love them less,
Because to thee they are not what they were.

To the Young Artist

Kayser! to whom, as to a second self,
Nature, or Nature's next-of-kin, the Elf,
Hight Genius, hath dispensed the happy skill
To cheer or soothe the parting friend's "Alas!"
Turning the blank scroll to a magic glass,   5
That makes the absent present at our will;
And to the shadowing of thy pencil gives
Such seeming substance, that it almost lives.

Well hast thou given the thoughtful Poet's face!
Yet hast thou on the tablet of his mind   10
A more delightful portrait left behind –
Even thy own youthful beauty, and artless grace,
Thy natural gladness and eyes bright with glee!
            Kayser! farewell!
Be wise! be happy! and forget not me.

II

CONVERSATION
POEMS

Conversation Poems

THIS DISTINCTIVE GROUP of nine blank-verse poems has slowly emerged as one of Coleridge's greatest poetic achievements. They were largely written in his mid-twenties, and concern the circle of family, friends and children which formed round him in the West Country between 1794 and 1798. The imaginary "conversations" are all held with particular people, and written in a new, intimate poetic form which Coleridge invented for the purpose. They are halfway between the traditional eighteenth-century verse-letter or "epistle", and a more psychological form of Romantic meditation or autobiography.

Most of the circle are named, or can easily be identified, in the poems: his wife Sara Coleridge and their little son Hartley; his elder brother George Coleridge; Charles and Mary Lamb; his great supporter, Tom Poole, the tanner of Nether Stowey; William and Dorothy Wordsworth; and young William Hazlitt, who visited them in the spring of 1798. The last poem of the group, "To William Wordsworth" (No. 30) forms a sort of coda, looking wistfully back at the circle when Coleridge was thirty-five, separated from his wife, and temporarily living in Leicestershire.

The Conversation poems began purely by chance in 1794, when Coleridge was writing to Lamb to say how frustrated he felt with the "elaborate and swelling" formalities of epic verse (see No. 22). But by 1798, Coleridge was more conscious of composing a linked series, and first used the term "a Conversational Poem" (see No. 29). In his collection *Sibylline Leaves* of 1817, he changed this to "a Conversation poem" and deliberately grouped seven of the nine pieces under the generic title "Meditative Poems in Blank Verse".

It is now clear that the Conversation Poems can be read as a single sequence, exploring an extending pastoral vision of friendship and family life, rooted in the countryside. Contrary to Coleridge's reputation for unfinished work, all the poems are beautifully polished and revised. Several exist in interesting early versions (see notes to Nos. 23, 27, and 30); some incorporate new material added as late as 1817. Altogether, the sequence runs to well over eight hundred lines of verse, the most substantial poetic structure that Coleridge ever created, larger even than "Christabel". It is nearly as long as the first two Books of Wordsworth's *Prelude* (begun in 1799 and addressed to Coleridge), which it partly inspired both in theme and style.

The pastoral vision is no longer an idealized or picturesque eighteenth-century one, a Claude Lorraine landscape of gods, nymphs and shepherds. The Conversation Poems are set in a recognizable English West Country, the North Somersetshire and Devon coastline between Bristol and Lynmouth, and the woods and moorlands of the Quantock hills. Coleridge recreates this landscape, with its weather and wild animals, as surely as the regional novelists of the later Victorian period. The whole pattern of his cottage life with Sara – walking, talking, lovemaking, baby-minding, meeting friends (especially the Wordsworths), sitting up at night writing – all appears as a recognizable domestic background. The poems constantly move out from this homely framework to explore long meditations on marriage (No. 23), work (No. 24), friendship and family (No. 25), life in the countryside (No. 26), childhood and memory (No. 27), public affairs (No. 28), or poetry itself (No. 29).

Filled with real people, Coleridge's poems are both psychologically acute and physically robust, at times even humorous (see the note to "This Lime-Tree Bower My Prison", No. 26). Wives complain, children cry, friends argue, husbands make a fuss, even nightingales get rowdy. The pastoral vision can sustain powerful outside forces: the demands of work and social duty (No. 24); the needs of children (Nos. 27, 29); the problems of politics and war (No. 28). It is a vision that reaches towards a consistent philosophy of man's harmonious place in Nature; the vision of a "One Life", in which people, children, animals and plants all share (see note to No. 23). Coleridge later wrote in a letter of 1802: "Nature has her proper interest; & he will know what it is, who believes & feels, that every Thing has a Life of its own, & that we are all *one Life*. A Poet's Heart & intellect should be *combined*, intimately combined & *unified*, with the great appearances in Nature – & not merely held in solution & loose mixture with them, in the shape of formal Similies." This is a central, and ultimately spiritual theme, of the Conversation Poems.

Coleridge developed his form from the blank verse of Mark

Akenside ("The Pleasures of the Imagination", 1744) and especially from William Cowper, whose poem "The Task" (1770) gave him a preliminary model for a domestic, conversational mode of autobiography – "the Divine Chit-Chat of Cowper". But he steadily transformed his eighteenth-century models throughout the sequence, his language growing rhythmically more colloquial, but visually more intense. It rises to those "quiet" epiphanies or revelations, when the whole landscape seems to radiate with transcendental power, as in the moonlit close of "Frost at Midnight" (No. 27).

Wordsworth himself went on to develop this form in "Tintern Abbey" (autumn 1798), and then in *The Prelude*, but in his more stately, monumental manner. Indeed it is the success of *The Prelude* which Coleridge celebrates in the last poem of the group (No. 30), while looking back at his own comparative failure to fulfil the promise of the time. But this "failure" (wholly contradicted by Coleridge's actual poetic output) is part of the dramatic structure of the Conversation Poems, in which the pastoral Paradise can never be recaptured, and thus becomes sacred: a Paradise Lost.

The poems often have a characteristic outward and return movement – starting at some specific location (the study, the garden arbour, Stowey wood), and performing some large physical or imaginative journey, before returning home. These home-comings, often accompanied by a moment of "blessing", have a kind of choral role in the sequence, which has attained great symbolic significance by the end, as the place of love. In this sense, Coleridge's outer landscapes move subtly to the condition of interior heartlands. The emphasis becomes increasingly psychological: with memory, meditation and prayer becoming dominant modes. Figuratively this is expressed by one remarkable transformation: the child of Nature, little Hartley Coleridge, who becomes the central channel of feelings in the early poems, is finally changed back into Coleridge himself as a child, even as a baby, in the closing passages of "To William Wordsworth" (No. 30). The Conversation sequence has performed a complete, symbolic life-cycle.

The Conversational mode, with its understated English style, was one of Coleridge's most fruitful creations (as against, say, the more rhetorical *Epistles* of Pope). Its influence can be variously traced in the intimate blank verse of Browning, Hardy, Edward Thomas, Robert Frost and Elizabeth Bishop.

To a Friend

[CHARLES LAMB]

TOGETHER WITH AN UNFINISHED POEM

Thus far my scanty brain hath built the rhyme
Elaborate and swelling: yet the heart
Not owns it. From thy spirit-breathing powers
I ask not now, my friend! the aiding verse,
Tedious to thee, and from thy anxious thought   5
Of dissonant mood. In fancy (well I know)
From business wandering far and local cares,
Thou creepest round a dear-lov'd Sister's bed
With noiseless step, and watchest the faint look,
Soothing each pang with fond solicitude,   10
And tenderest tones medicinal of love.
I too a Sister *had*, an only Sister –
She lov'd me dearly, and I doted on her!
To her I pour'd forth all my puny sorrows
(As a sick Patient in a Nurse's arms)   15
And of the heart those hidden maladies
That e'en from Friendship's eye will shrink asham'd.

O! I have wak'd at midnight, and have wept,
Because she was not! – Cheerily, dear Charles!
Thou thy best friend shalt cherish many a year: 20
Such warm presages feel I of high Hope.
For not uninterested the dear Maid
I've view'd – her soul affectionate yet wise,
Her polish'd wit as mild as lambent glories
That play around a sainted infant's head.   25
He knows (the Spirit that in secret sees,
Of whose omniscient and all-spreading Love
Aught to *implore* were impotence of mind)
That my mute thoughts are sad before his throne,
Prepar'd, when he his healing ray vouchsafes,   30
Thanksgiving to pour forth with lifted heart,
And praise Him Gracious with a Brother's Joy!

The Eolian Harp

COMPOSED AT CLEVEDON, SOMERSETSHIRE

My pensive Sara! thy soft cheek reclined
Thus on mine arm, most soothing sweet it is
To sit beside our Cot, our Cot o'ergrown
With white-flower'd Jasmin, and the broad-leav'd Myrtle,
(Meet emblems they of Innocence and Love!)   5
And watch the clouds, that late were rich with light,
Slow saddening round, and mark the star of eve
Serenely brilliant (such should Wisdom be)
Shine opposite! How exquisite the scents
Snatch'd from yon bean-field! and the world *so* hush'd!   10
The stilly murmur of the distant Sea
Tells us of silence.

          And that simplest Lute,
Placed length-ways in the clasping casement, hark!
How by the desultory breeze caress'd,
Like some coy maid half yielding to her lover,   15
It pours such sweet upbraiding, as must needs
Tempt to repeat the wrong! And now, its strings
Boldlier swept, the long sequacious notes
Over delicious surges sink and rise,
Such a soft floating witchery of sound   20
As twilight Elfins make, when they at eve
Voyage on gentle gales from Fairy-Land,
Where Melodies round honey-dropping flowers,
Footless and wild, like birds of Paradise,
Nor pause, nor perch, hovering on untam'd wing!   25
O! the one Life within us and abroad,
Which meets all motion and becomes its soul,
A light in sound, a sound-like power in light,
Rhythm in all thought, and joyance every where –
Methinks, it should have been impossible   30
Not to love all things in a world so fill'd;
Where the breeze warbles, and the mute still air
Is Music slumbering on her instrument.

And thus, my Love! as on the midway slope
Of yonder hill I stretch my limbs at noon,   35
Whilst through my half-clos'd eye-lids I behold
The sunbeams dance, like diamonds, on the main,
And tranquil muse upon tranquillity;
Full many a thought uncall'd and undetain'd,
And many idle flitting phantasies,   40
Traverse my indolent and passive brain,
As wild and various as the random gales
That swell and flutter on this subject Lute!

And what if all of animated nature
Be but organic Harps diversely fram'd,   45
That tremble into thought, as o'er them sweeps
Plastic and vast, one intellectual breeze,
At once the Soul of each, and God of all?

But thy more serious eye a mild reproof
Darts, O belovéd Woman! nor such thoughts   50
Dim and unhallow'd dost thou not reject,
And biddest me walk humbly with my God.
Meek Daughter in the family of Christ!
Well hast thou said and holily disprais'd
These shapings of the unregenerate mind;   55
Bubbles that glitter as they rise and break
On vain Philosophy's aye-babbling spring.
For never guiltless may I speak of him,
The Incomprehensible! save when with awe
I praise him, and with Faith that inly *feels*;   60
Who with his saving mercies healéd me,
A sinful and most miserable man,
Wilder'd and dark, and gave me to possess
Peace, and this Cot, and thee, heart-honour'd Maid!

Reflections on Having Left a Place of Retirement

Sermoni propriora. – HORACE

Low was our pretty Cot: our tallest Rose
Peep'd at the chamber-window. We could hear
At silent noon, and eve, and early morn,
The Sea's faint murmur. In the open air
Our Myrtles blossom'd; and across the porch   5
Thick Jasmins twined: the little landscape round
Was green and woody, and refresh'd the eye.
It was a spot which you might aptly call
The Valley of Seclusion! Once I saw
(Hallowing his Sabbath-day by quietness)   10
A wealthy son of Commerce saunter by,
Bristowa's citizen: methought, it calm'd
His thirst of idle gold, and made him muse
With wiser feelings: for he paus'd, and look'd
With a pleas'd sadness, and gaz'd all around,   15
Then eyed our Cottage, and gaz'd round again,
And sigh'd, and said, it was a Blesséd Place.
And we *were* bless'd. Oft with patient ear
Long-listening to the viewless sky-lark's note
(Viewless, or haply for a moment seen   20
Gleaming on sunny wings) in whisper'd tones
I've said to my Belovéd, "Such, sweet Girl!
The inobtrusive song of Happiness,
Unearthly minstrelsy! then only heard
When the Soul seeks to hear; when all is hush'd,   25
And the Heart listens!"

                           But the time, when first
From that low Dell, steep up the stony Mount
I climb'd with perilous toil and reach'd the top,
Oh! what a goodly scene! *Here* the bleak mount,
The bare bleak mountain speckled thin with sheep;   30
Grey clouds, that shadowing spot the sunny fields;
And river, now with bushy rocks o'er-brow'd,

Now winding bright and full, with naked banks;
And seats, and lawns, the Abbey and the wood,
And cots, and hamlets, and faint city-spire;   35
The Channel *there*, the Islands and white sails,
Dim coasts, and cloud-like hills, and shoreless Ocean –
It seem'd like Omnipresence! God, methought,
Had built him there a Temple: the whole World
Seem'd *imag'd* in its vast circumference: 40
No *wish* profan'd my overwhelméd heart.
Blest hour! It was a luxury, – to be!

  Ah! quiet Dell! dear Cot, and Mount sublime!
I was constrain'd to quit you. Was it right,
While my unnumber'd brethren toil'd and bled,   45
That I should dream away the entrusted hours
On rose-leaf beds, pampering the coward heart
With feelings all too delicate for use?
Sweet is the tear that from some Howard's eye
Drops on the cheek of one he lifts from earth: 50
And he that works me good with unmov'd face,
Does it but half: he chills me while he aids,
My benefactor, not my brother man!
Yet even this, this cold beneficence
Praise, praise it, O my Soul! oft as thou scann'st   55
The sluggard Pity's vision-weaving tribe!
Who sigh for Wretchedness, yet shun the Wretched,
Nursing in some delicious solitude
Their slothful loves and dainty sympathies!
I therefore go, and join head, heart, and hand,   60
Active and firm, to fight the bloodless fight
Of Science, Freedom, and the Truth in Christ.

  Yet oft when after honourable toil
Rests the tir'd mind, and waking loves to dream,
My spirit shall revisit thee, dear Cot!   65
Thy Jasmin and thy window-peeping Rose,
And Myrtles fearless of the mild sea-air.
And I shall sigh fond wishes – sweet Abode!
Ah! – had none greater! And that all had such!
It might be so – but the time is not yet.   70
Speed it, O Father! Let thy Kingdom come!

To the Rev. George Coleridge

OF OTTERY ST. MARY, DEVON

With some Poems

Notus in fratres animi paterni.
– HORACE *Carm.* lib. II. 2.

A blessèd lot hath he, who having passed
His youth and early manhood in the stir
And turmoil of the world, retreats at length,
With cares that move, not agitate the heart,
To the same dwelling where his father dwelt;   5
And haply views his tottering little ones
Embrace those agèd knees and climb that lap,
On which first kneeling his own infancy
Lisp'd its brief prayer. Such, O my earliest Friend!
Thy lot, and such thy brothers too enjoy.   10
At distance did ye climb Life's upland road,
Yet cheer'd and cheering: now fraternal love
Hath drawn you to one centre. Be your days
Holy, and blest and blessing may ye live!

    To me the Eternal Wisdom hath dispens'd   15
A different fortune and more different mind –
Me from the spot where first I sprang to light
Too soon transplanted, ere my soul had fix'd
Its first domestic loves; and hence through life
Chasing chance-started friendships. A brief while   20
Some have preserv'd me from life's pelting ills;
But, like a tree with leaves of feeble stem,
If the clouds lasted, and a sudden breeze
Ruffled the boughs, they on my head at once
Dropped the collected shower; and some most false,   25
False and fair-foliag'd as the Manchineel,
Have tempted me to slumber in their shade
E'en mid the storm; then breathing subtlest damps,
Mix'd their own venom with the rain from Heaven,
That I woke poison'd! But, all praise to Him   30
Who gives us all things, more have yielded me

Permanent shelter; and beside one Friend,
Beneath the impervious covert of one oak,
I've rais'd a lowly shed, and know the names
Of Husband and of Father; not unhearing   35
Of that divine and nightly-whispering Voice,
Which from my childhood to maturer years
Spake to me of predestinated wreaths,
Bright with no fading colours!

                              Yet at times
My soul is sad, that I have roam'd through life   40
Still most a stranger, most with naked heart
At mine own home and birth-place: chiefly then,
When I remember thee, my earliest Friend!
Thee, who didst watch my boyhood and my youth;
Didst trace my wanderings with a father's eye;   45
And boding evil yet still hoping good,
Rebuk'd each fault, and over all my woes
Sorrow'd in silence! He who counts alone
The beatings of the solitary heart,
That Being knows, how I have lov'd thee ever,   50
Lov'd as a brother, as a son rever'd thee!
Oh! 'tis to me an ever new delight,
To talk of thee and thine: or when the blast
Of the shrill winter, rattling our rude sash,
Endears the cleanly hearth and social bowl;   55
Or when, as now, on some delicious eve,
We in our sweet sequester'd orchard-plot
Sit on the tree crook'd earth-ward; whose old boughs,
That hang above us in an arborous roof,
Stirr'd by the faint gale of departing May,   60
Send their loose blossoms slanting o'er our heads!

    Nor dost not thou sometimes recall those hours,
When with the joy of hope thou gavest thine ear
To my wild firstling-lays. Since then my song
Hath sounded deeper notes, such as beseem   65
Or that sad wisdom folly leaves behind,
Or such as, tuned to these tumultuous times,
Cope with the tempest's swell!

These various strains,
Which I have fram'd in many a various mood,
Accept, my Brother! and (for some perchance   70
Will strike discordant on thy milder mind)
If aught of error or intemperate truth
Should meet thine ear, think thou that riper Age
Will calm it down, and let thy love forgive it!

26.

This Lime-Tree Bower My Prison

In the June of 1797 some long-expected friends paid a visit to the author's cottage; and on the morning of their arrival, he met with an accident, which disabled him from walking during the whole time of their stay. One evening, when they had left him for a few hours, he composed the following lines in the garden-bower.

Well, they are gone, and here must I remain,
This lime-tree bower my prison! I have lost
Beauties and feelings, such as would have been
Most sweet to my remembrance even when age
Had dimm'd mine eyes to blindness! They, meanwhile,   5
Friends, whom I never more may meet again,
On springy heath, along the hill-top edge,
Wander in gladness, and wind down, perchance,
To that still roaring dell, of which I told;
The roaring dell, o'erwooded, narrow, deep,   10
And only speckled by the mid-day sun;
Where its slim trunk the ash from rock to rock
Flings arching like a bridge; – that branchless ash,
Unsunn'd and damp, whose few poor yellow leaves
Ne'er tremble in the gale, yet tremble still,   15
Fann'd by the water-fall! and there my friends
Behold the dark green file of long lank weeds,
That all at once (a most fantastic sight!)
Still nod and drip beneath the dripping edge
Of the blue clay-stone.   20

          Now, my friends emerge
Beneath the wide wide Heaven – and view again
The many-steepled tract magnificent
Of hilly fields and meadows, and the sea,
With some fair bark, perhaps, whose sails light up
The slip of smooth clear blue betwixt two Isles   25

43

Of purple shadow! Yes! they wander on
In gladness all; but thou, methinks, most glad,
My gentle-hearted Charles! for thou hast pined
And hunger'd after Nature, many a year,
In the great City pent, winning thy way   30
With sad yet patient soul, through evil and pain
And strange calamity! Ah! slowly sink
Behind the western ridge, thou glorious Sun!
Shine in the slant beams of the sinking orb,
Ye purple heath-flowers! richlier burn, ye clouds!   35
Live in the yellow light, ye distant groves!
And kindle, thou blue Ocean! So my friend
Struck with deep joy may stand, as I have stood,
Silent with swimming sense; yea, gazing round
On the wide landscape, gaze till all doth seem   40
Less gross than bodily; and of such hues
As veil the Almighty Spirit, when yet he makes
Spirits perceive his presence.

                    A delight
Comes sudden on my heart, and I am glad
As I myself were there! Nor in this bower,   45
This little lime-tree bower, have I not mark'd
Much that has sooth'd me. Pale beneath the blaze
Hung the transparent foliage; and I watch'd
Some broad and sunny leaf, and lov'd to see
The shadow of the leaf and stem above   50
Dappling its sunshine! And that walnut-tree
Was richly ting'd, and a deep radiance lay
Full on the ancient ivy, which usurps
Those fronting elms, and now, with blackest mass
Makes their dark branches gleam a lighter hue   55
Through the late twilight: and though now the bat
Wheels silent by, and not a swallow twitters,
Yet still the solitary humble-bee
Sings in the bean-flower! Henceforth I shall know
That Nature ne'er deserts the wise and pure;   60
No plot so narrow, be but Nature there,
No waste so vacant, but may well employ
Each faculty of sense, and keep the heart
Awake to Love and Beauty! and sometimes

'Tis well to be bereft of promis'd good,   65
That we may lift the soul, and contemplate
With lively joy the joys we cannot share.
My gentle-hearted Charles! when the last rook
Beat its straight path along the dusky air
Homewards, I blest it! deeming its black wing   70
(Now a dim speck, now vanishing in light)
Had cross'd the mighty Orb's dilated glory,
While thou stood'st gazing; or, when all was still,
Flew creeking o'er thy head, and had a charm
For thee, my gentle-hearted Charles, to whom   75
No sound is dissonant which tells of Life.

27

Frost at Midnight

The Frost performs its secret ministry,
Unhelped by any wind. The owlet's cry
Came loud – and hark, again! loud as before.
The inmates of my cottage, all at rest,
Have left me to that solitude, which suits   5
Abstruser musings: save that at my side
My cradled infant slumbers peacefully.
'Tis calm indeed! so calm, that it disturbs
And vexes meditation with its strange
And extreme silentness. Sea, hill, and wood,   10
This populous village! Sea, and hill, and wood,
With all the numberless goings-on of life,
Inaudible as dreams! the thin blue flame
Lies on my low-burnt fire, and quivers not;
Only that film, which fluttered on the grate,   15
Still flutters there, the sole unquiet thing.
Methinks, its motion in this hush of nature
Gives it dim sympathies with me who live,
Making it a companionable form,
Whose puny flaps and freaks the idling Spirit   20
By its own moods interprets, every where
Echo or mirror seeking of itself,
And makes a toy of Thought.

                        But O! how oft,
How oft, at school, with most believing mind,
Presageful, have I gazed upon the bars,   25
To watch that fluttering *stranger*! and as oft
With unclosed lids, already had I dreamt
Of my sweet birth-place, and the old church-tower,
Whose bells, the poor man's only music, rang
From morn to evening, all the hot Fair-day,   30
So sweetly, that they stirred and haunted me

With a wild pleasure, falling on mine ear
Most like articulate sounds of things to come!
So gazed I, till the soothing things, I dreamt,
Lulled me to sleep, and sleep prolonged my dreams!   35
And so I brooded all the following morn,
Awed by the stern preceptor's face, mine eye
Fixed with mock study on my swimming book:
Save if the door half opened, and I snatched
A hasty glance, and still my heart leaped up,   40
For still I hoped to see the *stranger's* face,
Townsman, or aunt, or sister more beloved,
My play-mate when we both were clothed alike!

Dear Babe, that sleepest cradled by my side,
Whose gentle breathings, heard in this deep calm,   45
Fill up the interspersèd vacancies
And momentary pauses of the thought!
My babe so beautiful! it thrills my heart
With tender gladness, thus to look at thee,
And think that thou shalt learn far other lore,   50
And in far other scenes! For I was reared
In the great city, pent 'mid cloisters dim,
And saw nought lovely but the sky and stars.
But *thou*, my babe! shalt wander like a breeze
By lakes and sandy shores, beneath the crags   55
Of ancient mountain, and beneath the clouds,
Which image in their bulk both lakes and shores
And mountain crags: so shalt thou see and hear
The lovely shapes and sounds intelligible
Of that eternal language, which thy God   60
Utters, who from eternity doth teach
Himself in all, and all things in himself.
Great universal Teacher! he shall mould
Thy spirit, and by giving make it ask.

Therefore all seasons shall be sweet to thee,   65
Whether the summer clothe the general earth
With greenness, or the redbreast sit and sing
Betwixt the tufts of snow on the bare branch
Of mossy apple-tree, while the nigh thatch

Smokes in the sun-thaw; whether the eave-drops fall
Heard only in the trances of the blast,
Or if the secret ministry of frost
Shall hang them up in silent icicles,
Quietly shining to the quiet Moon.

28

Fears in Solitude

WRITTEN IN APRIL 1798,
DURING THE ALARM OF AN INVASION

A green and silent spot, amid the hills,
A small and silent dell! O'er stiller place
No singing sky-lark ever poised himself.
The hills are heathy, save that swelling slope,
Which hath a gay and gorgeous covering on,　　　5
All golden with the never-bloomless furze,
Which now blooms most profusely: but the dell,
Bathed by the mist, is fresh and delicate
As vernal corn-field, or the unripe flax,
When, through its half-transparent stalks, at eve,　　10
The level sunshine glimmers with green light.
Oh! 'tis a quiet spirit-healing nook!
Which all, methinks, would love; but chiefly he,
The humble man, who, in his youthful years,
Knew just so much of folly, as had made　　　15
His early manhood more securely wise!
Here he might lie on fern or withered heath,
While from the singing lark (that sings unseen
The minstrelsy that solitude loves best),
And from the sun, and from the breezy air,　　　20
Sweet influences trembled o'er his frame;
And he, with many feelings, many thoughts,
Made up a meditative joy, and found
Religious meanings in the forms of Nature!
And so, his senses gradually wrapt　　　25
In a half sleep, he dreams of better worlds,
And dreaming hears thee still, O singing lark,
That singest like an angel in the clouds!

　　My God! it is a melancholy thing
For such a man, who would full fain preserve　　30
His soul in calmness, yet perforce must feel
For all his human brethren – O my God!

49

It weighs upon the heart, that he must think
What uproar and what strife may now be stirring
This way or that way o'er these silent hills—   35
Invasion, and the thunder and the shout,
And all the crash of onset; fear and rage,
And undetermined conflict – even now,
Even now, perchance, and in his native isle:
Carnage and groans beneath this blessed sun!   40
We have offended, Oh! my countrymen!
We have offended very grievously,
And been most tyrannous. From east to west
A groan of accusation pierces Heaven!
The wretched plead against us; multitudes   45
Countless and vehement, the sons of God,
Our brethren! Like a cloud that travels on,
Steamed up from Cairo's swamps of pestilence,
Even so, my countrymen! have we gone forth
And borne to distant tribes slavery and pangs,   50
And, deadlier far, our vices, whose deep taint
With slow perdition murders the whole man,
His body and his soul! Meanwhile, at home,
All individual dignity and power
Engulfed in Courts, Committees, Institutions,   55
Associations and Societies,
A vain, speech-mouthing, speech-reporting Guild,
One Benefit-Club for mutual flattery,
We have drunk up, demure as at a grace,
Pollutions from the brimming cup of wealth;   60
Contemptuous of all honourable rule,
Yet bartering freedom and the poor man's life
For gold, as at a market! The sweet words
Of Christian promise, words that even yet
Might stem destruction, were they wisely preached,   65
Are muttered o'er by men, whose tones proclaim
How flat and wearisome they feel their trade:
Rank scoffers some, but most too indolent
To deem them falsehoods or to know their truth.
Oh! blasphemous! the Book of Life is made   70
A superstitious instrument, on which
We gabble o'er the oaths we mean to break;
For all must swear – all and in every place,

College and wharf, council and justice-court;
All, all must swear, the briber and the bribed,   75
Merchant and lawyer, senator and priest,
The rich, the poor, the old man and the young;
All, all make up one scheme of perjury,
That faith doth reel; the very name of God
Sounds like a juggler's charm; and, bold with joy,   80
Forth from his dark and lonely hiding-place,
(Portentous sight!) the owlet Atheism,
Sailing on obscene wings athwart the noon,
Drops his blue-fringéd lids, and holds them close,
And hooting at the glorious sun in Heaven,   85
Cries out, "Where is it?"

                               Thankless too for peace,
(Peace long preserved by fleets and perilous seas)
Secure from actual warfare, we have loved
To swell the war-whoop, passionate for war!
Alas! for ages ignorant of all   90
Its ghastlier workings, (famine or blue plague,
Battle, or siege, or flight through wintry snows,)
We, this whole people, have been clamorous
For war and bloodshed; animating sports,
The which we pay for as a thing to talk of,   95
Spectators and not combatants! No guess
Anticipative of a wrong unfelt,
No speculation on contingency,
However dim and vague, too vague and dim
To yield a justifying cause; and forth,   100
(Stuffed out with big preamble, holy names,
And adjurations of the God in Heaven,)
We send our mandates for the certain death
Of thousands and ten thousands! Boys and girls,
And women, that would groan to see a child   105
Pull off an insect's leg, all read of war,
The best amusement for our morning meal!
The poor wretch, who has learnt his only prayers
From curses, who knows scarcely words enough
To ask a blessing from his Heavenly Father,   110
Becomes a fluent phraseman, absolute
And technical in victories and defeats,

And all our dainty terms for fratricide;
Terms which we trundle smoothly o'er our tongues
Like mere abstractions, empty sounds to which   115
We join no feeling and attach no form!
As if the soldier died without a wound;
As if the fibres of this godlike frame
Were gored without a pang; as if the wretch,
Who fell in battle, doing bloody deeds,   120
Passed off to Heaven, translated and not killed;
As though he had no wife to pine for him,
No God to judge him! Therefore, evil days
Are coming on us, O my countrymen!
And what if all-avenging Providence,   125
Strong and retributive, should make us know
The meaning of our words, force us to feel
The desolation and the agony
Of our fierce doings?

      Spare us yet awhile,
Father and God! O! spare us yet awhile!   130
Oh! let not English women drag their flight
Fainting beneath the burthen of their babes,
Of the sweet infants, that but yesterday
Laughed at the breast! Sons, brothers, husbands, all
Who ever gazed with fondness on the forms   135
Which grew up with you round the same fire-side,
And all who ever heard the sabbath-bells
Without the infidel's scorn, make yourselves pure!
Stand forth! be men! repel an impious foe,
Impious and false, a light yet cruel race,   140
Who laugh away all virtue, mingling mirth
With deeds of murder; and still promising
Freedom, themselves too sensual to be free,
Poison life's amities, and cheat the heart
Of faith and quiet hope, and all that soothes,   145
And all that lifts the spirit! Stand we forth;
Render them back upon the insulted ocean,
And let them toss as idly on its waves
As the vile sea-weed, which some mountain-blast
Swept from our shores! And oh! may we return   150
Not with a drunken triumph, but with fear,

Repenting of the wrongs with which we stung
So fierce a foe to frenzy!

                    I have told,
O Britons! O my brethren! I have told
Most bitter truth, but without bitterness.   155
Nor deem my zeal or factious or mistimed;
For never can true courage dwell with them,
Who, playing tricks with conscience, dare not look
At their own vices. We have been too long
Dupes of a deep delusion! Some, belike,   160
Groaning with restless enmity, expect
All change from change of constituted power;
As if a Government had been a robe,
On which our vice and wretchedness were tagged
Like fancy-points and fringes, with the robe   165
Pulled off at pleasure. Fondly these attach
A radical causation to a few
Poor drudges of chastising Providence,
Who borrow all their hues and qualities
From our own folly and rank wickedness,   170
Which gave them birth and nursed them. Others, meanwhile,
Dote with a mad idolatry; and all
Who will not fall before their images,
And yield them worship, they are enemies
Even of their country!

                    Such have I been deemed. –   175
But, O dear Britain! O my Mother Isle!
Needs must thou prove a name most dear and holy
To me, a son, a brother, and a friend,
A husband, and a father! who revere
All bonds of natural love, and find them all   180
Within the limits of thy rocky shores.
O native Britain! O my Mother Isle!
How shouldst thou prove aught else but dear and holy
To me, who from thy lakes and mountain-hills,
Thy clouds, thy quiet dales, thy rocks and seas,   185
Have drunk in all my intellectual life,
All sweet sensations, all ennobling thoughts,
All adoration of the God in nature,

All lovely and all honourable things,
Whatever makes this mortal spirit feel   190
The joy and greatness of its future being?
There lives nor form nor feeling in my soul
Unborrowed from my country! O divine
And beauteous island! thou hast been my sole
And most magnificent temple, in the which   195
I walk with awe, and sing my stately songs,
Loving the God that made me! –

                                        May my fears,
My filial fears, be vain! and may the vaunts
And menace of the vengeful enemy
Pass like the gust, that roared and died away   200
In the distant tree: which heard, and only heard
In this low dell, bowed not the delicate grass.

   But now the gentle dew-fall sends abroad
The fruit-like perfume of the golden furze:
The light has left the summit of the hill,   205
Though still a sunny gleam lies beautiful,
Aslant the ivied beacon. Now farewell,
Farewell, awhile, O soft and silent spot!
On the green sheep-track, up the heathy hill,
Homeward I wind my way; and lo! recalled   210
From bodings that have well-nigh wearied me,
I find myself upon the brow, and pause
Startled! And after lonely sojourning
In such a quiet and surrounded nook,
This burst of prospect, here the shadowy main,   215
Dim-tinted, there the mighty majesty
Of that huge amphitheatre of rich
And elmy fields, seems like society –
Conversing with the mind, and giving it
A livelier impulse and a dance of thought!   220
And now, beloved Stowey! I behold
Thy church-tower, and, methinks, the four huge elms
Clustering, which mark the mansion of my friend;
And close behind them, hidden from my view,
Is my own lowly cottage, where my babe   225
And my babe's mother dwell in peace! With light

And quickened footsteps thitherward I tend,
Remembering thee, O green and silent dell!
And grateful, that by nature's quietness
And solitary musings, all my heart   230
Is softened, and made worthy to indulge
Love, and the thoughts that yearn for human kind.

29

The Nightingale

No cloud, no relique of the sunken day
Distinguishes the West, no long thin slip
Of sullen light, no obscure trembling hues.
Come, we will rest on this old mossy bridge!
You see the glimmer of the stream beneath,   5
But hear no murmuring: it flows silently,
O'er its soft bed of verdure. All is still,
A balmy night! and though the stars be dim,
Yet let us think upon the vernal showers
That gladden the green earth, and we shall find   10
A pleasure in the dimness of the stars.
And hark! the Nightingale begins its song,
"Most musical, most melancholy" bird!
A melancholy bird? Oh! idle thought!
In Nature there is nothing melancholy.   15
But some night-wandering man whose heart was pierced
With the remembrance of a grievous wrong,
Or slow distemper, or neglected love,
(And so, poor wretch! filled all things with himself,
And made all gentle sounds tell back the tale   20
Of his own sorrow) he, and such as he,
First named these notes a melancholy strain.
And many a poet echoes the conceit;
Poet who hath been building up the rhyme
When he had better far have stretched his limbs   25
Beside a brook in mossy forest-dell,
By sun or moon-light, to the influxes
Of shapes and sounds and shifting elements
Surrendering his whole spirit, of his song
And of his fame forgetful! so his fame   30
Should share in Nature's immortality,
A venerable thing! and so his song
Should make all Nature lovelier, and itself
Be loved like Nature! But 'twill not be so;

And youths and maidens most poetical,   35
Who lose the deepening twilights of the spring
In ball-rooms and hot theatres, they still
Full of meek sympathy must heave their sighs
O'er Philomela's pity-pleading strains.

My Friend, and thou, our Sister! we have learnt   40
A different lore: we may not thus profane
Nature's sweet voices, always full of love
And joyance! 'Tis the merry Nightingale
That crowds, and hurries, and precipitates
With fast thick warble his delicious notes,   45
As he were fearful that an April night
Would be too short for him to utter forth
His love-chant, and disburthen his full soul
Of all its music!

    And I know a grove
Of large extent, hard by a castle huge,   50
Which the great lord inhabits not; and so
This grove is wild with tangling underwood,
And the trim walks are broken up, and grass,
Thin grass and king-cups grow within the paths.
But never elsewhere in one place I knew   55
So many nightingales; and far and near,
In wood and thicket, over the wide grove,
They answer and provoke each other's song,
With skirmish and capricious passagings,
And murmurs musical and swift jug jug,   60
And one low piping sound more sweet than all –
Stirring the air with such a harmony,
That should you close your eyes, you might almost
Forget it was not day! On moonlight bushes,
Whose dewy leaflets are but half-disclosed,   65
You may perchance behold them on the twigs,
Their bright, bright eyes, their eyes both bright and full,
Glistening, while many a glow-worm in the shade
Lights up her love-torch.

    A most gentle Maid,
Who dwelleth in her hospitable home   70

Hard by the castle, and at latest eve
(Even like a Lady vowed and dedicate
To something more than Nature in the grove)
Glides through the pathways; she knows all their notes,
That gentle Maid! and oft, a moment's space,   75
What time the moon was lost behind a cloud,
Hath heard a pause of silence; till the moon
Emerging, hath awakened earth and sky
With one sensation, and those wakeful birds
Have all burst forth in choral minstrelsy,   80
As if some sudden gale had swept at once
A hundred airy harps! And she hath watched
Many a nightingale perch giddily
On blossomy twig still swinging from the breeze,
And to that motion tune his wanton song   85
Like tipsy Joy that reels with tossing head.

Farewell, O Warbler! till to-morrow eve,
And you, my friends! farewell, a short farewell!
We have been loitering long and pleasantly,
And now for our dear homes. – That strain again!   90
Full fain it would delay me! My dear babe,
Who, capable of no articulate sound,
Mars all things with his imitative lisp,
How he would place his hand beside his ear,
His little hand, the small forefinger up,   95
And bid us listen! And I deem it wise
To make him Nature's play-mate. He knows well
The evening-star; and once, when he awoke
In most distressful mood (some inward pain
Had made up that strange thing, an infant's dream –)   100
I hurried with him to our orchard-plot,
And he beheld the moon, and, hushed at once,
Suspends his sobs, and laughs most silently,
While his fair eyes, that swam with undropped tears,
Did glitter in the yellow moon-beam! Well! –   105
It is a father's tale: But if that Heaven
Should give me life, his childhood shall grow up
Familiar with these songs, that with the night
He may associate joy. – Once more, farewell,
Sweet Nightingale! once more, my friends! farewell.   110

58

To William Wordsworth

Friend of the wise! and Teacher of the Good!
Into my heart have I received that Lay
More than historic, that prophetic Lay
Wherein (high theme by thee first sung aright)
Of the foundations and the building up   5
Of a Human Spirit thou hast dared to tell
What may be told, to the understanding mind
Revealable; and what within the mind
By vital breathings secret as the soul
Of vernal growth, oft quickens in the heart   10
Thoughts all too deep for words! —

                         Theme hard as high!
Of smiles spontaneous, and mysterious fears
(The first-born they of Reason and twin-birth),
Of tides obedient to external force,
And currents self-determined, as might seem,   15
Or by some inner Power; of moments awful,
Now in thy inner life, and now abroad,
When power streamed from thee, and thy soul received
The light reflected, as a light bestowed —
Of fancies fair, and milder hours of youth,   20
Hyblean murmurs of poetic thought
Industrious in its joy, in vales and glens
Native or outland, lakes and famous hills!
Or on the lonely high-road, when the stars
Were rising; or by secret mountain-streams,   25
The guides and the companions of thy way!

Of more than Fancy, of the Social Sense
Distending wide, and man beloved as man,
Where France in all her towns lay vibrating
Like some becalméd bark beneath the burst   30
Of Heaven's immediate thunder, when no cloud

Is visible, or shadow on the main.
For thou wert there, thine own brows garlanded,
Amid the tremor of a realm aglow,
Amid a mighty nation jubilant,   35
When from the general heart of human kind
Hope sprang forth like a full-born Deity!
— Of that dear Hope afflicted and struck down,
So summoned homeward, thenceforth calm and sure
From the dread watch-tower of man's absolute self,   40
With light unwaning on her eyes, to look
Far on — herself a glory to behold,
The Angel of the vision! Then (last strain)
Of Duty, chosen Laws controlling choice,
Action and joy! – An Orphic song indeed,   45
A song divine of high and passionate thoughts
To their own music chaunted!

                              O great Bard!
Ere yet that last strain dying awed the air,
With stedfast eye I viewed thee in the choir
Of ever-enduring men. The truly great   50
Have all one age, and from one visible space
Shed influence! They, both in power and act,
Are permanent, and Time is not with them,
Save as it worketh for them, they in it.
Nor less a sacred Roll, than those of old,   55
And to be placed, as they, with gradual fame
Among the archives of mankind, thy work
Makes audible a linkéd lay of Truth,
Of Truth profound a sweet continuous lay,
Not learnt, but native, her own natural notes!   60
Ah! as I listened with a heart forlorn,
The pulses of my being beat anew:
And even as Life returns upon the drowned,
Life's joy rekindling roused a throng of pains —
Keen pangs of Love, awakening as a babe   65
Turbulent, with an outcry in the heart;
And fears self-willed, that shunned the eye of Hope;
And Hope that scarce would know itself from Fear;
Sense of past Youth, and Manhood come in vain,
And Genius given, and Knowledge won in vain;   70

And all which I had culled in wood-walks wild,
And all which patient toil had reared, and all,
Commune with thee had opened out – but flowers
Strewed on my corse, and borne upon my bier,
In the same coffin, for the self-same grave!   75

    That way no more! and ill beseems it me,
Who came a welcomer in herald's guise,
Singing of Glory, and Futurity,
To wander back on such unhealthful road,
Plucking the poisons of self-harm! And ill   80
Such intertwine beseems triumphal wreaths
Strew'd before thy advancing!

                    Nor do thou,
Sage Bard! impair the memory of that hour
Of thy communion with my nobler mind
By pity or grief, already felt too long!   85
Nor let my words import more blame than needs.
The tumult rose and ceased: for Peace is nigh
Where Wisdom's voice has found a listening heart.
Amid the howl of more than wintry storms,
The Halcyon hears the voice of vernal hours   90
Already on the wing.

              Eve following eve,
Dear tranquil time, when the sweet sense of Home
Is sweetest! moments for their own sake hailed
And more desired, more precious, for thy song,
In silence listening, like a devout child,   95
My soul lay passive, by thy various strain
Driven as in surges now beneath the stars,
With momentary stars of my own birth,
Fair constellated foam, still darting off
Into the darkness; now a tranquil sea,   100
Outspread and bright, yet swelling to the moon.

And when – O Friend! my comforter and guide!
Strong in thyself, and powerful to give strength! –
Thy long sustainéd Song finally closed,
And thy deep voice had ceased – yet thou thyself   105

Wert still before my eyes, and round us both
That happy vision of belovéd faces –
Scarce conscious, and yet conscious of its close
I sate, my being blended in one thought
(Thought was it? or aspiration? or resolve?)   110
Absorbed, yet hanging still upon the sound –
And when I rose, I found myself in prayer.

III

BALLADS

Ballads

PREFACE

COLERIDGE PUBLISHED SIX BALLADS over a period of thirty years. They are the most consciously experimental part of his work, and although three of them are unfinished, they total over two thousand lines of verse with many additional drafts and rejected versions. A number of shorter poems, collected in the Visionary Fragments section (VII), may also be sketches or openings for others. He developed the form through experiments in variable metre; the incantatory effects of rhyme and repetition; archaic and magical use of vocabulary; and the symbolic use of natural imagery.

The ballad always fascinated Coleridge as a popular type of story-telling which broke the conventions of eighteenth-century realism, and gave access to extreme and primitive emotions. Many of his ballads puzzled and shocked even his most perceptive contemporaries like Wordsworth and Hazlitt. At some symbolic level, they touched on the disturbing elements of human experience which are normally censored by the rational mind. All of them concern some violent or "forbidden" action or event, that has inexplicably terrible consequences.

In chapter 14 of the *Biographia Literaria*, Coleridge described his ballads as "directed to persons and characters supernatural". He later intended to write "a critical essay on the supernatural in poetry, and the principles that regulate its introduction"; but perhaps deliberately this was never done. Some of his ideas appear in the preface to "The Three Graves" (No. 31), and later scattered through his Notebooks and *Table Talk*. He said he had personally seen "far too many" ghosts actually to believe in them; and it is clear that it was the psychology and symbolism of the supernatural (closely related to that of dreams) which interested him.

The ballads are often thought of as uniformly "nightmare" pieces, whereas in fact their atmospheres and settings are diverse: an

65

eighteenth-century country village (No. 31), a seventeenth-century sea-voyage (No. 32), a fifteenth-century castle (No. 33), and other loosely medieval or courtly scenarios. Their literary sources are also various: folk tales, fairy tales, travellers' stories, legends, dreams. But all of them can be described as studies in irrational experiences, with a strong emphasis on ideas of enchantment or possession or violation.

Most of the six ballads present supernatural or "daemonic" forces in Nature, battoning on human protagonists, and subjecting them to extreme stress. Three of the victims are women, three are men, all are young. (Coleridge pointed out that even the Mariner was young at the time of his voyage.) Their experiences are not easily subject to rational, or even religious, explanation. The forces are given figurative (but not always human) shape and great psychological authenticity. Coleridge wanted "these shadows of the imagination" to produce what he called, in a famous phrase, "that willing suspension of disbelief for the moment, that constitutes poetic faith".

As a form, the popular or "gothick" ballad was not itself Coleridge's rediscovery. Wide interest had already been aroused by the collection of Border Ballads published by the folklorist Bishop Thomas Percy (who was also an expert on Oriental Tales and Icelandic Sagas) as *Reliques of Ancient English Poetry* (3 vols., 1765). This collection contained "Sir Patrick Spence" (referred to by Coleridge in "Dejection: An Ode", No. 50), "Barbara Allen", and "Sir Cauline" (whose heroine is "fayre Christabelle"). The forged medieval ballads of Thomas Chatterton (edited by Southey), and the horror-ballad "Lenore" (1774) by the German poet Gottfried Bürger, were also fashionable. Wordsworth originally suggested the form to Coleridge in 1797, perhaps not entirely seriously, as a way of making money from the magazines, and his first efforts were collaborations (see Nos. 31 and 75).

Coleridge took the popular themes of folklore – the demon lover, the nightmare voyage, the haunted castle, the *femme fatale* – and transformed them into sophisticated psychological dramas, which explore the dark side of his imagination. All kinds of childhood fears, adult obsessions, problems of identity, guilts, hallucinatory experiences, sexual fantasies, and religious doubts are released into the poems with most powerful effect. Time and again, it is evident that the protagonists of the ballads (of either sex) are, at some level, Coleridge himself.

But the very formality of the eighteenth-century ballad conventions encouraged Coleridge to transcend confessional restraints. The impetuous narrative movement, the use of framing voices, the archaic or naïve stylization, the daemonic figures, the gothick imagery, the chant-like phrasing, and the whole emphasis on direct dramatic presentation (rather than meditation) helped to free him from conscious censorship or poetic inhibitions. In an almost anthropological sense, he could enter into areas of the "taboo". Witchcraft (No. 31), paranoid delusions (No. 32), sexual violation (No. 33), possession (No. 35), and murderous jealousy (No. 36) are all touched on with extraordinary daring.

The artistic freedom with which Coleridge developed the basic four-line, four-stress pattern of the traditional ballad stanza is also remarkable. The visual and cosmic symbolism of the poems (which has received much study) also depends on certain music and cadence within the language, which produces magical effects of spell-binding incantation through repetition and internal rhyme:

> The harbour-bay was clear as glass
> So smoothly it was strewn!
> And on the bay the moonlight lay
> And the shadow of the Moon.

In a Preface to "Christabel" Coleridge also hinted how the sudden extending or contracting of syllabic structures, and stanza lengths, could express shifts of feeling. They were "not introduced wantonly, or for the mere ends of convenience, but in correspondence with some transition in the nature of the imagery or passion".

Though Coleridge began most of his ballads in the Stowey period, he worked on them for many years, quite contrary to the common belief that they were the product of a single inspired period of his life. "The Rime of the Ancient Mariner" went through at least three major versions, and took nineteen years to reach its final form (with the brilliant framing device of the prose "gloss") in 1817. The two parts of "Christabel" were composed over three years, and there is evidence for a lost third part which Coleridge was working on as late as 1816 (see No. 85). "The Three Graves", which first appeared in 1809, seems to have been reworked over a decade. "Alice Du Clos" was not written until the 1820s, but still shows new effects of narrative and imagery.

The literary impact of Coleridge's ballads was also extended over a considerable time, as they came to be better understood. It is most immediately evident in Scott's *Lay of the Last Minstrel* (1805); Keats's poems "La Belle Dame Sans Merci" and "St Agnes Eve" (1820); and Shelley's "Mask of Anarchy" (1819). The general revival of gothick and medieval styles in Victorian England, and the whole of the Pre-Raphaelite Movement, owes much to their settings and use of symbolism. Tennyson, Morris and Ruskin all learned from them; and even such a strange invention as Christina Rossetti's ballad "Goblin Market" shows their subtle influence. Nor should it be forgotten that when Byron read "Christabel" aloud at the Villa Diodati, one stormy night in June 1816, Shelley ran out in a fit and Mary Shelley began her novel *Frankenstein*.

The Three Graves

A FRAGMENT OF A SEXTON'S TALE

"The Author has published the following humble fragment, encouraged by the decisive recommendation of more than one of our most celebrated living Poets. The language was intended to be dramatic; that is, suited to the narrator; and the metre corresponds to the homeliness of the diction. It is therefore presented as the fragment, not of a Poem, but of a common Ballad-tale. Whether this is sufficient to justify the adoption of such a style, in any metrical composition not professedly ludicrous, the Author is himself in some doubt. At all events, it is not presented as poetry, and it is in no way connected with the Author's judgment concerning poetic diction. Its merits, if any, are exclusively psychological. The story which must be supposed to have been narrated in the first and second parts is as follows: –

"Edward, a young farmer, meets at the house of Ellen her bosom-friend Mary, and commences an acquaintance, which ends in a mutual attachment. With her consent, and by the advice of their common friend Ellen, he announces his hopes and intentions to Mary's mother, a widow-woman bordering on her fortieth year, and from constant health, the possession of a competent property, and from having had no other children but Mary and another daughter (the father died in their infancy), retaining for the greater part her personal attractions and comeliness of appearance; but a woman of low education and violent temper. The answer which she at once returned to Edward's application was remarkable – 'Well, Edward! you are a handsome young fellow, and you shall have my daughter.' From this time all their wooing passed under the mother's eye; and, in fine, she became herself enamoured of her future son-in-law, and practised every art, both of endearment and of calumny, to transfer his affections from her daughter to herself. (The outlines of the Tale are positive facts, and of no very distant date, though the author has purposely altered the names and the scene of action, as well as invented the characters of the parties and the detail of the incidents.) Edward, however, though perplexed by her strange detractions from her daughter's good qualities, yet in the innocence of his own heart still mistook her increasing fondness for motherly affection; she at length, overcome by her miserable passion, after much abuse of Mary's temper and moral tendencies, exclaimed with violent emotion – 'O Edward! indeed, indeed, she is not fit for you – she has not a heart to love you as you deserve. It is I that love you! Marry me, Edward! and I will this very day settle all my property on you.' The Lover's eyes were now opened; and thus taken by surprise, whether from the effect of the horror which he felt, acting as it were hysterically on his nervous system, or that at the first moment he lost the sense of the guilt of the proposal in the feeling of its strangeness and absurdity, he flung her from him and burst into a fit of laughter. Irritated by this almost to frenzy, the woman fell on her knees, and in a loud voice that approached to a scream, she prayed for a curse both on him and on her own child. Mary happened to be in the room directly above them, heard Edward's laugh, and her mother's blasphemous prayer, and fainted away. He, hearing the fall, ran upstairs, and taking her in his arms, carried her off to Ellen's home; and after some fruitless attempts on her part toward a reconciliation with her mother, she was married to him. – And here the third part of the Tale begins.

"I was not led to choose this story from any partiality to tragic, much less to monstrous events (though at the time that I composed the verses, somewhat more than twelve years ago, I was less averse to such subjects than at present), but from finding in it a striking proof of the possible effect on the imagination, from an idea violently and suddenly impressed on it. I had been reading Bryan Edwards's account of the effects of the *Oby* witchcraft on the Negroes in the West Indies, and Hearne's deeply interesting anecdotes of similar workings on the imagination of the Copper Indians (those of my readers who have it in their power will be well repaid for the trouble of referring to those works for the passages alluded to); and I conceived the design of shewing that instances of this kind are not peculiar to savage or barbarous tribes, and of illustrating the mode in which the mind is affected in these cases, and the progress and symptoms of the morbid action on the fancy from the beginning.

"The Tale is supposed to be narrated by an old Sexton, in a country church-yard, to a traveller whose curiosity had been awakened by the appearance of three graves, close by each other, to two only of which there were grave-stones. On the first of these was the name, and dates, as usual: on the second, no name, but only a date, and the words, 'The Mercy of God is infinite.'"

The grapes upon the Vicar's wall
 Were ripe as ripe could be;
And yellow leaves in sun and wind
 Were falling from the tree.

On the hedge-elms in the narrow lane   5
 Still swung the spikes of corn:
Dear Lord! it seems but yesterday –
 Young Edward's marriage-morn.

Up through that wood behind the church,
 There leads from Edward's door   10
A mossy track, all over boughed,
 For half a mile or more.

And from their house-door by that track
 The bride and bridegroom went;
Sweet Mary, though she was not gay,   15
 Seemed cheerful and content.

But when they to the church-yard came,
 I've heard poor Mary say,
As soon as she stepped into the sun,
 Her heart it died away.   20

And when the Vicar join'd their hands,
 Her limbs did creep and freeze:
But when they prayed, she thought she saw
 Her mother on her knees.

And o'er the church-path they returned –   25
 I saw poor Mary's back,
Just as she stepped beneath the boughs
 Into the mossy track.

Her feet upon the mossy track
 The married maiden set: 30
That moment – I have heard her say –
 She wished she could forget.

The shade o'er-flushed her limbs with heat —
    Then came a chill like death:
And when the merry bells rang out,   35
    They seemed to stop her breath.

Beneath the foulest mother's curse
    No child could ever thrive:
A mother is a mother still,
    The holiest thing alive.   40

So five months passed: the mother still
    Would never heal the strife;
But Edward was a loving man
    And Mary a fond wife.

"My sister may not visit us,   45
    My mother says her nay:
O Edward! you are all to me,
I wish for your sake I could be
    More lifesome and more gay.

"I'm dull and sad! indeed, indeed   50
    I know I have no reason!'
Perhaps I am not well in health,
    And 'tis a gloomy season."

'Twas a drizzly time — no ice, no snow!
    And on the few fine days   55
She stirred not out, lest she might meet
    Her mother in the ways.

But Ellen, spite of miry ways
    And weather dark and dreary,
Trudged every day to Edward's house,   60
    And made them all more cheery.

Oh! Ellen was a faithful friend,
    More dear than any sister!
As cheerful too as singing lark;
And she ne'er left them till 'twas dark,   65
    And then they always missed her.

And now Ash-Wednesday came – that day
    But few to church repair:
For on that day you know we read
    The Commination prayer.   70

Our late old Vicar, a kind man,
    Once, Sir, he said to me,
He wished that service was clean out
    Of our good Liturgy.

The mother walked into the church –   75
    To Ellen's seat she went:
Though Ellen always kept her church
    All church-days during Lent.

And gentle Ellen welcomed her
    With courteous looks and mild: 80
Thought she, "What if her heart should melt,
    And all be reconciled!"

The day was scarcely like a day –
    The clouds were black outright:
And many a night, with half a moon,   85
    I've seen the church more light.

The wind was wild; against the glass
    The rain did beat and bicker;
The church-tower swinging over head,
    You scarce could hear the Vicar!   90

And then and there the mother knelt,
    And audibly she cried –
"Oh! may a clinging curse consume
    This woman by my side!

"O hear me, hear me, Lord in Heaven,   95
    Although you take my life –
O curse this woman, at whose house
    Young Edward woo'd his wife.

"By night and day, in bed and bower,
    O let her curséd be!!!"
So having prayed, steady and slow,
    She rose up from her knee!
And left the church, nor e'er again
    The church-door entered she.

I saw poor Ellen kneeling still,   105
    So pale! I guessed not why:
When she stood up, there plainly was
    A trouble in her eye.

And when the prayers were done, we all
    Came round and asked her why: 110
Giddy she seemed, and sure, there was
    A trouble in her eye.

But ere she from the church-door stepped
    She smiled and told us why:
"It was a wicked woman's curse,"   115
    Quoth she, "and what care I?"

She smiled, and smiled, and passed it off
    Ere from the door she stept –
But all agree it would have been
    Much better had she wept.   120

And if her heart was not at ease,
    This was her constant cry –
"It was a wicked woman's curse –
    God's good, and what care I?"

There was a hurry in her looks,   125
    Her struggles she redoubled:
"It was a wicked woman's curse,
    And why should I be troubled?"

These tears will come – I dandled her
    When 'twas the merest fairy –   130
Good creature! and she hid it all:
    She told it not to Mary.

But Mary heard the tale: her arms
   Round Ellen's neck she threw;
"O Ellen, Ellen, she cursed me,   135
   And now she hath cursed you!"

I saw young Edward by himself
   Stalk fast adown the lee,
He snatched a stick from every fence,
   A twig from every tree.   140

He snapped them still with hand or knee,
   And then away they flew!
As if with his uneasy limbs
   He knew not what to do!

You see, good sir! that single hill?   145
   His farm lies underneath:
He heard it there, he heard it all,
   And only gnashed his teeth.

Now Ellen was a darling love
   In all his joys and cares: 150
And Ellen's name and Mary's name
Fast-linked they both together came,
   Whene'er he said his prayers.

And in the moment of his prayers
   He loved them both alike: 155
Yea, both sweet names with one sweet joy
   Upon his heart did strike!

He reach'd his home, and by his looks
   They saw his inward strife:
And they clung round him with their arms,   160
   Both Ellen and his wife.

And Mary could not check her tears,
   So on his breast she bowed;
Then frenzy melted into grief,
   And Edward wept aloud.   165

Dear Ellen did not weep at all,
    But closelier did she cling,
And turned her face and looked as if
    She saw some frightful thing.

PART IV

To see a man tread over graves   170
    I hold it no good mark;
'Tis wicked in the sun and moon,
    And bad luck in the dark!

You see that grave? The Lord he gives,
    The Lord, he takes away: 175
O Sir! the child of my old age
    Lies there as cold as clay.

Except that grave, you scarce see one
    That was not dug by me;
I'd rather dance upon 'em all   180
    Than tread upon these three!

"Aye, Sexton! 'tis a touching tale."
    You, Sir! are but a lad;
This month I'm in my seventieth year,
    And still it makes me sad.   185

And Mary's sister told it me,
    For three good hours and more;
Though I had heard it, in the main,
    From Edward's self, before.

Well! it passed off! the gentle Ellen   190
    Did well nigh dote on Mary;
And she went oftener than before,
And Mary loved her more and more:
    She managed all the dairy.

To market she on market-days,   195
    To church on Sundays came;
All seemed the same: all seemed so, Sir!
    But all was not the same!

Had Ellen lost her mirth? Oh! no!
   But she was seldom cheerful;   200
And Edward looked as if he thought
   That Ellen's mirth was fearful.

When by herself, she to herself
   Must sing some merry rhyme;
She could not now be glad for hours,   205
   Yet silent all the time.

And when she soothed her friend, through all
   Her soothing words 'twas plain
She had a sore grief of her own,
   A haunting in her brain.   210

And oft she said, I'm not grown thin!
   And then her wrist she spanned;
And once when Mary was down-cast,
   She took her by the hand,
And gazed upon her, and at first   215
   She gently pressed her hand;

Then harder, till her grasp at length
   Did gripe like a convulsion!
"Alas!" said she, "we ne'er can be
   Made happy by compulsion!"   220

And once her both arms suddenly
   Round Mary's neck she flung,
And her heart panted, and she felt
   The words upon her tongue.

She felt them coming, but no power   225
   Had she the words to smother;
And with a kind of shriek she cried,
   "Oh Christ! you're like your mother!"

So gentle Ellen now no more
   Could make this sad house cheery;   230
And Mary's melancholy ways
   Drove Edward wild and weary.

Lingering he raised his latch at eve,
    Though tired in heart and limb:
He loved no other place, and yet   235
    Home was no home to him.

One evening he took up a book,
    And nothing in it read;
Then flung it down, and groaning cried,
    "O! Heaven! that I were dead."   240

Mary looked up into his face,
    And nothing to him said;
She tried to smile, and on his arm
    Mournfully leaned her head.

And he burst into tears, and fell   245
    Upon his knees in prayer:
"Her heart is broke! O God! my grief,
    It is too great to bear!"

'Twas such a foggy time as makes
    Old sextons, Sir! like me,   250
Rest on their spades to cough; the spring
    Was late uncommonly.

And then the hot days, all at once,
    They came, we knew not how:
You looked about for shade, when scarce   255
    A leaf was on a bough.

It happened then ('twas in the bower,
    A furlong up the wood:
Perhaps you know the place, and yet
    I scarce know how you should,)   260

No path leads thither, 'tis not nigh
    To any pasture-plot;
But clustered near the chattering brook,
    Lone hollies marked the spot.

Those hollies of themselves a shape   265
    As of an arbour took,
A close, round arbour; and it stands
    Not three strides from a brook.

Within this arbour, which was still
    With scarlet berries hung,   270
Were these three friends, one Sunday morn,
    Just as the first bell rung.

'Tis sweet to hear a brook, 'tis sweet
    To hear the Sabbath-bell,
'Tis sweet to hear them both at once,   275
    Deep in a woody dell.

His limbs along the moss, his head
    Upon a mossy heap,
With shut-up senses, Edward lay:
That brook e'en on a working day   280
    Might chatter one to sleep.

And he had passed a restless night,
    And was not well in health;
The women sat down by his side,
    And talked as 'twere by stealth.   285

"The Sun peeps through the close thick leaves,
    See, dearest Ellen! see!
'Tis in the leaves, a little sun,
    No bigger than your ee;

"A tiny sun, and it has got   290
    A perfect glory too;
Ten thousand threads and hairs of light,
Make up a glory gay and bright
    Round that small orb, so blue."

And then they argued of those rays,   295
    What colour they might be;
Says this, "They're mostly green"; says that,
    "They're amber-like to me."

So they sat chatting, while bad thoughts
    Were troubling Edward's rest;   300
But soon they heard his hard quick pants,
    And the thumping in his breast.

"A mother too!" these self-same words
    Did Edward mutter plain;
His face was drawn back on itself,   305
    With horror and huge pain.

Both groaned at once, for both knew well
    What thoughts were in his mind;
When he waked up, and stared like one
    That hath been just struck blind.   310

He sat upright; and ere the dream
    Had had time to depart,
"O God, forgive me!" (he exclaimed)
    "I have torn out her heart."

Then Ellen shrieked, and forthwith burst   315
    Into ungentle laughter;
And Mary shivered, where she sat,
    And never she smiled after.

32

The Rime of the Ancient Mariner

IN SEVEN PARTS

Facile credo, plures esse Naturas invisibiles quam visibiles in rerum univer-sitate. Sed horum omnium familiam quis nobis enarrabit, et gradus et cognationes et discrimina et singulorum munera? Quid agunt? quæ loca habitant? Harum rerum notitiam semper ambivit ingenium humanum, nun-quam attigit. Juvat, interea, non diffiteor, quandoque in animo, tanquam in tabula, majoris et melioris mundi imaginem contemplari: ne mens assuefacta hodiernæ vitæ minutiis se contrahat nimis, et tota subsidat in pusillas cogit-ationes. Sed veritati interea invigilandum est, modusque servandus, ut certa ab incertis, diem a nocte, distinguamus.

T. Burnet, *Archæol. Phil.* p. 68.

[I can easily believe that there are more invisible creatures in the universe than visible ones. But who will tell us what family each belongs to, what their ranks and relationships are, and what their respective distinguishing characters may be? What do they do? Where do they live? Human wit has always circled around a knowledge of these things without ever attaining it. But I do not doubt that it is beneficial sometimes to contemplate in the mind, as in a picture, the image of a grander and better world; for if the mind grows used to the trivia of daily life, it may dwindle too much and decline altogether into worthless thoughts. Meanwhile, however, we must be on the watch for the truth, keeping a sense of proportion so that we can tell what is certain from what is uncertain and day from night.]

PART I

An ancient Mariner meeteth three Gallants bidden to a wedding-feast, and detaineth one.

It is an ancient Mariner,
And he stoppeth one of three.
"By thy long grey beard and glittering eye,
Now wherefore stopp'st thou me?

The Bridegroom's doors are opened wide,   5
And I am next of kin;
The guests are met, the feast is set:
May'st hear the merry din."

He holds him with his skinny hand,
"There was a ship," quoth he.
"Hold off! unhand me, grey-beard loon!"
Eftsoons his hand dropt he.   10

The Wedding Guest is spellbound by the eye of the old sea-faring man, and constrained to hear his tale.
He holds him with his glittering eye —
The Wedding-Guest stood still,
And listens like a three years' child: 15
The Mariner hath his will.

The Wedding-Guest sat on a stone:
He cannot choose but hear;
And thus spake on that ancient man,
The bright-eyed Mariner.   20

"The ship was cheered, the harbour cleared,
Merrily did we drop
Below the kirk, below the hill,
Below the lighthouse top.

The Mariner tells how the ship sailed southward with a good wind and fair weather, till it reached the line.
The Sun came up upon the left,   25
Out of the sea came he!
And he shone bright, and on the right
Went down into the sea.

Higher and higher every day,
Till over the mast at noon —"   30
The Wedding-Guest here beat his breast,
For he heard the loud bassoon.

The Wedding Guest heareth the bridal music; but the Mariner continueth his tale.
The bride hath paced into the hall,
Red as a rose is she;
Nodding their heads before her goes   35
The merry minstrelsy.

The Wedding-Guest he beat his breast,
Yet he cannot choose but hear;
And thus spake on that ancient man,
The bright-eyed Mariner.   40

The ship drawn by a storm toward the south pole.

"And now the STORM-BLAST came, and he
Was tyrannous and strong:
He struck with his o'ertaking wings,
And chased us south along.

With sloping masts and dipping prow,   45
As who pursued with yell and blow
Still treads the shadow of his foe,
And forward bends his head,
The ship drove fast, loud roared the blast,
And southward aye we fled.   50

And now there came both mist and snow,
And it grew wondrous cold:
And ice, mast-high, came floating by,
As green as emerald.

The land of ice, and of fearful sounds where no living thing was to be seen.

And through the drifts the snowy clifts   55
Did send a dismal sheen:
Nor shapes of men nor beasts we ken –
The ice was all between.

The ice was here, the ice was there,
The ice was all around: 60
It cracked and growled, and roared and howled,
Like noises in a swound!

Till a great sea-bird, called the Albatross, came through the snow-fog, and was received with great joy and hospitality.

At length did cross an Albatross,
Thorough the fog it came;
As if it had been a Christian soul,   65
We hailed it in God's name.

It ate the food it ne'er had eat,
And round and round it flew.
The ice did split with a thunder-fit;
The helmsman steered us through!   70

And lo! the Albatross proveth a bird of good omen, and followeth the ship as it returned northward through fog and floating ice.

And a good south wind sprung up behind;
The Albatross did follow,
And every day, for food or play,
Came to the mariner's hollo!

In mist or cloud, on mast or shroud,   75
It perched for vespers nine;
Whiles all the night, through fog-smoke white,
Glimmered the white Moon-shine."

The ancient
Mariner
inhospitably
killeth the pious
bird of good
omen.

"God save thee, ancient Mariner!
From the fiends, that plague thee thus! —   80
Why look'st thou so?" — With my cross-bow
I shot the ALBATROSS.

PART II

The Sun now rose upon the right:
Out of the sea came he,
Still hid in mist, and on the left   85
Went down into the sea.

And the good south wind still blew behind,
But no sweet bird did follow,
Nor any day for food or play
Came to the mariners' hollo!   90

His shipmates cry
out against the
ancient Mariner,
for killing the bird
of good luck.

And I had done a hellish thing,
And it would work 'em woe:
For all averred, I had killed the bird
That made the breeze to blow.
Ah wretch! said they, the bird to slay,   95
That made the breeze to blow!

But when the fog
cleared off, they
justify the same,
and thus make
themselves
accomplices in
the crime.

Nor dim nor red, like God's own head,
The glorious Sun uprist:
Then all averred, I had killed the bird
That brought the fog and mist.   100
'Twas right, said they, such birds to slay,
That bring the fog and mist.

The fair breeze
continues; the
ship enters the
Pacific Ocean, and
sails northward,
even till it reaches
the Line.

The fair breeze blew, the white foam flew,
The furrow followed free;
We were the first that ever burst   105
Into that silent sea.

The ship hath been suddenly becalmed.

Down dropt the breeze, the sails dropt down,
'Twas sad as sad could be;
And we did speak only to break
The silence of the sea!   110

All in a hot and copper sky,
The bloody Sun, at noon,
Right up above the mast did stand,
No bigger than the Moon.

Day after day, day after day,   115
We stuck, nor breath nor motion;
As idle as a painted ship
Upon a painted ocean.

And the Albatross begins to be avenged.

Water, water, every where,
And all the boards did shrink;   120
Water, water, every where,
Nor any drop to drink.

The very deep did rot: O Christ!
That ever this should be!
Yea, slimy things did crawl with legs   125
Upon the slimy sea.

About, about, in reel and rout
The death-fires danced at night;
The water, like a witch's oils,
Burnt green, and blue and white.   130

A Spirit had followed them; one of the invisible inhabitants of this planet, neither departed souls nor angels; concerning whom the learned Jew, Josephus, and the Platonic Constantinopolitan, Michael Psellus, may be consulted. They are very numerous, and there is no climate or element without one or more.

And some in dreams assuréd were
Of the spirit that plagued us so;
Nine fathom deep he had followed us
From the land of mist and snow.

And every tongue, through utter drought,   135
Was withered at the root;
We could not speak, no more than if
We had been choked with soot.

The shipmates, in their sore distress, would fain throw the whole guilt on the ancient Mariner: in sign whereof they hang the dead sea-bird round his neck.

Ah! well a-day! what evil looks
Had I from old and young!   140
Instead of the cross, the Albatross
About my neck was hung.

PART III

There passed a weary time. Each throat
Was parched, and glazed each eye.
A weary time! a weary time!   145
How glazed each weary eye,
The ancient Mariner beholdeth a sign in the element afar off.
When looking westward, I beheld
A something in the sky.

At first it seemed a little speck,
And then it seemed a mist;   150
It moved and moved, and took at last
A certain shape, I wist.

A speck, a mist, a shape, I wist!
And still it neared and neared:
As if it dodged a water-sprite,   155
It plunged and tacked and veered.

At its nearer approach, it seemeth him to be a ship; and at a dear ransom he freeth his speech from the bonds of thirst.
With throats unslaked, with black lips baked,
We could nor laugh nor wail;
Through utter drought all dumb we stood!
I bit my arm, I sucked the blood,   160
And cried, A sail! a sail!

With throats unslaked, with black lips baked,
Agape they heard me call:
A flash of joy;
Gramercy! they for joy did grin,
And all at once their breath drew in,   165
As they were drinking all.

And horror follows. For can it be a ship that comes onward without wind or tide?
See! see! (I cried) she tacks no more!
Hither to work us weal;
Without a breeze, without a tide,
She steadies with upright keel!   170

86

The western wave was all a-flame.
The day was well nigh done!
Almost upon the western wave
Rested the broad bright Sun;
When that strange shape drove suddenly   175
Betwixt us and the Sun.

And straight the Sun was flecked with bars,
(Heaven's Mother send us grace!)
As if through a dungeon-grate he peered
With broad and burning face.   180

Alas! (thought I, and my heart beat loud)
How fast she nears and nears!

Are those *her* sails that glance in the Sun,
Like restless gossameres?

Are those *her* ribs through which the Sun   185
Did peer, as through a grate?
And is that Woman all her crew?
Is that a DEATH? and are there two?
Is DEATH that woman's mate?

Her lips were red, *her* looks were free,   190
Her locks were yellow as gold:
Her skin was as white as leprosy,
The Night-mare LIFE-IN-DEATH was she,
Who thicks man's blood with cold.

The naked hulk alongside came,   195
And the twain were casting dice;
"The game is done! I've won! I've won!"
Quoth she, and whistles thrice.

The Sun's rim dips; the stars rush out:
At one stride comes the dark;   200
With far-heard whisper, o'er the sea,
Off shot the spectre-bark.

87

At the rising of the Moon,

We listened and looked sideways up!
Fear at my heart, as at a cup,
My life-blood seemed to sip!   205
The stars were dim, and thick the night,
The steersman's face by his lamp gleamed white;
From the sails the dew did drip —
Till clomb above the eastern bar
The hornéd Moon, with one bright star   210
Within the nether tip.

One after another,

One after one, by the star-dogged Moon,
Too quick for groan or sigh,
Each turned his face with a ghastly pang,
And cursed me with his eye.   215

His shipmates drop down dead.

Four times fifty living men,
(And I heard nor sigh nor groan)
With heavy thump, a lifeless lump,
They dropped down one by one.

But Life-in-Death begins her work on the ancient Mariner.

The souls did from their bodies fly, —   220
They fled to bliss or woe!
And every soul, it passed me by,
Like the whizz of my cross-bow!

PART IV

The Wedding Guest feareth that a Spirit is talking to him.

"I fear thee, ancient Mariner!
I fear thy skinny hand!   225
And thou art long, and lank, and brown,
As is the ribbed sea-sand.

I fear thee and thy glittering eye,
And thy skinny hand, so brown." —

But the ancient Mariner assureth him of his bodily life, and proceedeth to relate his horrible penance.

Fear not, fear not, thou Wedding-Guest!   230
This body dropt not down.

Alone, alone, all, all alone,
Alone on a wide wide sea!
And never a saint took pity on
My soul in agony.   235

He despiseth the creatures of the calm.

The many men, so beautiful!
And they all dead did lie:
And a thousand thousand slimy things
Lived on; and so did I.

And envieth that they should live, and so many lie dead.

I looked upon the rotting sea,   240
And drew my eyes away;
I looked upon the rotting deck,
And there the dead men lay.

I looked to heaven, and tried to pray;
But or ever a prayer had gusht,   245
A wicked whisper came, and made
My heart as dry as dust.

I closed my lids, and kept them close,
And the balls like pulses beat;
For the sky and the sea, and the sea and the sky   250
Lay like a load on my weary eye,
And the dead were at my feet.

But the curse liveth for him in the eye of the dead men.

The cold sweat melted from their limbs,
Nor rot nor reek did they:
The look with which they looked on me   255
Had never passed away.

An orphan's curse would drag to hell
A spirit from on high;
But oh! more horrible than that
Is the curse in a dead man's eye!   260
Seven days, seven nights, I saw that curse,
And yet I could not die.

In his loneliness and fixedness he yearneth towards the journeying Moon, and the stars that still sojourn, yet still move onward; and every where the blue sky belongs to them, and is their appointed rest, and their native country and their own natural homes, which they enter unannounced, as lords that are certainly expected and yet there is a silent joy at their arrival.

The moving Moon went up the sky,
And no where did abide:
Softly she was going up,   265
And a star or two beside —

Her beams bemocked the sultry main,
Like April hoar-frost spread;
But where the ship's huge shadow lay,
The charméd water burnt alway   270
A still and awful red.

By the light of the
Moon he
beholdeth God's
creatures of the
great calm.
Beyond the shadow of the ship,
I watched the water-snakes:
They moved in tracks of shining white,
And when they reared, the elfish light   275
Fell off in hoary flakes.

Within the shadow of the ship
I watched their rich attire:
Blue, glossy green, and velvet black,
They coiled and swam; and every track   280
Was a flash of golden fire.

Their beauty and
their happiness.
O happy living things! no tongue
Their beauty might declare:
A spring of love gushed from my heart,
He blesseth them
in his heart.
And I blessed them unaware: 285
Sure my kind saint took pity on me,
And I blessed them unaware.

The spell begins to
break.
The selfsame moment I could pray;
And from my neck so free
The Albatross fell off, and sank   290
Like lead into the sea.

PART V

Oh sleep! it is a gentle thing,
Beloved from pole to pole!
To Mary Queen the praise be given!
She sent the gentle sleep from Heaven,   295
That slid into my soul.

By grace of the
holy Mother, the
ancient Mariner is
refreshed with rain.
The silly buckets on the deck,
That had so long remained,
I dreamt that they were filled with dew;
And when I awoke, it rained.   300

My lips were wet, my throat was cold,
My garments all were dank;
Sure I had drunken in my dreams,
And still my body drank.

I moved, and could not feel my limbs: 305
I was so light – almost
I thought that I had died in sleep,
And was a blessèd ghost.

He heareth sounds and seeth strange sights and commotions in the sky and the element.

And soon I heard a roaring wind:
It did not come anear;   310
But with its sound it shook the sails,
That were so thin and sere.

The upper air burst into life!
And a hundred fire-flags sheen,
To and fro they were hurried about!   315
And to and fro, and in and out,
The wan stars danced between.

And the coming wind did roar more loud,
And the sails did sigh like sedge;
And the rain poured down from one black
   cloud;   320
The Moon was at its edge.

The thick black cloud was cleft, and still
The Moon was at its side:
Like waters shot from some high crag,
The lightning fell with never a jag,   325
A river steep and wide.

The bodies of the ship's crew are inspired, and the ship moves on;

The loud wind never reached the ship,
Yet now the ship moved on!
Beneath the lightning and the Moon
The dead men gave a groan.   330

They groaned, they stirred, they all uprose,
Nor spake, nor moved their eyes;
It had been strange, even in a dream,
To have seen those dead men rise.

The helmsman steered, the ship moved on;   335
Yet never a breeze up blew;
The mariners all 'gan work the ropes,
Where they were wont to do;
They raised their limbs like lifeless tools –
We were a ghastly crew.   340

The body of my brother's son
Stood by me, knee to knee:
The body and I pulled at one rope,
But he said nought to me.

But not by the
souls of the men,
nor by daemons of
earth or middle
air, but by a blessed
troop of angelic
spirits, sent down
by the invocation
of the guardian
saint.
"I fear thee, ancient Mariner!"   345
Be calm, thou Wedding-Guest!
'Twas not those souls that fled in pain,
Which to their corses came again,
But a troop of spirits blest:

For when it dawned – they dropped their arms,   350
And clustered round the mast;
Sweet sounds rose slowly through their mouths,
And from their bodies passed.

Around, around, flew each sweet sound,
Then darted to the Sun;   355
Slowly the sounds came back again,
Now mixed, now one by one.

Sometimes a-dropping from the sky
I heard the sky-lark sing;
Sometimes all little birds that are,   360
How they seemed to fill the sea and air
With their sweet jargoning!

And now 'twas like all instruments,
Now like a lonely flute;
And now it is an angel's song,   365
That makes the heavens be mute.

It ceased; yet still the sails made on
A pleasant noise till noon,
A noise like of a hidden brook
In the leafy month of June,   370
That to the sleeping woods all night
Singeth a quiet tune.

Till noon we quietly sailed on,
Yet never a breeze did breathe:
Slowly and smoothly went the ship,   375
Moved onward from beneath.

The lonesome
Spirit from the
south-pole carries
on the ship as far as
the Line, in
obedience to the
angelic troop, but
still requireth
vengeance.

Under the keel nine fathom deep,
From the land of mist and snow,
The spirit slid: and it was he
That made the ship to go.   380
The sails at noon left off their tune,
And the ship stood still also.

The Sun, right up above the mast,
Had fixed her to the ocean:
But in a minute she 'gan stir,   385
With a short uneasy motion –
Backwards and forwards half her length
With a short uneasy motion.

Then like a pawing horse let go,
She made a sudden bound: 390
It flung the blood into my head,
And I fell down in a swound.

The Polar Spirit's
fellow daemons,
the invisible
inhabitants of the
element, take part
in his wrong; and
two of them relate,
one to the other,
that penance long
and heavy for the
ancient Mariner
hath been
accorded to the
Polar Spirit, who
returneth
southward.

How long in that same fit I lay,
I have not to declare;
But ere my living life returned,   395
I heard and in my soul discerned
Two voices in the air.

"Is it he?" quoth one, "Is this the man?
By him who died on cross,
With his cruel bow he laid full low   400
The harmless Albatross.

93

The spirit who bideth by himself
In the land of mist and snow,
He loved the bird that loved the man
Who shot him with his bow." 405

The other was a softer voice,
As soft as honey-dew:
Quoth he, "The man hath penance done,
And penance more will do."

PART VI

FIRST VOICE

"But tell me, tell me! speak again, 410
Thy soft response renewing –
What makes that ship drive on so fast?
What is the ocean doing?"

SECOND VOICE

"Still as a slave before his lord,
The ocean hath no blast; 415
His great bright eye most silently
Up to the Moon is cast –

If he may know which way to go;
For she guides him smooth or grim.
See, brother, see! how graciously 420
She looketh down on him."

FIRST VOICE

*The Mariner hath
been cast into a
trance; for the
angelic power
causeth the vessel
to drive northward
faster than human
life could endure.*

"But why drives on that ship so fast,
Without or wave or wind?"

SECOND VOICE

"The air is cut away before,
And closes from behind. 425

94

Fly, brother, fly! more high, more high!
Or we shall be belated:
For slow and slow that ship will go,
When the Mariner's trance is abated."

The supernatural motion is retarded; the Mariner awakes, and his penance begins anew.

I woke, and we were sailing on   430
As in a gentle weather:
'Twas night, calm night, the Moon was high;
The dead men stood together.

All stood together on the deck,
For a charnel-dungeon fitter: 435
All fixed on me their stony eyes,
That in the Moon did glitter.

The pang, the curse, with which they died,
Had never passed away:
I could not draw my eyes from theirs,   440
Nor turn them up to pray.

The curse is finally expiated.

And now this spell was snapt: once more
I viewed the ocean green,
And looked far forth, yet little saw
Of what had else been seen –   445

Like one, that on a lonesome road
Doth walk in fear and dread,
And having once turned round walks on,
And turns no more his head;
Because he knows, a frightful fiend   450
Doth close behind him tread.

But soon there breathed a wind on me,
Nor sound nor motion made:
Its path was not upon the sea,
In ripple or in shade.   455

It raised my hair, it fanned my cheek
Like a meadow-gale of spring –
It mingled strangely with my fears,
Yet it felt like a welcoming.

Swiftly, swiftly flew the ship,   460
Yet she sailed softly too:
Sweetly, sweetly blew the breeze –
On me alone it blew.

And the ancient
Mariner
beholdeth his
native country.
Oh! dream of joy! is this indeed
The light-house top I see?   465
Is this the hill? is this the kirk?
Is this mine own countree?

We drifted o'er the harbour-bar,
And I with sobs did pray –
O let me be awake, my God!   470
Or let me sleep alway.

The harbour-bay was clear as glass,
So smoothly it was strewn!
And on the bay the moonlight lay,
And the shadow of the Moon.   475

The rock shone bright, the kirk no less,
That stands above the rock:
The moonlight steeped in silentness
The steady weathercock.

And the bay was white with silent light,   480
Till rising from the same,
The angelic spirits
leave the dead
bodies,
Full many shapes, that shadows were,
In crimson colours came.

And appear in
their own forms
of light.
A little distance from the prow
Those crimson shadows were: 485
I turned my eyes upon the deck –
Oh, Christ! what saw I there!

Each corse lay flat, lifeless and flat,
And, by the holy rood!
A man all light, a seraph-man,   490
On every corse there stood.

96

This seraph-band, each waved his hand:
It was a heavenly sight!
They stood as signals to the land,
Each one a lovely light;   495

This seraph-band, each waved his hand,
No voice did they impart –
No voice; but oh! the silence sank
Like music on my heart.

But soon I heard the dash of oars,   500
I heard the Pilot's cheer;
My head was turned perforce away,
And I saw a boat appear.

The Pilot and the Pilot's boy,
I heard them coming fast: 505
Dear Lord in Heaven! it was a joy
The dead men could not blast.

I saw a third – I heard his voice:
It is the Hermit good!
He singeth loud his godly hymns   510
That he makes in the wood.
He'll shrieve my soul, he'll wash away
The Albatross's blood.

PART VII

This Hermit good lives in that wood
Which slopes down to the sea.   515
How loudly his sweet voice he rears!
He loves to talk with marineres
That come from a far countree.

He kneels at morn, and noon, and eve –
He hath a cushion plump: 520
It is the moss that wholly hides
The rotted old oak-stump.

97

The skiff-boat neared: I heard them talk,
"Why, this is strange, I trow!
Where are those lights so many and fair,   525
That signal made but now?"

Approacheth the
ship with wonder.
"Strange, by my faith!" the Hermit said –
"And they answered not our cheer!
The planks looked warped! and see those sails,
How thin they are and sere!   530
I never saw aught like to them,
Unless perchance it were

Brown skeletons of leaves that lag
My forest-brook along;
When the ivy-tod is heavy with snow,   535
And the owlet whoops to the wolf below,
That eats the she-wolf's young."

"Dear Lord! it hath a fiendish look –
(The Pilot made reply)
I am a-feared" – "Push on, push on!"   540
Said the Hermit cheerily.

The boat came closer to the ship,
But I nor spake nor stirred;
The boat came close beneath the ship,
And straight a sound was heard.   545

The ship suddenly
sinketh.
Under the water it rumbled on,
Still louder and more dread:
It reached the ship, it split the bay;
The ship went down like lead.

The ancient
Mariner is saved in
the Pilot's boat.
Stunned by that loud and dreadful sound,   550
Which sky and ocean smote,
Like one that hath been seven days drowned
My body lay afloat;
But swift as dreams, myself I found
Within the Pilot's boat.   555

Upon the whirl, where sank the ship,
The boat spun round and round;
And all was still, save that the hill
Was telling of the sound.

I moved my lips – the Pilot shrieked   560
And fell down in a fit;
The holy Hermit raised his eyes,
And prayed where he did sit.

I took the oars: the Pilot's boy,
Who now doth crazy go,   565
Laughed loud and long, and all the while
His eyes went to and fro.
"Ha! ha!" quoth he, "full plain I see,
The Devil knows how to row."

And now, all in my own countree,   570
I stood on the firm land!
The Hermit stepped forth from the boat,
And scarcely he could stand.

The ancient Mariner earnestly entreateth the Hermit to shrieve him; and the penance of life falls on him.

"O shrieve me, shrieve me, holy man!"
The Hermit crossed his brow.   575
"Say quick," quoth he, "I bid thee say –
What manner of man art thou?"

Forthwith this frame of mine was wrenched
With a woful agony,
Which forced me to begin my tale;   580
And then it left me free.

And ever and anon throughout his future life an agony constraineth him to travel from land to land;

Since then, at an uncertain hour,
That agony returns:
And till my ghastly tale is told,
This heart within me burns.   585

I pass, like night, from land to land;
I have strange power of speech;
That moment that his face I see,
I know the man that must hear me:
To him my tale I teach.   590

99

What loud uproar bursts from that door!
The wedding-guests are there:
But in the garden-bower the bride
And bride-maids singing are:
And hark the little vesper bell,   595
Which biddeth me to prayer!

O Wedding-Guest! this soul hath been
Alone on a wide wide sea:
So lonely 'twas, that God himself
Scarce seeméd there to be.   600

O sweeter than the marriage-feast,
'Tis sweeter far to me,
To walk together to the kirk
With a goodly company! –

To walk together to the kirk,   605
And all together pray,
While each to his great Father bends,
Old men, and babes, and loving friends,
And youths and maidens gay!

And to teach, by
his own example,
love and reverence
to all things that
God made and
loveth.

Farewell, farewell! but this I tell   610
To thee, thou Wedding-Guest!
He prayeth well, who loveth well
Both man and bird and beast.

He prayeth best, who loveth best
All things both great and small;   615
For the dear God who loveth us,
He made and loveth all.

The Mariner, whose eye is bright,
Whose beard with age is hoar,
Is gone: and now the Wedding-Guest   620
Turned from the bridegroom's door.

He went like one that hath been stunned,
And is of sense forlorn:
A sadder and a wiser man,
He rose the morrow morn.   625

33

Christabel

PREFACE

The first part of the following poem was written in the year 1797, at Stowey, in the county of Somerset. The second part, after my return from Germany, in the year 1800, at Keswick, Cumberland. It is probable that if the poem had been finished at either of the former periods, or if even the first and second part had been published in the year 1800, the impression of its originality would have been much greater than I dare at present expect. But for this I have only my own indolence to blame. The dates are mentioned for the exclusive purpose of precluding charges of plagiarism or servile imitation from myself. For there is amongst us a set of critics, who seem to hold, that every possible thought and image is traditional; who have no notion that there are such things as fountains in the world, small as well as great; and who would therefore charitably derive every rill they behold flowing, from a perforation made in some other man's tank. I am confident, however, that as far as the present poem is concerned, the celebrated poets whose writings I might be suspected of having imitated, either in particular passages, or in the tone and the spirit of the whole, would be among the first to vindicate me from the charge, and who, on any striking coincidence, would permit me to address them in this doggerel version of two monkish Latin hexameters.

> 'Tis mine and it is likewise yours;
> But an if this will not do;
> Let it be mine, good friend! for I
> Am the poorer of the two.

I have only to add that the metre of Christabel is not, properly speaking, irregular, though it may seem so from its being founded on a new principle: namely, that of counting in each line the accents, not the syllables. Though the latter may vary from seven to twelve, yet in each line the accents will be found to be only four. Nevertheless, this occasional variation in number of syllables is not introduced wantonly, or for the mere ends of convenience, but in correspondence with some transition in the nature of the imagery or passion.

PART I

'Tis the middle of night by the castle clock,
And the owls have awakened the crowing cock;
Tu – whit!—Tu – whoo!
And hark, again! the crowing cock,
How drowsily it crew.   5

Sir Leoline, the Baron rich,
Hath a toothless mastiff bitch;
From her kennel beneath the rock
She maketh answer to the clock,
Four for the quarters, and twelve for the hour;   10
Ever and aye, by shine and shower,
Sixteen short howls, not over loud;
Some say, she sees my lady's shroud.

Is the night chilly and dark?
The night is chilly, but not dark.   15
The thin gray cloud is spread on high,
It covers but not hides the sky.
The moon is behind, and at the full;
And yet she looks both small and dull.
The night is chill, the cloud is gray: 20
'Tis a month before the month of May,
And the Spring comes slowly up this way.

The lovely lady, Christabel,
Whom her father loves so well,
What makes her in the wood so late,   25
A furlong from the castle gate?
She had dreams all yesternight
Of her own betrothéd knight;
And she in the midnight wood will pray
For the weal of her lover that's far away.   30

She stole along, she nothing spoke,
The sighs she heaved were soft and low,
And naught was green upon the oak
But moss and rarest misletoe:

She kneels beneath the huge oak tree,   35
And in silence prayeth she.

The lady sprang up suddenly,
The lovely lady, Christabel!
It moaned as near, as near can be,
But what it is she cannot tell. –   40
On the other side it seems to be,
Of the huge, broad-breasted, old oak tree.

The night is chill; the forest bare;
Is it the wind that moaneth bleak?
There is not wind enough in the air   45
To move away the ringlet curl
From the lovely lady's cheek –
There is not wind enough to twirl
The one red leaf, the last of its clan,
That dances as often as dance it can,   50
Hanging so light, and hanging so high,
On the topmost twig that looks up at the sky.

Hush, beating heart of Christabel!
Jesu, Maria, shield her well!
She folded her arms beneath her cloak,   55
And stole to the other side of the oak.
            What sees she there?

There she sees a damsel bright,
Drest in a silken robe of white,
That shadowy in the moonlight shone: 60
The neck that made that white robe wan,
Her stately neck, and arms were bare;
Her blue-veined feet unsandal'd were,
And wildly glittered here and there
The gems entangled in her hair.   65
I guess, 'twas frightful there to see
A lady so richly clad as she –
Beautiful exceedingly!

Mary mother, save me now!
(Said Christabel,) And who art thou?   70

The lady strange made answer meet,
And her voice was faint and sweet: —
Have pity on my sore distress,
I scarce can speak for weariness:
Stretch forth thy hand, and have no fear!   75
Said Christabel, How camest thou here?
And the lady, whose voice was faint and sweet,
Did thus pursue her answer meet: —

My sire is of a noble line,
And my name is Geraldine: 80
Five warriors seized me yestermorn,
Me, even me, a maid forlorn:
They choked my cries with force and fright,
And tied me on a palfrey white.
The palfrey was as fleet as wind,   85
And they rode furiously behind.

They spurred amain, their steeds were white:
And once we crossed the shade of night.
As sure as Heaven shall rescue me,
I have no thought what men they be;   90
Nor do I know how long it is
(For I have lain entranced I wis)
Since one, the tallest of the five,
Took me from the palfrey's back,
A weary woman, scarce alive.   95
Some muttered words his comrades spoke:
He placed me underneath this oak;
He swore they would return with haste;
Whither they went I cannot tell —
I thought I heard, some minutes past,   100
Sounds as of a castle bell.
Stretch forth thy hand (thus ended she),
And help a wretched maid to flee.

Then Christabel stretched forth her hand,
And comforted fair Geraldine: 105
O well, bright dame! may you command
The service of Sir Leoline;
And gladly our stout chivalry

Will he send forth and friends withal
To guide and guard you safe and free   110
Home to your noble father's hall.

She rose: and forth with steps they passed
That strove to be, and were not, fast.
Her gracious stars the lady blest,
And thus spake on sweet Christabel: 115
All our household are at rest,
The hall as silent as the cell;
Sir Leoline is weak in health,
And may not well awakened be,
But we will move as if in stealth,   120
And I beseech your courtesy,
This night, to share your couch with me.

They crossed the moat, and Christabel
Took the key that fitted well;
A little door she opened straight,   125
All in the middle of the gate;
The gate that was ironed within and without,
Where an army in battle array had marched out.
The lady sank, belike through pain,
And Christabel with might and main   130
Lifted her up, a weary weight,
Over the threshold of the gate:
Then the lady rose again,
And moved, as she were not in pain.

So free from danger, free from fear,   135
They crossed the court: right glad they were.
And Christabel devoutly cried
To the lady by her side,
Praise we the Virgin all divine
Who hath rescued thee from thy distress!   140
Alas, alas! said Geraldine,
I cannot speak for weariness.
So free from danger, free from fear,
They crossed the court: right glad they were.

Outside her kennel, the mastiff old   145
Lay fast asleep, in moonshine cold.
The mastiff old did not awake,
Yet she an angry moan did make!
And what can ail the mastiff bitch?
Never till now she uttered yell   150
Beneath the eye of Christabel.
Perhaps it is the owlet's scritch:
For what can ail the mastiff bitch?

They passed the hall, that echoes still,
Pass as lightly as you will!   155
The brands were flat, the brands were dying,
Amid their own white ashes lying;
But when the lady passed, there came
A tongue of light, a fit of flame;
And Christabel saw the lady's eye,   160
And nothing else saw she thereby,
Save the boss of the shield of Sir Leoline tall,
Which hung in a murky old niche in the wall.
O softly tread, said Christabel,
My father seldom sleepeth well.   165

Sweet Christabel her feet doth bare,
And jealous of the listening air
They steal their way from stair to stair,
Now in glimmer, and now in gloom,
And now they pass the Baron's room,   170
As still as death, with stifled breath!
And now have reached her chamber door;
And now doth Geraldine press down
The rushes of the chamber floor.

The moon shines dim in the open air,   175
And not a moonbeam enters here.
But they without its light can see
The chamber carved so curiously,
Carved with figures strange and sweet,
All made out of the carver's brain,   180
For a lady's chamber meet:

The lamp with twofold silver chain
Is fastened to an angel's feet.

The silver lamp burns dead and dim;
But Christabel the lamp will trim.   185
She trimmed the lamp, and made it bright,
And left it swinging to and fro,
While Geraldine, in wretched plight,
Sank down upon the floor below.

O weary lady, Geraldine,   190
I pray you, drink this cordial wine!
It is a wine of virtuous powers;
My mother made it of wild flowers.

And will your mother pity me,
Who am a maiden most forlorn?   195
Christabel answered – Woe is me!
She died the hour that I was born.
I have heard the grey-haired friar tell
How on her death-bed she did say,
That she should hear the castle-bell   200
Strike twelve upon my wedding-day.
O mother dear! that thou wert here!
I would, said Geraldine, she were!

But soon with altered voice, said she –
"Off, wandering mother! Peak and pine!   205
I have power to bid thee flee."
Alas! what ails poor Geraldine?
Why stares she with unsettled eye?
Can she the bodiless dead espy?
And why with hollow voice cries she,   210
"Off, woman, off! this hour is mine –
Though thou her guardian spirit be,
Off, woman, off! 'tis given to me."

Then Christabel knelt by the lady's side,
And raised to heaven her eyes so blue –   215
Alas! said she, this ghastly ride –
Dear lady! it hath wildered you!

The lady wiped her moist cold brow,
And faintly said, "'tis over now!"

Again the wild-flower wine she drank: 220
Her fair large eyes 'gan glitter bright,
And from the floor whereon she sank,
The lofty lady stood upright:
She was most beautiful to see,
Like a lady of a far countree.   225

And thus the lofty lady spake –
"All they who live in the upper sky,
Do love you, holy Christabel!
And you love them, and for their sake
And for the good which me befel,   230
Even I in my degree will try,
Fair maiden, to requite you well.
But now unrobe yourself; for I
Must pray, ere yet in bed I lie."

Quoth Christabel, So let it be!   235
And as the lady bade, did she.
Her gentle limbs did she undress,
And lay down in her loveliness.

But through her brain of weal and woe
So many thoughts moved to and fro,   240
That vain it were her lids to close;
So half-way from the bed she rose,
And on her elbow did recline
To look at the lady Geraldine.

Beneath the lamp the lady bowed,   245
And slowly rolled her eyes around;
Then drawing in her breath aloud,
Like one that shuddered, she unbound
The cincture from beneath her breast:
Her silken robe, and inner vest,   250
Dropt to her feet, and full in view,
Behold! her bosom and half her side—

A sight to dream of, not to tell!
O shield her! shield sweet Christabel!

Yet Geraldine nor speaks nor stirs;   255
Ah! what a stricken look was hers!
Deep from within she seems half-way
To lift some weight with sick assay,
And eyes the maid and seeks delay;
Then suddenly, as one defied,   260
Collects herself in scorn and pride,
And lay down by the Maiden's side! –
And in her arms the maid she took,
            Ah wel-a-day!
And with low voice and doleful look   265
These words did say:
"In the touch of this bosom there worketh a spell,
Which is lord of thy utterance, Christabel!
Thou knowest to-night, and wilt know to-morrow,
This mark of my shame, this seal of my sorrow;   270
        But vainly thou warrest,
            For this is alone in
        Thy power to declare,
            That in the dim forest
            Thou heard'st a low moaning,   275
And found'st a bright lady, surpassingly fair;
And didst bring her home with thee in love and in charity,
To shield her and shelter her from the damp air."

THE CONCLUSION TO PART I

It was a lovely sight to see
The lady Christabel, when she   280
Was praying at the old oak tree.
        Amid the jaggéd shadows
        Of mossy leafless boughs,
        Kneeling in the moonlight,
        To make her gentle vows;   285
Her slender palms together prest,
Heaving sometimes on her breast;
Her face resigned to bliss or bale –
Her face, oh call it fair not pale,

And both blue eyes more bright than clear, 290
Each about to have a tear.

With open eyes (ah woe is me!)
Asleep, and dreaming fearfully,
Fearfully dreaming, yet, I wis,
Dreaming that alone, which is — 295
O sorrow and shame! Can this be she,
The lady, who knelt at the old oak tree?
And lo! the worker of these harms,
That holds the maiden in her arms,
Seems to slumber still and mild, 300
As a mother with her child.

A star hath set, a star hath risen,
O Geraldine! since arms of thine
Have been the lovely lady's prison.
O Geraldine! one hour was thine — 305
Thou'st had thy will! By tairn and rill,
The night-birds all that hour were still.
But now they are jubilant anew,
From cliff and tower, tu—whoo! tu—whoo!
Tu—whoo! tu—whoo! from wood and fell! 310

And see! the lady Christabel
Gathers herself from out her trance;
Her limbs relax, her countenance
Grows sad and soft; the smooth thin lids
Close o'er her eyes; and tears she sheds — 315
Large tears that leave the lashes bright!
And oft the while she seems to smile
As infants at a sudden light!

Yea, she doth smile, and she doth weep,
Like a youthful hermitess, 320
Beauteous in a wilderness,
Who, praying always, prays in sleep.
And, if she move unquietly,
Perchance, 'tis but the blood so free
Comes back and tingles in her feet. 325
No doubt, she hath a vision sweet.

What if her guardian spirit 'twere,
What if she knew her mother near?
But this she knows, in joys and woes,
That saints will aid if men will call: 330
For the blue sky bends over all!

PART II

Each matin bell, the Baron saith,
Knells us back to a world of death.
These words Sir Leoline first said,
When he rose and found his lady dead: 335
These words Sir Leoline will say
Many a morn to his dying day!

And hence the custom and law began
That still at dawn the sacristan,
Who duly pulls the heavy bell,   340
Five and forty beads must tell
Between each stroke – a warning knell,
Which not a soul can choose but hear
From Bratha Head to Wyndermere.

Saith Bracy the bard, So let it knell!   345
And let the drowsy sacristan
Still count as slowly as he can!
There is no lack of such, I ween,
As well fill up the space between.
In Langdale Pike and Witch's Lair,   350
And Dungeon-ghyll so foully rent,
With ropes of rock and bells of air
Three sinful sextons' ghosts are pent,
Who all give back, one after t'other,
The death-note to their living brother;   355
And oft too, by the knell offended,
Just as their one! two! three! is ended,
The devil mocks the doleful tale
With a merry peal from Borodale.

The air is still! through mist and cloud   360
That merry peal comes ringing loud;

And Geraldine shakes off her dread,
And rises lightly from the bed;
Puts on her silken vestments white,
And tricks her hair in lovely plight, 365
And nothing doubting of her spell
Awakens the lady Christabel.
"Sleep you, sweet lady Christabel?
I trust that you have rested well."

And Christabel awoke and spied 370
The same who lay down by her side –
O rather say, the same whom she
Raised up beneath the old oak tree!
Nay, fairer yet! and yet more fair!
For she belike hath drunken deep 375
Of all the blessedness of sleep!
And while she spake, her looks, her air
Such gentle thankfulness declare,
That (so it seemed) her girded vests
Grew tight beneath her heaving breasts. 380
"Sure I have sinn'd!" said Christabel,
"Now heaven be praised if all be well!"
And in low faltering tones, yet sweet,
Did she the lofty lady greet
With such perplexity of mind 385
As dreams too lively leave behind.

So quickly she rose, and quickly arrayed
Her maiden limbs, and having prayed
That He, who on the cross did groan,
Might wash away her sins unknown, 390
She forthwith led fair Geraldine
To meet her sire, Sir Leoline.

The lovely maid and the lady tall
Are pacing both into the hall,
And pacing on through page and groom, 395
Enter the Baron's presence-room.

The Baron rose, and while he prest
His gentle daughter to his breast,
With cheerful wonder in his eyes
The lady Geraldine espies,   400
And gave such welcome to the same,
As might beseem so bright a dame!

But when he heard the lady's tale,
And when she told her father's name,
Why waxed Sir Leoline so pale,   405
Murmuring o'er the name again,
Lord Roland de Vaux of Tryermaine?

Alas! they had been friends in youth;
But whispering tongues can poison truth;
And constancy lives in realms above;   410
And life is thorny; and youth is vain;
And to be wroth with one we love
Doth work like madness in the brain.
And thus it chanced, as I divine,
With Roland and Sir Leoline.   415
Each spake words of high disdain
And insult to his heart's best brother:
They parted – ne'er to meet again!
But never either found another
To free the hollow heart from paining –   420
They stood aloof, the scars remaining,
Like cliffs which had been rent asunder;
A dreary sea now flows between; –
But neither heat, nor frost, nor thunder,
Shall wholly do away, I ween,   425
The marks of that which once hath been.

Sir Leoline, a moment's space,
Stood gazing on the damsel's face:
And the youthful Lord of Tryermaine
Came back upon his heart again.   430

O then the Baron forgot his age,
His noble heart swelled high with rage;
He swore by the wounds in Jesu's side

He would proclaim it far and wide,
With trump and solemn heraldry,   435
That they, who thus had wronged the dame,
Were base as spotted infamy!
"And if they dare deny the same,
My herald shall appoint a week,
And let the recreant traitors seek   440
My tourney court – that there and then
I may dislodge their reptile souls
From the bodies and forms of men!"
He spake: his eye in lightning rolls!
For the lady was ruthlessly seized; and he kenned   445
In the beautiful lady the child of his friend!

And now the tears were on his face,
And fondly in his arms he took
Fair Geraldine, who met the embrace,
Prolonging it with joyous look.   450
Which when she viewed, a vision fell
Upon the soul of Christabel,
The vision of fear, the touch and pain!
She shrunk and shuddered, and saw again –
(Ah, woe is me! Was it for thee,   455
Thou gentle maid! such sights to see?)

Again she saw that bosom old,
Again she felt that bosom cold,
And drew in her breath with a hissing sound:
Whereat the Knight turned wildly round,   460
And nothing saw, but his own sweet maid
With eyes upraised, as one that prayed.

The touch, the sight, had passed away,
And in its stead that vision blest,
Which comforted her after-rest   465
While in the lady's arms she lay,
Had put a rapture in her breast,
And on her lips and o'er her eyes
Spread smiles like light!
                              With new surprise,
"What ails then my belovéd child?"   470

The Baron said – His daughter mild
Made answer, "All will yet be well!"
I ween, she had no power to tell
Aught else: so mighty was the spell.

Yet he, who saw this Geraldine,   475
Had deemed her sure a thing divine:
Such sorrow with such grace she blended,
As if she feared she had offended
Sweet Christabel, that gentle maid!
And with such lowly tones she prayed   480
She might be sent without delay
Home to her father's mansion.
                                   "Nay!
Nay, by my soul!" said Leoline.
"Ho! Bracy the bard, the charge be thine!
Go thou, with music sweet and loud,   485
And take two steeds with trappings proud,
And take the youth whom thou lov'st best
To bear thy harp, and learn thy song,
And clothe you both in solemn vest,
And over the mountains haste along,   490
Lest wandering folk, that are abroad,
Detain you on the valley road.

"And when he has crossed the Irthing flood,
My merry bard! he hastes, he hastes
Up Knorren Moor, through Halegarth Wood,   495
And reaches soon that castle good
Which stands and threatens Scotland's wastes.

"Bard Bracy! bard Bracy! your horses are fleet,
Ye must ride up the hall, your music so sweet,
More loud than your horses' echoing feet!   500
And loud and loud to Lord Roland call,
Thy daughter is safe in Langdale hall!
Thy beautiful daughter is safe and free –
Sir Leoline greets thee thus through me!
He bids thee come without delay   505
With all thy numerous array
And take thy lovely daughter home:

And he will meet thee on the way
With all his numerous array
White with their panting palfreys' foam: 510
And, by mine honour! I will say,
That I repent me of the day
When I spake words of fierce disdain
To Roland de Vaux of Tryermaine! —
— For since that evil hour hath flown,   515
Many a summer's sun hath shone;
Yet ne'er found I a friend again
Like Roland de Vaux of Tryermaine."

The lady fell, and clasped his knees,
Her face upraised, her eyes o'erflowing;   520
And Bracy replied, with faltering voice,
His gracious Hail on all bestowing! —
"Thy words, thou sire of Christabel,
Are sweeter than my harp can tell;
Yet might I gain a boon of thee,   525
This day my journey should not be,
So strange a dream hath come to me,
That I had vowed with music loud
To clear yon wood from thing unblest,
Warned by a vision in my rest!   530
For in my sleep I saw that dove,
That gentle bird, whom thou dost love,
And call'st by thy own daughter's name —
Sir Leoline! I saw the same
Fluttering, and uttering fearful moan,   535
Among the green herbs in the forest alone.
Which when I saw and when I heard,
I wonder'd what might ail the bird;
For nothing near it could I see,
Save the grass and green herbs underneath the old tree. 540

"And in my dream methought I went
To search out what might there be found;
And what the sweet bird's trouble meant,
That thus lay fluttering on the ground.
I went and peered, and could descry   545
No cause for her distressful cry;

But yet for her dear lady's sake
I stooped, methought, the dove to take,
When lo! I saw a bright green snake
Coiled around its wings and neck.   550
Green as the herbs on which it couched,
Close by the dove's its head it crouched;
And with the dove it heaves and stirs,
Swelling its neck as she swelled hers!
I woke; it was the midnight hour,   555
The clock was echoing in the tower;
But though my slumber was gone by,
This dream it would not pass away —
It seems to live upon my eye!
And thence I vowed this self-same day   560
With music strong and saintly song
To wander through the forest bare,
Lest aught unholy loiter there."

Thus Bracy said: the Baron, the while,
Half-listening heard him with a smile;   565
Then turned to Lady Geraldine,
His eyes made up of wonder and love;
And said in courtly accents fine,
"Sweet maid, Lord Roland's beauteous dove,
With arms more strong than harp or song,   570
Thy sire and I will crush the snake!"
He kissed her forehead as he spake,
And Geraldine in maiden wise
Casting down her large bright eyes,
With blushing cheek and courtesy fine   575
She turned her from Sir Leoline;
Softly gathering up her train,
That o'er her right arm fell again;
And folded her arms across her chest,
And couched her head upon her breast,   580
And looked askance at Christabel —
Jesu, Maria, shield her well!

A snake's small eye blinks dull and shy;
And the lady's eyes they shrunk in her head,
Each shrunk up to a serpent's eye,   585

And with somewhat of malice, and more of dread,
At Christabel she looked askance! —
One moment — and the sight was fled!
But Christabel in dizzy trance
Stumbling on the unsteady ground   590
Shuddered aloud, with a hissing sound;
And Geraldine again turned round,
And like a thing, that sought relief,
Full of wonder and full of grief,
She rolled her large bright eyes divine   595
Wildly on Sir Leoline.

The maid, alas! her thoughts are gone,
She nothing sees — no sight but one!
The maid, devoid of guile and sin,
I know not how, in fearful wise,   600
So deeply had she drunken in
That look, those shrunken serpent eyes,
That all her features were resigned
To this sole image in her mind:
And passively did imitate   605
That look of dull and treacherous hate!
And thus she stood, in dizzy trance,
Still picturing that look askance
With forced unconscious sympathy
Full before her father's view —   610
As far as such a look could be
In eyes so innocent and blue!

And when the trance was o'er, the maid
Paused awhile, and inly prayed:
Then falling at the Baron's feet,   615
"By my mother's soul do I entreat
That thou this woman send away!"
She said: and more she could not say:
For what she knew she could not tell,
O'er-mastered by the mighty spell.   620

Why is thy cheek so wan and wild,
Sir Leoline? Thy only child
Lies at thy feet, thy joy, thy pride,

So fair, so innocent, so mild;
The same, for whom thy lady died!   625
O by the pangs of her dear mother
Think thou no evil of thy child!
For her, and thee, and for no other,
She prayed the moment ere she died:
Prayed that the babe for whom she died,   630
Might prove her dear lord's joy and pride!
    That prayer her deadly pangs beguiled,
        Sir Leoline!
    And wouldst thou wrong thy only child,
        Her child and thine?   635

Within the Baron's heart and brain
If thoughts, like these, had any share,
They only swelled his rage and pain,
And did but work confusion there.
His heart was cleft with pain and rage,   640
His cheeks they quivered, his eyes were wild,
Dishonoured thus in his old age;
Dishonoured by his only child,
And all his hospitality
To the wronged daughter of his friend   645
By more than woman's jealousy
Brought thus to a disgraceful end –
He rolled his eye with stern regard
Upon the gentle minstrel bard,
And said in tones abrupt, austere –   650
"Why, Bracy! dost thou loiter here?
I bade thee hence!" The bard obeyed;
And turning from his own sweet maid,
The agéd knight, Sir Leoline,
Led forth the lady Geraldine!   655

THE CONCLUSION TO PART II

A little child, a limber elf,
Singing, dancing to itself,
A fairy thing with red round cheeks,
That always finds, and never seeks,
Makes such a vision to the sight   660

As fills a father's eyes with light;
And pleasures flow in so thick and fast
Upon his heart, that he at last
Must needs express his love's excess
With words of unmeant bitterness.   665
Perhaps 'tis pretty to force together
Thoughts so all unlike each other;
To mutter and mock a broken charm,
To dally with wrong that does no harm.
Perhaps 'tis tender too and pretty   670
At each wild word to feel within
A sweet recoil of love and pity.
And what, if in a world of sin
(O sorrow and shame should this be true!)
Such giddiness of heart and brain   675
Comes seldom save from rage and pain,
So talks as it's most used to do.

The Ballad of the Dark Ladié

A FRAGMENT

Beneath yon birch with silver bark,
And boughs so pendulous and fair,
The brook falls scatter'd down the rock:
 And all is mossy there!

And there upon the moss she sits, 5
The Dark Ladié in silent pain;
The heavy tear is in her eye,
 And drops and swells again.

Three times she sends her little page
Up the castled mountain's breast, 10
If he might find the Knight that wears
 The Griffin for his crest.

The sun was sloping down the sky,
And she had linger'd there all day,
Counting moments, dreaming fears – 15
 Oh wherefore can he stay?

She hears a rustling o'er the brook,
She sees far off a swinging bough!
"'Tis, He! 'Tis my betrothéd Knight!
 Lord Falkland, it is Thou!" 20

She springs, she clasps him round the neck,
She sobs a thousand hopes and fears,
Her kisses glowing on his cheeks
 She quenches with her tears.

* * *

"My friends with rude ungentle words 25
They scoff and bid me fly to thee!
O give me shelter in thy breast!
 O shield and shelter me!

"My Henry, I have given thee much,
I gave what I can ne'er recall,
I gave my heart, I gave my peace,
    O Heaven! I gave thee all." 30

The Knight made answer to the Maid,
While to his heart he held her hand,
"Nine castles hath my noble sire,
    None statelier in the land. 35

"The fairest one shall be my love's,
The fairest castle of the nine!
Wait only till the stars peep out,
    The fairest shall be thine: 40

"Wait only till the hand of eve
Hath wholly closed yon western bars,
And through the dark we two will steal
    Beneath the twinkling stars!" –

"The dark? the dark? No! not the dark?
The twinkling stars? How, Henry? How?" 45
O God! 'twas in the eye of noon
    He pledged his sacred vow!

And in the eye of noon my love
Shall lead me from my mother's door,
Sweet boys and girls all clothed in white 50
    Strewing flowers before:

But first the nodding minstrels go
With music meet for lordly bowers,
The children next in snow-white vests, 55
    Strewing buds and flowers!

And then my love and I shall pace,
My jet black hair in pearly braids,
Between our comely bachelors
    And blushing bridal maids. 60

*   *   *

Love

All thoughts, all passions, all delights,
Whatever stirs this mortal frame,
All are but ministers of Love,
    And feed his sacred flame.

Oft in my waking dreams do I   5
Live o'er again that happy hour,
When midway on the mount I lay,
    Beside the ruined tower.

The moonshine, stealing o'er the scene
Had blended with the lights of eve;   10
And she was there, my hope, my joy,
    My own dear Genevieve!

She leant against the arméd man,
The statue of the arméd knight;
She stood and listened to my lay,   15
    Amid the lingering light.

Few sorrows hath she of her own,
My hope! my joy! my Genevieve!
She loves me best, whene'er I sing
    The songs that make her grieve.   20

I played a soft and doleful air,
I sang an old and moving story –
An old rude song, that suited well
    That ruin wild and hoary.

She listened with a flitting blush,   25
With downcast eyes and modest grace;
For well she knew, I could not choose
    But gaze upon her face.

I told her of the Knight that wore
Upon his shield a burning brand;
And that for ten long years he wooed
        The Lady of the Land.

I told her how he pined: and ah!
The deep, the low, the pleading tone
With which I sang another's love,
        Interpreted my own.

She listened with a flitting blush,
With downcast eyes, and modest grace;
And she forgave me, that I gazed
        Too fondly on her face!

But when I told the cruel scorn
That crazed that bold and lovely Knight,
And that he crossed the mountain-woods,
        Nor rested day nor night;

That sometimes from the savage den,
And sometimes from the darksome shade,
And sometimes starting up at once
        In green and sunny glade, –

There came and looked him in the face
An angel beautiful and bright;
And that he knew it was a Fiend,
        This miserable Knight!

And that unknowing what he did,
He leaped amid a murderous band,
And saved from outrage worse than death
        The Lady of the Land!

And how she wept, and clasped his knees;
And how she tended him in vain –
And ever strove to expiate
        The scorn that crazed his brain; –

And that she nursed him in a cave;
And how his madness went away,
When on the yellow forest-leaves
 A dying man he lay; –

His dying words – but when I reached   65
That tenderest strain of all the ditty,
My faultering voice and pausing harp
 Disturbed her soul with pity!

All impulses of soul and sense
Had thrilled my guileless Genevieve;   70
The music and the doleful tale,
 The rich and balmy eve;

And hopes, and fears that kindle hope,
An undistinguishable throng,
And gentle wishes long subdued,   75
 Subdued and cherished long!

She wept with pity and delight,
She blushed with love, and virgin-shame;
And like the murmur of a dream,
 I heard her breathe my name.   80

Her bosom heaved – she stepped aside,
As conscious of my look she stepped –
Then suddenly, with timorous eye
 She fled to me and wept.

She half enclosed me with her arms,   85
She pressed me with a meek embrace;
And bending back her head, looked up,
 And gazed upon my face.

'Twas partly love, and partly fear,
And partly 'twas a bashful art,   90
That I might rather feel, than see,
 The swelling of her heart.

I calmed her fears, and she was calm,
And told her love with virgin pride;
And so I won my Genevieve,
    My bright and beauteous Bride.

Alice Du Clos

OR THE FORKED TONGUE

A BALLAD
"One word with two meanings is the traitor's shield and
shaft: and a slit tongue be his blazon!"
Caucasian Proverb.

"The Sun is not yet risen,
But the dawn lies red on the dew:
Lord Julian has stolen from the hunters away,
Is seeking, Lady! for you.
Put on your dress of green,   5
   Your buskins and your quiver;
Lord Julian is a hasty man,
   Long waiting brook'd he never.
I dare not doubt him, that he means
   To wed you on a day,   10
Your lord and master for to be,
   And you his lady gay.
O Lady! throw your book aside!
I would not that my Lord should chide."

Thus spake Sir Hugh the vassal knight   15
   To Alice, child of old Du Clos,
As spotless fair, as airy light
   As that moon-shiny doe,
The gold star on its brow, her sire's ancestral crest!
For ere the lark had left his nest,   20
   She in the garden bower below
Sate loosely wrapt in maiden white,
Her face half drooping from the sight,
   A snow-drop on a tuft of snow!

O close your eyes, and strive to see   25
The studious maid, with book on knee, –
   Ah! earliest-open'd flower;
While yet with keen unblunted light

The morning star shone opposite
    The lattice of her bower –   30
Alone of all the starry host,
    As if in prideful scorn
Of flight and fear he stay'd behind,
    To brave th' advancing morn.

O! Alice could read passing well,   35
    And she was conning then
Dan Ovid's mazy tale of loves,
    And gods, and beasts, and men.

The vassal's speech, his taunting vein,
It thrill'd like venom thro' her brain;   40
    Yet never from the book
She rais'd her head, nor did she deign
    The knight a single look.

"Off, traitor friend! how dar'st thou fix
    Thy wanton gaze on me?   45
And why, against my earnest suit,
    Does Julian send by thee?

"Go, tell thy Lord, that slow is sure:
    Fair speed his shafts to-day!
I follow here a stronger lure,   50
    And chase a gentler prey."

She said: and with a baleful smile
    The vassal knight reel'd off –
Like a huge billow from a bark
    Toil'd in the deep sea-trough,   55
That shouldering sideways in mid plunge,
    Is travers'd by a flash.
And staggering onward, leaves the ear
    With dull and distant crash.

And Alice sate with troubled mien   60
A moment; for the scoff was keen,
    And thro' her veins did shiver!
Then rose and donn'd her dress of green,
    Her buskins and her quiver.

There stands the flow'ring may-thorn tree! 65
From thro' the veiling mist you see
    The black and shadowy stem; –
Smit by the sun the mist in glee
Dissolves to lightsome jewelry –
    Each blossom hath its gem! 70

With tear-drop glittering to a smile,
The gay maid on the garden-stile
    Mimics the hunter's shout.
"Hip! Florian, hip! To horse, to horse!
    Go, bring the palfrey out. 75

"My Julian's out with all his clan,
    And, bonny boy, you wis,
Lord Julian is a hasty man,
    Who comes late, comes amiss."

Now Florian was a stripling squire, 80
    A gallant boy of Spain,
That toss'd his head in joy and pride,
Behind his Lady fair to ride,
    But blush'd to hold her train.

The huntress is in her dress of green – 85
And forth they go; she with her bow,
    Her buskins and her quiver! –
The squire – no younger e'er was seen –
With restless arm and laughing een,
    He makes his javelin quiver. 90

And had not Alice stay'd the race,
And stopp'd to see, a moment's space,
    The whole great globe of light
Give the last parting kiss-like touch
To the eastern ridge, it lack'd not much, 95
    They had o'erta'en the knight.

It chanced that up the covert lane,
    Where Julian waiting stood,
A neighbour knight prick'd on to join
    The huntsmen in the wood. 100

And with him must Lord Julian go,
   Tho' with an anger'd mind:
Betroth'd not wedded to his bride,
   In vain he sought, 'twixt shame and pride,
     Excuse to stay behind.   105

He bit his lip, he wrung his glove,
He look'd around, he look'd above,
   But pretext none could find or frame.
Alas! alas! and well-a-day!
It grieves me sore to think, to say,   110
That names so seldom meet with Love,
   Yet Love wants courage without a name!

Straight from the forest's skirt the trees
   O'er-branching, made an aisle,
Where hermit old might pace and chaunt   115
   As in a minster's pile.

From underneath its leafy screen,
   And from the twilight shade,
You pass at once into a green,
   A green and lightsome glade.   120

And there Lord Julian sate on steed;
   Behind him, in a round,
Stood knight and squire, and menial train;
Against the leash the greyhounds strain;
   The horses paw'd the ground.   125

When up the alley green, Sir Hugh
   Spurr'd in upon the sward,
And mute, without a word, did he
   Fall in behind his lord.

Lord Julian turn'd his steed half round, –   130
   "What! doth not Alice deign
To accept your loving convoy, knight?
Or doth she fear our woodland sleight,
   And join us on the plain?"

With stifled tones the knight replied,   135
And look'd askance on either side, –
   "Nay, let the hunt proceed! –
The Lady's message that I bear,
I guess would scantly please your ear,
   And less deserves your heed.   140

"You sent betimes. Not yet unbarr'd
   I found the middle door; –
Two stirrers only met my eyes,
   Fair Alice, and one more.

"I came unlook'd for; and, it seem'd,   145
   In an unwelcome hour;
And found the daughter of Du Clos
   Within the lattic'd bower.

"But hush! the rest may wait. If lost,
   No great loss, I divine;   150
And idle words will better suit
   A fair maid's lips than mine."

"God's wrath! speak out, man," Julian cried,
   O'ermaster'd by the sudden smart; –
And feigning wrath, sharp, blunt, and rude,   155
The knight his subtle shift pursued. –
"Scowl not at me; command my skill,
To lure your hawk back, if you will,
   But not a woman's heart.

"'Go! (said she) tell him, – slow is sure;   160
   Fair speed his shafts to-day!
I follow here a stronger lure,
   And chase a gentler prey."

"The game, pardie, was full in sight,
That then did, if I saw aright,   165
   The fair dame's eyes engage;
For turning, as I took my ways,
I saw them fix'd with steadfast gaze
   Full on her wanton page."

The last word of the traitor knight   170
  It had but entered Julian's ear, –
From two o'erarching oaks between,
With glist'ning helm-like cap is seen,
  Borne on in giddy cheer,

A youth, that ill his steed can guide;   175
Yet with reverted face doth ride,
  As answering to a voice,
That seems at once to laugh and chide –
"Not mine, dear mistress," still he cried,
  "'Tis this mad filly's choice."   180

With sudden bound, beyond the boy,
See! see! that face of hope and joy,
  That regal front! those cheeks aglow!
Thou needed'st but the crescent sheen,
A quiver'd Dian to have been,   185
  Thou lovely child of old Du Clos!

Dark as a dream Lord Julian stood,
Swift as a dream, from forth the wood,
  Sprang on the plighted Maid!
With fatal aim, and frantic force,   190
The shaft was hurl'd! – a lifeless corse,
Fair Alice from her vaulting horse,
  Lies bleeding on the glade.

IV

HILL WALKING
POEMS

Hill Walking Poems

IT IS EASY TO THINK of Coleridge's passion for "Nature" as some sort of metaphysical abstraction (see No. 18). Yet he was the son of a country vicar, was uneasy in cities, and for the first forty years of his life he gardened, rambled, botanized, climbed and sea-bathed as often as he could. The outdoor world was vital to him. Wordsworth describes him carrying magnifying glasses and special coloured filters to view plants and insects. His Notebooks, certainly up to 1812, are filled with minute descriptions of wildlife, effects of wind and sunlight, studies of clouds and birds, and the subtlest impressions of flowing water. (Many of his library books still contain pressed flowers, gathered as he read in some field.)

But Coleridge's greatest passion was for hill walking: whether rambling, scrambling, long-distance hiking, tramping, yomping, peak climbing or simply idling on a grassy slope (No. 42). He had walked over the Welsh mountains (including Snowdon); over the Mendip, Exmoor and Quantock hills in the west of England; over the Hartz Mountains and the Brocken in Germany; over most of the major peaks in the Lake District (including Skiddaw, Helvellyn, and Scafell); over much of the Highlands of Scotland; and even over Mount Etna in Sicily. It is this open-air theme that unites the otherwise varied poems of this group, all written during the decade of his greatest expeditions between 1794 and 1804, when he became one of the pioneers of fell-walking.

Their style is various, leisurely or energetic. They include amorous meditations (Nos. 37 and 44), uplifting invitations (No. 38), quick sketches (No. 40), tender inscriptions (No. 41), rhetorical adaptations (No. 43) and wild hillside fantasies (No. 42). But all vividly display Coleridge's tireless early enthusiasm for exploring the countryside, which after a long middle period of illness, came back to him again in old age when he used to perambulate over Hampstead Heath at his "after-dinner alderman-like pace" (according to Keats) and bowl gently along the beaches of Kent and Sussex (see "Youth and Age", No. 69).

Physically, young Coleridge was a formidable walker, and this drive had a particular shaping effect on his poetry. It should not be forgotten that in 1796 he walked from Stowey to Bristol (a distance of some forty miles) in one day; and then walked back the following day, "not much tired"; while seven years later in 1803 he walked through the Scottish Highlands alone, carrying a small canvas bag, and covering 263 miles in eight days. He once said he could never remember a single occasion on which he turned back from a hill walk because of bad weather.

This impetuous movement through a changing landscape, often up towards some commanding peak or viewpoint, becomes a structural principle in his writing. Hazlitt (another enthusiastic walker) noticed this in his fine essay, "On Going on a Journey", in which he recalls how Coleridge "could go on in the most delightful explanatory way, over hill and dale, a summer's day, and convert a landscape into a didactic poem or a Pindaric ode." The imaginative, "explanatory" journeys of the Hill Walking Poems all tend to use this open, dynamic form in which the mobile details of landscape are gradually "converted" into some sort of cumulative enchantment or vision.

The classical trope behind this highly Romantic structure is perhaps the seventeenth-century philosopher Francis Bacon's conception of knowledge as a winding, upward path, only achieved with much effort and digression (see No. 38). The same instinctive movement towards a commanding "viewpoint" is found in the plein-air painters of the time, notably Caspar David Friedrich and J.M.W. Turner. But in Coleridge it becomes deeply internalized, far beyond the scope of these early poems, and is eventually responsible for the digressive structure of prose works like the *Biographia Literaria* and *The Friend*.

For Coleridge, the early experience of hill walking remained something fresh and astonishing, and a profound spiritual discovery. In 1803 he wrote this rousing declaration to his friend Tom Wedgwood, an invalid whom he was trying to rally and encourage:

"In simple earnest, I never find myself alone within the embracement of rocks & hills, a traveller up an alpine road, but my spirit courses, drives, and eddies, like a Leaf in Autumn. A wild activity, of thoughts, imaginations, feelings, and impulses of motion, rises up from within me . . . I think, that my soul must have pre-existed in the body of a Chamois-chaser . . . The farther I ascend from animated Nature, from men, and cattle, & the common birds of the woods, & fields, the greater becomes in me the Intensity of the feeling of Life . . . I do not think it possible, that any bodily pains could eat out the love & joy, that is so substantially part of me, towards hills, & rocks, & steep waters! And I have had some Trial.

(*Letters*, 14 January 1803.)

There is a sense in which Coleridge hill-walked his way into much of his early poetry. Again it was Hazlitt, in another essay, "My First Meeting with Poets", who pointed out that Coleridge's blank verse line often reflected his physical pace over the ground, and was actually composed while walking. "Coleridge has told me he himself liked to compose in walking over uneven ground, or breaking through the straggling branches of a copse-wood . . ."

As this impulse declined (see Nos. 43 and 44) the nature of Coleridge's inspiration changed, and his landscapes moved inwards. But the upward, striding, airy quality of these poems remain; while the sport he helped to pioneer has also become an intrinsic aspect of the English sensibility. His influence in this stretches from Alfred Lord Tennyson to Alfred Wainwright.

Lines Composed while Climbing the Left Ascent of Brockley Coomb, Somersetshire, May 1795

With many a pause and oft reverted eye
I climb the Coomb's ascent: sweet songsters near
Warble in shade their wild-wood melody:
Far off the unvarying Cuckoo soothes my ear.
Up scour the startling stragglers of the flock   5
That on green plots o'er precipices browze:
From the deep fissures of the naked rock
The Yew-tree bursts! Beneath its dark green boughs
(Mid which the May-thorn blends its blossoms white)
Where broad smooth stones jut out in mossy seats,   10
I rest: – and now have gain'd the topmost site.
Ah! what a luxury of landscape meets
My gaze! Proud towers, and Cots more dear to me,
Elm-shadow'd Fields, and prospect-bounding Sea!
Deep sighs my lonely heart: I drop the tear: 15
Enchanting spot! O were my Sara here!

To a Young Friend on his Proposing to Domesticate with the Author

A mount, not wearisome and bare and steep,
  But a green mountain variously up-piled,
Where o'er the jutting rocks soft mosses creep,
Or colour'd lichens with slow oozing weep;
    Where cypress and the darker yew start wild;   5
And, 'mid the summer torrent's gentle dash
Dance brighten'd the red clusters of the ash;
  Beneath whose boughs, by those still sounds beguil'd,
Calm Pensiveness might muse herself to sleep;
    Till haply startled by some fleecy dam,   10
That rustling on the bushy cliff above
With melancholy bleat of anxious love,
  Made meek enquiry for her wandering lamb:
  Such a green mountain 'twere most sweet to climb,
E'en while the bosom ach'd with loneliness –   15
How more than sweet, if some dear friend should bless
  The adventurous toil, and up the path sublime
Now lead, now follow: the glad landscape round,
Wide and more wide, increasing without bound!

  O then 'twere loveliest sympathy, to mark   20
The berries of the half-uprooted ash
Dripping and bright; and list the torrent's dash, –
  Beneath the cypress, or the yew more dark,
Seated at ease, on some smooth mossy rock;
In social silence now, and now to unlock   25
The treasur'd heart; arm linked in friendly arm,
Save if the one, his muse's witching charm
Muttering brow-bent, at unwatch'd distance lag;
  Till high o'er head his beckoning friend appears,
And from the forehead of the topmost crag   30
  Shouts eagerly: for haply *there* uprears
That shadowing Pine its old romantic limbs,

Which latest shall detain the enamour'd sight
Seen from below, when eve the valley dims,
    Tinged yellow with the rich departing light;   35
    And haply, bason'd in some unsunn'd cleft,
A beauteous spring, the rock's collected tears,
Sleeps shelter'd there, scarce wrinkled by the gale!
    Together thus, the world's vain turmoil left,
Stretch'd on the crag, and shadow'd by the pine,   40
    And bending o'er the clear delicious fount,
Ah! dearest youth! it were a lot divine
To cheat our noons in moralising mood,
While west-winds fann'd our temples toil-bedew'd:
    Then downwards slope, oft pausing, from the mount,   45
To some lone mansion, in some woody dale,
Where smiling with blue eye, Domestic Bliss
Gives *this* the Husband's, *that* the Brother's kiss!

    Thus rudely vers'd in allegoric lore,
The Hill of Knowledge I essayed to trace;   50
That verdurous hill with many a resting-place,
And many a stream, whose warbling waters pour
    To glad, and fertilise the subject plains;
That hill with secret springs, and nooks untrod,
And many a fancy-blest and holy sod   55
    Where Inspiration, his diviner strains
Low-murmuring, lay; and starting from the rock's
Stiff evergreens, (whose spreading foliage mocks
Want's barren soil, and the bleak frosts of age,
And Bigotry's mad fire-invoking rage!)   60
O meek retiring spirit! we will climb,
Cheering and cheered, this lovely hill sublime;
    And from the stirring world up-lifted high
(Whose noises, faintly wafted on the wind,
To quiet musings shall attune the mind,   65
    And oft the melancholy *theme* supply),
    There, while the prospect through the gazing eye
    Pours all its healthful greenness on the soul,
We'll smile at wealth, and learn to smile at fame,
Our hopes, our knowledge, and our joys the same,   70
    As neighbouring fountains image each the whole:

Then when the mind hath drunk its fill of truth
   We'll discipline the heart to pure delight,
Rekindling sober joy's domestic flame.
They whom I love shall love thee, honour'd youth!   75
   Now may Heaven realise this vision bright!

Lines Written in the Album at Elbingerode, in the Hartz Forest

I stood on Brocken's sovran height, and saw
Woods crowding upon woods, hills over hills,
A surging scene, and only limited
By the blue distance. Heavily my way
Downward I dragged through fir groves evermore,   5
Where bright green moss heaves in sepulchral forms
Speckled with sunshine; and, but seldom heard,
The sweet bird's song became a hollow sound;
And the breeze, murmuring indivisibly,
Preserved its solemn murmur most distinct   10
From many a note of many a waterfall,
And the brook's chatter; 'mid whose islet-stones
The dingy kidling with its tinkling bell
Leaped frolicsome, or old romantic goat
Sat, his white beard slow waving. I moved on   15
In low and languid mood: for I had found
That outward forms, the loftiest, still receive
Their finer influence from the Life within; –
Fair cyphers else: fair, but of import vague
Or unconcerning, where the heart not finds   20
History or prophecy of friend, or child,
Or gentle maid, our first and early love,
Or father, or the venerable name
Of our adoréd country! O thou Queen,
Thou delegated Deity of Earth,   25
O dear, dear England! how my longing eye
Turned westward, shaping in the steady clouds
Thy sands and high white cliffs!

                    My native Land!
Filled with the thought of thee this heart was proud,
Yea, mine eye swam with tears: that all the view   30
From sovran Brocken, woods and woody hills,
Floated away, like a departing dream,

Feeble and dim! Stranger, these impulses
Blame thou not lightly; nor will I profane,
With hasty judgment or injurious doubt,   35
That man's sublimer spirit, who can feel
That God is everywhere! the God who framed
Mankind to be one mighty family,
Himself our Father, and the World our Home.

A Thought Suggested by a View of Saddleback in Cumberland

On stern Blencartha's perilous height
  The winds are tyrannous and strong;
And flashing forth unsteady light
From stern Blencartha's skiey height,
  As loud the torrents throng!   5
Beneath the moon, in gentle weather,
  They bind the earth and sky together.
But oh! the sky and all its forms, how quiet!
The things that seek the earth, how full of noise and riot!

Inscription for a
Fountain on a Heath

This Sycamore, oft musical with bees, –
Such tents the Patriarchs loved! O long unharmed
May all its agéd boughs o'er-canopy
The small round basin, which this jutting stone
Keeps pure from falling leaves! Long may the Spring, 5
Quietly as a sleeping infant's breath,
Send up cold waters to the traveller
With soft and even pulse! Nor ever cease
Yon tiny cone of sand its soundless dance,
Which at the bottom, like a Fairy's Page, 10
As merry and no taller, dances still,
Nor wrinkles the smooth surface of the Fount.
Here Twilight is and Coolness: here is moss,
A soft seat, and a deep and ample shade.
Thou may'st toil far and find no second tree. 15
Drink, Pilgrim, here; Here rest! and if thy heart
Be innocent, here too shalt thou refresh
Thy spirit, listening to some gentle sound,
Or passing gale or hum of murmuring bees!

A Stranger Minstrel

WRITTEN TO MRS ROBINSON,
A FEW WEEKS BEFORE HER DEATH

As late on Skiddaw's mount I lay supine,
Midway th' ascent, in that repose divine
When the soul centred in the heart's recess
Hath quaff'd its fill of Nature's loveliness,
Yet still beside the fountain's marge will stay   5
    And fain would thirst again, again to quaff;
Then when the tear, slow travelling on its way,
    Fills up the wrinkles of a silent laugh –
In that sweet mood of sad and humorous thought
A form within me rose, within me wrought   10
With such strong magic, that I cried aloud,
"Thou ancient Skiddaw by thy helm of cloud,
And by thy many-colour'd chasms deep,
And by their shadows that for ever sleep,
By yon small flaky mists that love to creep   15
Along the edges of those spots of light,
Those sunny islands on thy smooth green height,
    And by yon shepherds with their sheep,
    And dogs and boys, a gladsome crowd,
    That rush e'en now with clamour loud   20
Sudden from forth thy topmost cloud,
And by this laugh, and by this tear,
I would, old Skiddaw, she were here!
A lady of sweet song is she,
Her soft blue eye was made for thee!   25
O ancient Skiddaw, by this tear,
I would, I would that she were here!"

Then ancient Skiddaw, stern and proud,
    In sullen majesty replying,
Thus spake from out his helm of cloud   30
    (His voice was like an echo dying!): –
"She dwells belike in scenes more fair,
And scorns a mount so bleak and bare."

I only sigh'd when this I heard,
Such mournful thoughts within me stirr'd   35
That all my heart was faint and weak,
    So sorely was I troubled!
No laughter wrinkled on my cheek,
    But O the tears were doubled!
But ancient Skiddaw green and high   40
Heard and understood my sigh;
And now, in tones less stern and rude,
As if he wish'd to end the feud,
Spake he, the proud response renewing
(His voice was like a monarch wooing): –   45
"Nay, but thou dost not know her might,
    The pinions of her soul how strong!
But many a stranger in my height
    Hath sung to me her magic song,
        Sending forth his ecstasy   50
        In her divinest melody,
    And hence I know her soul is free,
    She is where'er she wills to be,
    Unfetter'd by mortality!
Now to the 'haunted beach' can fly,   55
    Beside the threshold scourged with waves,
    Now where the maniac wildly raves,
'*Pale moon, thou spectre of the sky!*'
    No wind that hurries o'er my height
    Can travel with so swift a flight.   60
        I too, methinks, might merit
        The presence of her spirit!
        To me too might belong
    The honour of her song and witching melody,
        Which most resembles me,   65
        Soft, various, and sublime,
        Exempt from wrongs of Time!"

Thus spake the mighty Mount, and I
Made answer, with a deep-drawn sigh: –
"Thou ancient Skiddaw, by this tear,   70
I would, I would that she were here!"

Hymn before Sun-Rise, in the Vale of Chamouni

Besides the Rivers, Arve and Arveiron, which have their
sources in the foot of Mont Blanc, five conspicuous torrents
rush down its sides; and within a few paces of the Glaciers,
the Gentiana Major grows in immense numbers, with its
"flowers of loveliest blue."

Hast thou a charm to stay the morning-star
In his steep course? So long he seems to pause
On thy bald awful head, O sovran BLANC,
The Arve and Arveiron at thy base
Rave ceaselessly; but thou, most awful Form!   5
Risest from forth thy silent sea of pines,
How silently! Around thee and above
Deep is the air and dark, substantial, black,
An ebon mass: methinks thou piercest it,
As with a wedge! But when I look again,   10
It is thine own calm home, thy crystal shrine,
Thy habitation from eternity!
O dread and silent Mount! I gazed upon thee,
Till thou, still present to the bodily sense,
Didst vanish from my thought: entranced in prayer   15
I worshipped the Invisible alone.

Yet, like some sweet beguiling melody,
So sweet, we know not we are listening to it,
Thou, the meanwhile, wast blending with my Thought,
Yea, with my Life and Life's own secret joy: 20
Till the dilating Soul, enrapt, transfused,
Into the mighty vision passing – there
As in her natural form, swelled vast to Heaven!

Awake, my soul! not only passive praise
Thou owest! not alone these swelling tears,   25
Mute thanks and secret ecstasy! Awake,
Voice of sweet song! Awake, my heart, awake!
Green vales and icy cliffs, all join my Hymn.

Thou first and chief, sole sovereign of the Vale!
O struggling with the darkness all the night,   30
And visited all night by troops of stars,
Or when they climb the sky or when they sink:
Companion of the morning-star at dawn,
Thyself Earth's rosy star, and of the dawn
Co-herald: wake, O wake, and utter praise!   35
Who sank thy sunless pillars deep in Earth?
Who filled thy countenance with rosy light?
Who made thee parent of perpetual streams?

And you, ye five wild torrents fiercely glad!
Who called you forth from night and utter death,   40
From dark and icy caverns called you forth,
Down those precipitous, black, jaggéd rocks,
For ever shattered and the same for ever?
Who gave you your invulnerable life,
Your strength, your speed, your fury, and your joy,   45
Unceasing thunder and eternal foam?
And who commanded (and the silence came),
Here let the billows stiffen, and have rest?

Ye Ice-falls! ye that from the mountain's brow
Adown enormous ravines slope amain –   50
Torrents, methinks, that heard a mighty voice,
And stopped at once amid their maddest plunge!
Motionless torrents! silent cataracts!
Who made you glorious as the Gates of Heaven
Beneath the keen full moon? Who bade the sun   55
Clothe you with rainbows? Who, with living flowers
Of loveliest blue, spread garlands at your feet? –
GOD! let the torrents, like a shout of nations,
Answer! and let the ice-plains echo, GOD!
GOD! sing ye meadow-streams with gladsome voice!   60
Ye pine-groves, with your soft and soul-like sounds!
And they too have a voice, yon piles of snow,
And in their perilous fall shall thunder, GOD!

Ye living flowers that skirt the eternal frost!
Ye wild goats sporting round the eagle's nest!   65
Ye eagles, play-mates of the mountain-storm!

Ye lightnings, the dread arrows of the clouds!
Ye signs and wonders of the element!
Utter forth God, and fill the hills with praise!

    Thou too, hoar Mount! with thy sky-pointing peaks,   70
Oft from whose feet the avalanche, unheard,
Shoots downward, glittering through the pure serene
Into the depth of clouds, that veil thy breast –
Thou too again, stupendous Mountain! thou
That as I raise my head, awhile bowed low   75
In adoration, upward from thy base
Slow travelling with dim eyes suffused with tears,
Solemnly seemest, like a vapoury cloud,
To rise before me – Rise, O ever rise,
Rise like a cloud of incense from the Earth!   80
Thou kingly Spirit throned among the hills,
Thou dread ambassador from Earth to Heaven,
Great Hierarch! tell thou the silent sky,
And tell the stars, and tell yon rising sun
Earth, with her thousand voices, praises GOD.   85

The Picture, or The Lover's Resolution

Through weeds and thorns, and matted underwood
I force my way; now climb, and now descend
O'er rocks, or bare or mossy, with wild foot
Crushing the purple whorts; while oft unseen,
Hurrying along the drifted forest-leaves, 5
The scared snake rustles. Onward still I toil,
I know not, ask not whither! A new joy,
Lovely as light, sudden as summer gust,
And gladsome as the first-born of the spring,
Beckons me on, or follows from behind, 10
Playmate, or guide! The master-passion quelled,
I feel that I am free. With dun-red bark
The fir-trees, and the unfrequent slender oak,
Forth from this tangle wild of bush and brake
Soar up, and form a melancholy vault 15
High o'er me, murmuring like a distant sea.

Here Wisdom might resort, and here Remorse;
Here too the love-lorn man, who, sick in soul,
And of this busy human heart aweary,
Worships the spirit of unconscious life 20
In tree or wild-flower. – Gentle lunatic!
If so he might not wholly cease to be,
He would far rather not be that he is;
But would be something that he knows not of,
In winds or waters, or among the rocks! 25

But hence, fond wretch! breathe not contagion here!
No myrtle-walks are these: these are no groves
Where Love dare loiter! If in sullen mood
He should stray hither, the low stumps shall gore
His dainty feet, the briar and the thorn 30
Make his plumes haggard. Like a wounded bird
Easily caught, ensnare him, O ye Nymphs,
Ye Oreads chaste, ye dusky Dryades!

And you, ye Earth-winds! you that make at morn
The dew-drops quiver on the spiders' webs!   35
You, O ye wingless Airs! that creep between
The rigid stems of heath and bitten furze,
Within whose scanty shade, at summer-noon,
The mother-sheep hath worn a hollow bed –
Ye, that now cool her fleece with dropless damp,   40
Now pant and murmur with her feeding lamb.
Chase, chase him, all ye Fays, and elfin Gnomes!
With prickles sharper than his darts bemock
His little Godship, making him perforce
Creep through a thorn-bush on yon hedgehog's back.   45

   This is my hour of triumph! I can now
With my own fancies play the merry fool,
And laugh away worse folly, being free.
Here will I seat myself, beside this old,
Hollow, and weedy oak, which ivy-twine   50
Clothes as with net-work: here will I couch my limbs,
Close by this river, in this silent shade,
As safe and sacred from the step of man
As an invisible world – unheard, unseen,
And listening only to the pebbly brook   55
That murmurs with a dead, yet tinkling sound;
Or to the bees, that in the neighbouring trunk
Make honey-hoards. The breeze, that visits me,
Was never Love's accomplice, never raised
The tendril ringlets from the maiden's brow,   60
And the blue, delicate veins above her cheek;
Ne'er played the wanton – never half disclosed
The maiden's snowy bosom, scattering thence
Eye-poisons for some love-distempered youth,
Who ne'er henceforth may see an aspen-grove   65
Shiver in sunshine, but his feeble heart
Shall flow away like a dissolving thing.

Sweet breeze! thou only, if I guess aright,
Liftest the feathers of the robin's breast,
That swells its little breast, so full of song,   70
Singing above me, on the mountain-ash.
And thou too, desert stream! no pool of thine,

Though clear as lake in latest summer-eve,
Did e'er reflect the stately virgin's robe,
The face, the form divine, the downcast look   75
Contemplative! Behold! her open palm
Presses her cheek and brow! her elbow rests
On the bare branch of half-uprooted tree,
That leans towards its mirror! Who erewhile
Had from her countenance turned, or looked by stealth,   80
(For Fear is true-love's cruel nurse), he now
With steadfast gaze and unoffending eye,
Worships the watery idol, dreaming hopes
Delicious to the soul, but fleeting, vain,
E'en as that phantom-world on which he gazed,   85
But not unheeded gazed: for see, ah! see,
The sportive tyrant with her left hand plucks
The heads of tall flowers that behind her grow,
Lychnis, and willow-herb, and fox-glove bells:
And suddenly, as one that toys with time,   90
Scatters them on the pool! Then all the charm
Is broken – all that phantom world so fair
Vanishes, and a thousand circlets spread,
And each mis-shape the other. Stay awhile,
Poor youth, who scarcely dar'st lift up thine eyes!   95
The stream will soon renew its smoothness, soon
The visions will return! And lo! he stays:
And soon the fragments dim of lovely forms
Come trembling back, unite, and now once more
The pool becomes a mirror; and behold   100
Each wildflower on the marge inverted there,
And there the half-uprooted tree – but where,
O where the virgin's snowy arm, that leaned
On its bare branch? He turns, and she is gone!
Homeward she steals through many a woodland maze   105
Which he shall seek in vain. Ill-fated youth!
Go, day by day, and waste thy manly prime
In mad love-yearning by the vacant brook,
Till sickly thoughts bewitch thine eyes, and thou
Behold'st her shadow still abiding there,   110
The Naiad of the mirror!
                          Not to thee,
O wild and desert stream! belongs this tale:

Gloomy and dark art thou – the crowded firs
Spire from thy shores, and stretch across thy bed,
Making thee doleful as a cavern-well: 115
Save when the shy king-fishers build their nest
On thy steep banks, no loves hast thou, wild stream!

    This be my chosen haunt – emancipate
From Passion's dreams, a freeman, and alone,
I rise and trace its devious course. O lead,   120
Lead me to deeper shades and lonelier glooms.
Lo! stealing through the canopy of firs,
How fair the sunshine spots that mossy rock,
Isle of the river, whose disparted waves
Dart off asunder with an angry sound,   125
How soon to re-unite! And see! they meet,
Each in the other lost and found: and see
Placeless, as spirits, one soft water-sun
Throbbing within them, heart at once and eye!
With its soft neighbourhood of filmy clouds,   130
The stains and shadings of forgotten tears,
Dimness o'erswum with lustre! Such the hour
Of deep enjoyment, following love's brief feuds;
And hark, the noise of a near waterfall!
I pass forth into light – I find myself   135
Beneath a weeping birch (most beautiful
Of forest trees, the Lady of the Woods),
Hard by the brink of a tall weedy rock
That overbrows the cataract. How bursts
The landscape on my sight! Two crescent hills   140
Fold in behind each other, and so make
A circular vale, and land-locked, as might seem,
With brook and bridge, and grey stone cottages,
Half hid by rocks and fruit-trees. At my feet,
The whortle-berries are bedewed with spray,   145
Dashed upwards by the furious waterfall.
How solemnly the pendent ivy-mass
Swings in its winnow: All the air is calm.
The smoke from cottage-chimneys, tinged with light,
Rises in columns; from this house alone,   150
Close by the water-fall, the column slants,
And feels its ceaseless breeze. But what is this?

That cottage, with its slanting chimney-smoke,
And close beside its porch a sleeping child,
His dear head pillowed on a sleeping dog—   155
One arm between its fore-legs, and the hand
Holds loosely its small handful of wild-flowers,
Unfilletted, and of unequal lengths.
A curious picture, with a master's haste
Sketched on a strip of pinky-silver skin,   160
Peeled from the birchen bark! Divinest maid!
Yon bark her canvas, and those purple berries
Her pencil! See, the juice is scarcely dried
On the fine skin! She has been newly here;
And lo! yon patch of heath has been her couch—   165
The pressure still remains! O blesséd couch!
For this may'st thou flower early, and the sun,
Slanting at eve, rest bright, and linger long
Upon thy purple bells! O Isabel!
Daughter of genius! stateliest of our maids!   170
More beautiful than whom Alcaeus wooed,
The Lesbian woman of immortal song!
O child of genius! stately, beautiful,
And full of love to all, save only me,
And not ungentle e'en to me! My heart,   175
Why beats it thus? Through yonder coppice-wood
Needs must the pathway turn, that leads straightway
On to her father's house. She is alone!
The night draws on – such ways are hard to hit—
And fit it is I should restore this sketch,   180
Dropt unawares, no doubt. Why should I yearn
To keep the relique? 'twill but idly feed
The passion that consumes me. Let me haste!
The picture in my hand which she has left;
She cannot blame me that I followed her: 185
And I may be her guide the long wood through.

V

ASRA POEMS

Asra Poems

PREFACE

THESE FOURTEEN LOVE POEMS were all inspired by Coleridge's long affair with Sara Hutchinson between 1799 and 1810. The story of this passionate, but probably unconsummated, relationship has only been fully revealed through the recent publication of Coleridge's later Notebooks. It is perhaps still not wholly understood, and various mysteries remain, to which the poems may provide clues. The wider literary significance of the Asra Poems has barely been recognized. They alter our sense of Coleridge's emotional range as a poet, and provide a largely new context for his great poem "Dejection: An Ode" (No. 50).

Sara Hutchinson (1775–1835) was the younger sister of Wordsworth's wife, Mary Hutchinson. She came from a large, hospitable, hard-working family of Yorkshire farmers, and had grown up in the countryside. The family were prosperous – Sara's brothers became successful "gentlemen" farmers – and she was a well-educated, animated young woman with an independence and originality of mind all her own. She had been partly brought up in Cumberland in the house of a strange, kindly, autodidact relative known as James Patrick of Kendal, "the Intellectual Pedlar", whom Wordsworth would use as a model for the figure of the Wanderer in "The Excursion". She was a great walker, and loved watercolour painting and poetry (see also "The Picture", No. 44). But she was not a conventionally romantic, dreamy Muse. She was cheerful and outgoing, a small energetic figure with a mass of auburn hair, quick and neat in the house, and daring and eager on country walks (see "The Keepsake", No. 45). Many of Coleridge's tenderest memories of her are in a snug, firelit farmhouse kitchen (see "A Day-Dream: My Eyes Make Pictures", No. 47).

Coleridge first met Sara Hutchinson at her brother Tom's manor house farm near Sockburn-on-Tees in the winter of 1799, during his first momentous visit to the north of England and the Lake District with Wordsworth (see "The Keepsake", No. 45 and note). Coleridge was then twenty-seven, and had been married for four years; Sara was twenty-four with no attachments, nor did she ever subsequently marry. Coleridge felt he had fallen in love at first sight (see "The Language of Birds", No. 46), but also feared it was a catastrophe (see also the ballad "Love", No. 35). In his Notebooks he transposed the letters of Sara's name to form "Asra", his muse-figure or "moorish maid".

For the next four years they lived in close proximity, visiting each other in Cumberland and Yorkshire, while Coleridge continued his increasingly difficult family life at Keswick. These periods of rapturous meetings, followed by stricken separations, are reflected in the "Day-Dream" poems (Nos. 47 and 48). The unbearable unhappiness of this situation, coupled with Coleridge's illness and opium addiction, finally produced in April 1802 his great outburst of love and despair, "A Letter to Sara Hutchinson" (No. 49). With extraordinary skill, Coleridge shaped and edited this verse letter into one of his most famous poems, "Dejection: An Ode" (No. 50), which he felt he could publish and show to friends. But many of the other Asra poems had to be disguised, or kept in manuscript.

In an attempt to sort out his professional life and break off with Asra, Coleridge disappeared to the Mediterranean between 1804 and 1806 (see "Separation", No. 51, and "Phantom", No. 52). But when he returned, he separated from his wife and lived with Asra and the Wordsworths, first in Leicestershire and then back in Cumberland, for various periods between 1806 and 1810. Sara acted successfully as his amanuensis, during the writing of his periodical The Friend, but this was a time of great tension and jealousy (see "Ad Vilmum Axiolorum", No. 54, a Latin poem which reveals a great deal about the emotional complexities of the household; see also "The Tropic Tree", No. 80). The moments of lyrical happiness had become rare (see "Recollections of Love", No. 57).

When Coleridge quarrelled with Wordsworth in 1810, he left the Lake District and was never again intimate with Sara Hutchinson. She moved in permanently with Wordsworth's household, and settled herself as her sister's and brother-in-law's companion. Coleridge's subsequent reflections on what the disastrous love affair had really signified, "Constancy to an Ideal Object" (No. 58), forms the last poem of the Asra group, though disguised references to her appear in several of the Confessional Poems. In old age, Coleridge renewed a cheerful correspondence with her from Highgate, and met her on occasions in London and Ramsgate. When he died, she was one of the very few people to whom he left a small gold "mourning ring", as was the custom between intimate friends.

The suggestion that the Asra Poems form a distinctive group was first made by the Coleridge scholar George Whalley in 1955. His selection was rather wider and more speculative than this one, and includes for example "Love" (No. 35), "The Picture" (No. 44) and "To Two Sisters" (No. 61). Coleridge himself never collected the poems separately, but tried to disguise them or hide them from his friends. Surprisingly, it was Sara who put many of them together in a manuscript scrapbook entitled "Sara's Poets", though these also included poems by Wordsworth. (The possibility that she was half in love with both men may also be considered; but her real feelings remain a mystery to this day, as most of her early letters were destroyed.)

But the fourteen poems printed here – together of course with the heart-breaking sonnet "To Asra" (No. 14), written just before Coleridge's departure for Malta – do form a powerfully unified if fragmented sequence. They are held together by certain patterns of imagery and obsessive feeling, rather than by any particular poetic form. The story they tell is, perhaps, a tragedy of longing and self-deception (the terrible possibility finally faced in No. 58), rather than a conventional love affair. Certainly Sara Hutchinson seems to have suffered as much as Coleridge. Yet strangely "Asra" herself emerges as one of Coleridge's most haunting creations, like Christabel or the mysterious Abyssinian maid.

The Keepsake

The tedded hay, the first fruits of the soil,
The tedded hay and corn-sheaves in one field,
Show summer gone, ere come. The foxglove tall
Sheds its loose purple bells, or in the gust,
Or when it bends beneath the up-springing lark,   5
Or mountain-finch alighting. And the rose
(In vain the darling of successful love)
Stands, like some boasted beauty of past years,
The thorns remaining, and the flowers all gone.
Nor can I find, amid my lonely walk   10
By rivulet, or spring, or wet roadside,
That blue and bright-eyed floweret of the brook,
Hope's gentle gem, the sweet Forget-me-not!
So will not fade the flowers which Emmeline
With delicate fingers on the snow-white silk   15
Has worked (the flowers which most she knew I loved),
And, more beloved than they, her auburn hair.

  In the cool morning twilight, early waked
By her full bosom's joyous restlessness,
Softly she rose, and lightly stole along,   20
Down the slope coppice to the woodbine bower,
Whose rich flowers, swinging in the morning breeze,
Over their dim fast-moving shadows hung,
Making a quiet image of disquiet
In the smooth, scarcely moving river-pool.   25
There, in that bower where first she owned her love,
And let me kiss my own warm tear of joy
From off her glowing cheek, she sate and stretched
The silk upon the frame, and worked her name
Between the Moss-Rose and Forget-me-not –   30
Her own dear name, with her own auburn hair!
That forced to wander till sweet spring return,
I yet might ne'er forget her smile, her look,

Her voice, (that even in her mirthful mood
Has made me wish to steal away and weep,)   35
Nor yet the entrancement of that maiden kiss
With which she promised, that when spring returned,
She would resign one half of that dear name,
And own thenceforth no other name but mine!

The Language of Birds

Do you ask what the birds say? The Sparrow, the Dove,
The Linnet and Thrush say, "I love and I love!"
In the winter they're silent – the wind is so strong;
What it says, I don't know, but it sings a loud song.
But green leaves, and blossoms, and sunny warm weather,   5
And singing, and loving – all come back together.
But the Lark is so brimful of gladness and love,
The green fields below him, the blue sky above,
That he sings, and he sings; and for ever sings he –
"I love my Love, and my Love loves me!"   10

A Day-Dream:
My Eyes Make Pictures

My eyes make pictures, when they are shut:
    I see a fountain, large and fair,
A willow and a ruined hut,
    And thee, and me and Mary there.
O Mary! make thy gentle lap our pillow!   5
Bend o'er us, like a bower, my beautiful green willow!

A wild-rose roofs the ruined shed,
    And that and summer well agree:
And lo! where Mary leans her head,
    Two dear names carved upon the tree!   10
And Mary's tears, they are not tears of sorrow:
Our sister and our friend will both be here to-morrow.

'Twas day! but now few, large, and bright,
    The stars are round the crescent moon!
And now it is a dark warm night,   15
    The balmiest of the month of June!
A glow-worm fall'n, and on the marge remounting
Shines, and its shadow shines, fit stars for our sweet fountain.

O ever – ever be thou blest!
    For dearly, Asra! love I thee!   20
This brooding warmth across my breast,
    This depth of tranquil bliss – ah, me!
Fount, tree and shed are gone, I know not whither,
But in one quiet room we three are still together.

The shadows dance upon the wall,   25
    By the still dancing fire-flames made;
And now they slumber, moveless all!
    And now they melt to one deep shade!
But not from me shall this mild darkness steal thee:
I dream thee with mine eyes, and at my heart I feel thee!   30

Thine eyelash on my cheek doth play—
    'Tis Mary's hand upon my brow!
But let me check this tender lay
    Which none may hear but she and thou!
Like the still hive at quiet midnight humming,   35
Murmur it to yourselves, ye two beloved women!

The Day-Dream:
If Thou Wert Here

If thou wert here, these tears were tears of light!
   But from as sweet a vision did I start
As ever made these eyes grow idly bright!
   And though I weep, yet still around my heart
A sweet and playful tenderness doth linger,   5
Touching my heart as with an infant's finger.

My mouth half open, like a witless man,
   I saw our couch, I saw our quiet room,
   Its shadows heaving by the fire-light gloom;
And o'er my lips a subtle feeling ran,   10
All o'er my lips a soft and breeze-like feeling –
I know not what – but had the same been stealing

Upon a sleeping mother's lips, I guess
   It would have made the loving mother dream
That she was softly bending down to kiss   15
   Her babe, that something more than babe did seem,
A floating presence of its darling father,
And yet its own dear baby self far rather!

Across my chest there lay a weight, so warm!
   As if some bird had taken shelter there;   20
And lo! I seemed to see a woman's form –
   Thine, Sara, thine? O joy, if thine it were!
I gazed with stifled breath, and feared to stir it,
   No deeper trance e'er wrapt a yearning spirit!

And now, when I seemed sure thy face to see,   25
   Thy own dear self in our own quiet home;
There came an elfish laugh, and wakened me:
   'Twas Frederic, who behind my chair had clomb,
And with his bright eyes at my face was peeping.
I blessed him, tried to laugh, and fell a-weeping!   30

A Letter to Sara Hutchinson

1

Well! if the Bard was weather-wise who made
The dear old Ballad of Sir Patrick Spence,
This Night, so tranquil now, will not go hence
Unrous'd by Winds, that ply a busier trade
Than that, which moulds yon clouds in lazy flakes,   5
Or the dull sobbing Draft, that drones and rakes
Upon the strings of this Eolian Lute,
Which better far were mute.
For lo! the New-Moon, winter-bright!
And all suffus'd with phantom Light   10
(With swimming phantom Light o'erspread,
But rimm'd and circled with a silver Thread)
I see the Old Moon in her Lap foretelling
The coming-on of Rain and squally Blast. –
Ah Sara! That the gust ev'n now were swelling   15
And the slant Night-shower driving loud and fast.

2

A Grief without a Pang, void, dark, and drear,
A stifling, drowsy, unimpassioned Grief,
That finds no natural Outlet, no Relief
In word or sigh, or tear –   20
This, Sara! well thou know'st,
Is that sore Evil which I dread the most
And oft'nest suffer. In this heartless Mood,
To other Thoughts by yonder Throstle woo'd,
That pipes within the Larch-tree not unseen   25
(The Larch which pushes out in Tassels green
It's bundled Leafits) woo'd to mild Delights
By all the tender Sounds and gentle Sights
Of this sweet Primrose-month – and *vainly* woo'd!
O dearest Sara! in this heartless mood   30

All this long Eve so balmy and serene
Have I been gazing on the Western Sky
And it's peculiar Tint of yellow Green:
And still I gaze – and with how blank an eye!
And those thin Clouds above, in flakes and bars,　　　　35
That give away their motion to the Stars;
Those Stars, that glide behind them and between,
Now sparkling, now bedimm'd, but always seen;
Yon crescent Moon, as fixed as if it grew
In it's own cloudless, starless Lake of Blue,　　　　40
A Boat becalm'd! dear William's Sky-Canoe!
I see them all, so excellently fair,
I *see*, not *feel*, how beautiful they are!

My genial Spirits fail –
And what can these avail　　　　45
To lift the smoth'ring weight from off my breast?
It were a vain Endeavour,
Tho' I should gaze for ever
On that green Light, that lingers in the West –
I may not hope from outward Forms to win　　　　50
The Passion and the Life, whose Fountains are within!
Those lifeless Shapes, around, below, above,
O dearest Sara! what can they impart?
Even when the gentle Thought, that thou, my Love,
Art gazing now, like me　　　　55
And see'st the Heaven, I see,
Sweet Thought it is – yet feebly stirs my Heart.

Feebly, O! feebly! – Yet
(I well remember it)
In my first dawn of Youth, that Fancy stole,　　　　60
With many gentle Yearnings, on my Soul!
At eve, Sky-gazing in "ecstatic fit"
(Alas! far-cloister'd in a city school

The Sky was all I knew of Beautiful)
At the barr'd window often did I sit,   65
And often on the leaded School-roof lay
    And to myself would say –
There does not live the Man so stripp'd of good Affections
As not to love to see a Maiden's quiet Eyes
Uprais'd and linking on sweet dreams by dim Connexions 70
To Moon, or Evening Star, or glorious Western Skies!
While yet a Boy, this thought would so pursue me,
That often it became a kind of Vision to me!

6

Sweet Thought! and dear of old
To Hearts of finer Mould!   75
Ten thousand times by Friends and Lovers blest!
    I spake with rash Despair
    And 'ere I was aware,
The weight was somewhat lifted from my Breast.
Dear Sara! in the weather-fended wood,   80
Thy lov'd Haunt, where the stock-doves coo at Noon,
    I guess that thou hast stood
And watch'd yon Crescent and that ghost-like Moon!
    And yet far rather, in my present mood,
I would that thou'dst been sitting all this while   85
Upon the sod-built seat of Camomile –
And tho' thy Robin may have ceas'd to sing,
Yet needs for *my* sake must thou love to hear
    – The Bee-hive murmuring near,
That ever-busy and most quiet Thing   90
Which I have heard at Midnight murmuring!

7

    I feel my Spirit moved –
    And, wheresoe'er thou be,
    O Sister! O beloved!
Thy dear mild Eyes, that see   95
The very Heaven, *I* see,
There is a Prayer in them! It is for *me*!
And I dear Sara! *I* am blessing thee!

It was as calm as this, – the happy Night
When Mary, Thou and I, together were,   100
The low-decaying Fire our only Light,
And listen'd to the stillness of the Air!
O that affectionate and blameless Maid,
Dear, Mary! – on her Lap my Head she lay'd –
    Her hand was on my Brow,   105
  Even as my own is now;
And on my Cheek I felt thy Eye-lash play –
Such joy I had that I may truly say,
My Spirit was awe-stricken with the Excess
And trance-like depth of its brief Happiness.   110

9

Ah fair Remembrances, that so revive
My Heart, and fill it with a living power,
Where were they Sara? – or did I not strive
To win them to me? – on the fretting Hour,
Then when I wrote thee that complaining Scroll   115
Which even to bodily sickness bruis'd thy Soul!
And yet thou blam'st thyself alone! and yet
    Forbidd'st me all Regret!

10

And must I not *regret*, that I distrest
Thee, Best-loved! who lovest me the Best!   120
My better mind had fled, I know not whither –
For O! was this an absent Friend's Employ
To send from far both Pain and Sorrow thither,
Where still his Blessings should have call'd down Joy?
I read thy guileless Letter o'er again –
I hear thee of thy blameless Self complain –   125
And only this I learn – and this, alas! I know,
That thou art weak and pale with Sickness, Grief, and Pain,
And *I – I* made thee so!

11

O *for my own sake*, I regret, *perforce*,   130
Whatever turns *thee*, Sara! from the course
Of calm well-being and a heart at rest.
When thou, and with thee those, whom thou lov'sd best
Shall dwell together in one quiet Home,
One Home the sure *Abiding* Home of All!   135
I too will crown me with a Coronal,
Nor shall this Heart in idle wishes roam,
    Morbidly soft!
No! let me trust, that I shall wear away
In no inglorious Toils the manly Day;   140
And only now and then, and not too oft,
Some dear and memorable Eve shall bless,
Dreaming of all your Love and Happiness.

12

Be happy, and I need thee not in sight!
Peace in thy Heart and Quiet in thy dwelling,   145
Health in thy Limbs, and in thy Eyes the Light
Of Love, and Hope, and honourable Feeling,
Where'er I am, I needs must be content!
Not near thee, haply shall be more content!
To all things I prefer the Permanent;   150
And better seems it for a Heart like mine,
Always to *know* than sometimes to *behold*,
    Their Happiness and thine:
For change doth trouble me with Pangs untold!
To see thee, hear thee, feel thee, then to part –   155
    O! it weighs down the Heart!
To *visit* those, I love, as I love *thee*,
Mary, William and dear Dorothy,
It is but a temptation to repine!
The Transientness is Poison in the Wine,   160
Eats out the Pith of Joy, makes all Joy hollow!
All Pleasure a dim dream of Pain to follow!
My own peculiar Lot, my household Life
It is, and will remain Indifference or Strife –
While ye are well and happy, 'twould but wrong you,   165

If I should fondly yearn to be among you –
Wherefore, O! wherefore, should I wish to be
A wither'd Branch upon a blossoming Tree?

13

But, – (let me say it – for I vainly strive
To beat away the Thought) *but* if thou pin'd,   170
Whate'er the cause, in body or in mind,
I were the miserablest Man alive
To know it, and be absent! Thy Delights
Far off, or near, alike shall I partake –
But O! to mourn for thee, and to forsake
All power, all hope of giving comfort to thee!
To know that thou are weak and worn with pain,
And not to hear thee, Sara! not to view thee –
    Not sit beside thy Bed,
    Not press thy aching Head –   180
    Not bring thee Health again –
  (At least to hope, to try,)
By this Voice, which thou lov'st, and by this *earnest* Eye –

14

Nay – wherefore did I let it haunt my Mind,
    This dark distressful Dream!   185
I turn from it, and listen to the Wind,
Which long has howl'd unnoticed! What a Scream
Of Agony by Torture lengthen'd out
That Lute sent forth! O thou wild storm without!
Or Crag, or Tairn, or lightning-blasted Tree,   190
Or Pinegrove, whither Woodman never clomb,
Or lonely House long held the Witches' Home,
Methinks were fitter Instruments for thee,
Mad Lutanist! That in this Month of Showers,
Or dark-brown Gardens, and of peeping Flowers   195
Mak'st Devil's Yule, with worse than wintry song
The Blooms and Buds and timorous Leaves among!
Thou Actor perfect in all Tragic Sounds!
Thou mighty Poet, even to frenzy bold!
  What tell'st thou now about?   200

Tis of a rushing of an Host in rout,
And many Groans from Men with smarting wounds
That groan at once from Smart, and shudder with the cold!
But hush: there is a break of deepest silence –
Again! – but that dread sound as of a rushing Crowd,   205
With Groans and tremulous Shuddering, all are over –
And it has other Sounds, and all less deep, less loud!
    A Tale of less Affright.
  And tempered with delight,
As William's self had made the tender lay!   210
    Tis of a little Child
   Upon a heathy wild
Not far from home; but it has lost its way!
And now moans low in utter grief and fear,
And now screams loud and hopes to make its Mother hear!

15

Tis midnight! and small thought have I of sleep!
Full seldom may my Friend such Vigils keep!
O breathe she softly in her gentle Sleep!
Cover her, gentle Sleep! with wings of Healing,
And be this Tempest but a mountain Birth!   220
May all the stars hang bright above her dwelling
Silent as tho' they watch'd the sleeping Earth,
Like elder Sisters, with love-twinkling Eyes!
Healthful, and light my Darling! may'st thou rise,
And of the same good Tidings to me send!   225
For O! beloved Friend!
I am not the buoyant Thing, I was of yore,
When like an own Child, I to Joy belong'd,
For others mourning oft, myself oft sorely wrong'd,
Yet bearing all things then, as if I nothing bore.   230

16

E'er I was wedded, tho' my path was rough,
The joy within me dallied with distress.
And all misfortunes were but as the Stuff
Whence Fancy made me Dreams of Happiness:
For Hope grew round me, like the climbing Vine,   235

175

And Leaves and Fruitage, not my own, seem'd mine!
But now Ill-tidings bow me down to Earth –
Nor care I, that they rob me of my Mirth;
    But O! each Visitation
Suspends, what Nature gave me at my Birth,   240
My shaping Spirit of Imagination!
I speak not now of those habitual Ills,
That wear out Life, when two unequal minds
Meet in one House, and two discordant Wills –
    This leaves me, where it finds,   245
Past cure and past Complaint! A fate Austere,
Too fixed and hopeless to partake of Fear!

17

But thou, DEAR Sara! (Dear indeed thou art)
My Comforter! A Heart within my Heart!
Thou and the Few, we love, tho' Few ye be,   250
Make up a world of Hopes and Fears for me.
And when Affliction, or distempering Pain,
Or wayward Chance befall you, I complain.
Not that I mourn – O Friends, most dear, most true,
    Methinks to weep with you   255
Were better far than to rejoice alone –
But that my coarse domestic life has known
No Griefs, but such as dull and deaden me,
No Habits of heart-nursing Sympathy,
No mutual mild enjoyments of it's own,   260
No Hopes of it's own Vintage, none, O! none –
Whence, when I mourn for you, my heart must borrow
Fair forms and living motions for it's Sorrow,
For not to think of what I needs must feel,
But to be still and patient all I can;   265
And haply by abstruse Research to steal
From my own Nature all the Natural Man;
This was my sole Resource, my wisest Plan!
And that, which suits a part, infects the whole,
And now is almost grown the temper of my Soul!   270

18

My little children are a Joy, a Love,
    A good Gift from above!
But what is Bliss, that ever calls up Woe,
    And makes it doubly keen?
Compelling me to feel what well I know,   275
What a most blessed Lot mine *might* have been!
Those little Angel children (woe is me!)
There have been hours, when feeling how they bind
And pluck out the wing-feathers of my mind,
Turning my Error to Necessity,   280
I have half-wished, they never had been born.
THAT – *seldom*; but sad Thought they always bring,
And like the Poet's Nightingale, I sing
My Love-song with my breast against a Thorn.

19

With no unthankful Spirit I confess,   285
This clinging Grief too in it's turn awakes,
That Love and Father's Joy; but O! it makes
The Love the greater, and the Joy far less!
These Mountains too, these Vales, these Woods, these Lakes,
Scenes full of Beauty and of Loftiness   290
Where all my Life I fondly hope to live –
I were sunk low indeed, did they *no* solace give!
But oft I seem to feel, and evermore to fear,
They are not to me now the Things, which once they were.

20

O Sara! we receive but what we give   295
And in *our* Life alone does Nature live –
Our's is her Wedding-garment, our's her Shroud!
And would we aught behold of higher worth
Than that inanimate cold World allow'd
To the poor loveless, ever-anxious Crowd,   300
Ah! from the Soul itself must issue forth
A Light, a Glory, and a luminous Cloud,
    Enveloping the Earth!

And from the Soul itself must there be sent
A sweet and potent Voice of it's own Birth,   305
Of all sweet sounds the Life and Element.
O pure of Heart! thou need'st not ask of me,
What this strange music in the Soul may be,
What and wherein it doth exist,
This Light, this Glory, this fair luminous Mist,   310
This beautiful and beauty-making Power!
Joy, innocent Sara! Joy, that ne'er was given
Save to the pure and in their purest Hour,
JOY, Sara! is the Spirit and the Power
That wedding Nature to us gives in dower,   315
   A new Earth and new Heaven,
Undreamt of by the Sensual and the Proud!
JOY is that sweet Voice, JOY that luminous cloud!
      We, we ourselves rejoice –
And thence flows all that charms or ear or sight,   320
All Melodies the Echoes of that Voice,
All Colors a *Suffusion* from that Light.
Sister and Friend of my devoutest Choice!
Thou being innocent and full of Love,
And nested with the Darlings of thy Love,   325
And feeling in thy Soul, Heart, Lips, and Arms
Even what the conjugal and Mother Dove
That borrows genial warmth from these, she warms,
Feels in her thrill'd wings, blessedly outspread!
Thou, free'd awhile from Cares and human Dread   330
By the immenseness of the Good and Fair,
    Which thou see'st every where –
Thus, thus would'st thou rejoice!
To thee would all things *live* from pole to pole,
Their Life the Eddying of thy living Soul.   335
O dear! O Innocent! O full of Love!
Sara! thou Friend of my devoutest Choice!
As dear as Light and Impulse from above!
So may'st thou ever, evermore rejoice!

Dejection: An Ode

Late, late yestreen I saw the new Moon,
With the old Moon in her arms;
And I fear, I fear, my Master dear!
We shall have a deadly storm.
Ballad of Sir Patrick Spence.

I

Well! If the Bard was weather-wise, who made
  The grand old ballad of Sir Patrick Spence,
   This night, so tranquil now, will not go hence
Unroused by winds, that ply a busier trade
Than those which mould yon cloud in lazy flakes,   5
Or the dull sobbing draft, that moans and rakes
Upon the strings of this Æolian lute,
    Which better far were mute.
  For lo! the New-moon winter-bright!
  And overspread with phantom light,   10
  (With swimming phantom light o'erspread
  But rimmed and circled by a silver thread)
I see the old Moon in her lap, foretelling
  The coming-on of rain and squally blast.
And oh! that even now the gust were swelling,   15
  And the slant night-shower driving loud and fast!
Those sounds which oft have raised me, whilst they awed,
  And sent my soul abroad,
Might now perhaps their wonted impulse give,
Might startle this dull pain, and make it move and live!   20

II

A grief without a pang, void, dark, and drear,
  A stifled, drowsy, unimpassioned grief,
  Which finds no natural outlet, no relief,
    In word, or sigh, or tear –

O Lady! in this wan and heartless mood,   25
To other thoughts by yonder throstle woo'd,
   All this long eve, so balmy and serene,
Have I been gazing on the western sky,
   And its peculiar tint of yellow green:
And still I gaze – and with how blank an eye!   30
And those thin clouds above, in flakes and bars,
That give away their motion to the stars;
Those stars, that glide behind them or between,
Now sparkling, now bedimmed, but always seen:
Yon crescent Moon, as fixed as if it grew   35
In its own cloudless, starless lake of blue;
I see them all so excellently fair,
I see, not feel, how beautiful they are!

III

   My genial spirits fail;
      And what can these avail   40
To lift the smothering weight from off my breast?
      It were a vain endeavour,
      Though I should gaze for ever
On that green light that lingers in the west:
I may not hope from outward forms to win   45
The passion and the life, whose fountains are within.

IV

O Lady! we receive but what we give,
And in our life alone does Nature live:
Ours is her wedding garment, ours her shroud!
   And would we aught behold, of higher worth,   50
Than that inanimate cold world allowed
To the poor loveless ever-anxious crowd,
   Ah! from the soul itself must issue forth
A light, a glory, a fair luminous cloud
      Enveloping the Earth –   55
And from the soul itself must there be sent
   A sweet and potent voice, of its own birth,
Of all sweet sounds the life and element!

O pure of heart! thou need'st not ask of me
What this strong music in the soul may be!   60
What, and wherein it doth exist,
This light, this glory, this fair luminous mist,
This beautiful and beauty-making power.
   Joy, virtuous Lady! Joy that ne'er was given,
Save to the pure, and in their purest hour,   65
Life, and Life's effluence, cloud at once and shower,
Joy, Lady! is the spirit and the power,
 Which wedding Nature to us gives in dower
   A new Earth and new Heaven,
Undreamt of by the sensual and the proud –   70
Joys is the sweet voice, Joy the luminous cloud –
    We in ourselves rejoice!
And thence flows all that charms or ear or sight,
   All melodies the echoes of that voice,
All colours a suffusion from that light.   75

VI

There was a time when, though my path was rough,
   This joy within me dallied with distress,
And all misfortunes were but as the stuff
   Whence Fancy made me dreams of happiness:
For hope grew round me, like the twining vine,   80
And fruits, and foliage, not my own, seemed mine.
But now afflictions bow me down to earth:
Nor care I that they rob me of my mirth;
   But oh! each visitation
Suspends what nature gave me at my birth,   85
   My shaping spirit of Imagination.
For not to think of what I needs must feel,
   But to be still and patient, all I can;
And haply by abstruse research to steal
   From my own nature all the natural man—   90
   This was my sole resource, my only plan:
Till that which suits a part infects the whole,
And now is almost grown the habit of my soul.

Hence, viper thoughts, that coil around my mind,
 Reality's dark dream!   95
I turn from you, and listen to the wind,
 Which long has raved unnoticed. What a scream
Of agony by torture lengthened out
That lute sent forth! Thou Wind, that rav'st without,
 Bare crag, or mountain-tairn, or blasted tree,   100
Or pine-grove whither woodman never clomb,
Or lonely house, long held the witches' home,
 Methinks were fitter instruments for thee,
Mad Lutanist! who in this month of showers,
Of dark-brown gardens, and of peeping flowers,   105
Mak'st Devils' yule, with worse than wintry song,
The blossoms, buds, and timorous leaves among.

 Thou Actor, perfect in all tragic sounds!
Thou mighty Poet, e'en to frenzy bold!
  What tell'st thou now about?   110
  'Tis of the rushing of an host in rout,
 With groans, of trampled men, with smarting wounds—
At once they groan with pain, and shudder with the cold!
But hush! there is a pause of deepest silence!
 And all that noise, as of a rushing crowd,   115
With groans, and tremulous shudderings – all is over—
 It tells another tale, with sounds less deep and loud!
  A tale of less affright,
  And tempered with delight,
As Otway's self had framed the tender lay,—   120
  'Tis of a little child
  Upon a lonesome wild,
Not far from home, but she hath lost her way:
And now moans low in bitter grief and fear,
And now screams loud, and hopes to make her mother hear.

'Tis midnight, but small thoughts have I of sleep:
Full seldom may my friend such vigils keep!
Visit her, gentle Sleep! with wings of healing,
 And may this storm be but a mountain-birth,

May all the stars hang bright above her dwelling,   130
   Silent as though they watched the sleeping Earth!
    With light heart may she rise,
    Gay fancy, cheerful eyes,
  Joy lift her spirit, joy attune her voice;
To her may all things live, from pole to pole,   135
Their life the eddying of her living soul!
  O simple spirit, guided from above,
Dear Lady! friend devoutest of my choice,
Thus mayest thou ever, evermore rejoice.

Separation

A sworded man whose trade is blood,
   In grief, in anger, and in fear,
Thro' jungle, swamp, and torrent flood,
   I seek the wealth you hold so dear!

The dazzling charm of outward form,   5
   The power of gold, the pride of birth,
Have taken Woman's heart by storm—
   Usurp'd the place of inward worth.

Is not true Love of higher price
   Than outward Form, though fair to see,   10
Wealth's glittering fairy-dome of ice,
   Or echo of proud ancestry?—

O! Asra, Asra! couldst thou see
   Into the bottom of my heart,
There's such a mine of Love for thee,   15
   As almost might supply desert!

(This separation is, alas!
   Too great a punishment to bear;
O! take my life, or let me pass
   That life, that happy life, with her!)   20

The perils, erst with steadfast eye
   Encounter'd, now I shrink to see—
Oh! I have heart enough to die—
   Not half enough to part from Thee!

Phantom

All look and likeness caught from earth,
All accident of kin and birth,
Had pass'd away. There was no trace
Of aught on that illumined face,
Uprais'd beneath the rifted stone   5
But of one spirit all her own;—
She, she herself, and only she,
Shone through her body visibly.

O Sara! Never Rashly Let Me Go

O Sara! never rashly let me go
Beyond the precincts of this holy Place,
Where streams as pure as in Elysium flow
And flowrets view reflected Grace:
What though in vain the melted Metals glow,   5
We die, and dying own a more than mortal Love.

Ad Vilmum Axiologum

Me n' Asræ perferre jubes oblivia? et Asræ
  Me aversos oculos posse videre meæ?
Scire et eam falsam, crudelem, quæ mihi semper
  Cara fuit, semper cara futura mihi?
Meque pati lucem, cui vanam perdite amanti,   5
  Quicquid Naturæ est, omne tremit, titubat?
Cur non ut patiarque fodi mea viscera ferro,
  Dissimulato etiam, Vilme, dolore jubes?
Quin Cor, quin Oculosque meos, quin erue vel quod
  Carius est, si quid carius esse potest!   10
Deficientem animam, quod vis, tolerare jubebo,
  Asræ dum superet, me moriente, fides.
At Fidis Inferias vidi! et morior! – Ratione
  Victum iri facili, me *Ratione*, putas?
Ah pereat, qui, in Amore potest rationibus uti!   15
  Ah pereat, qui, ni perdite, amare potest!
Quid deceat, quid non, videant quibus integra mens est!
  Vixi! vivit adhuc immemor Asra mei.

[*Translation*: TO WILLIAM WORDSWORTH

  Do you command me to endure Asra's neglect? and to be able to see the eyes
of my Asra averted? And to know her as false and cruel who always was, always
will be dear to me? And me to suffer the daylight when, since I desperately love
one who is false, the whole of Nature trembles and shudders? Why do you not
also command me, William, to suffer my bowels to be pierced with a sword and
then to pretend that it does not hurt? Nay, why not pluck out my heart and eyes
or whatever is dearer, if anything can be dearer? I shall command my failing spirit
to tolerate anything as long as Asra's faith remains, even if I die. But I have seen
the last rites of her faithfulness! and I die! Do you think that I am to be overcome
by mere Reason? by *Reason*? Ah, perish the man who can make use of reasons in
matters of love – perish he who can love except desperately! What may be fitting,
what not, let them consider who are whole of mind! My life is done! Yet Asra still
lives, unmindful of me.]

You Mould My Hopes

You mould my Hopes you fashion me within:
And to the leading love-throb in the heart,
Through all my being, through my pulses beat;
You lie in all my many thoughts like Light,
Like the fair light of Dawn, or summer Eve,   5
On rippling stream, or cloud-reflecting lake;
And looking to the Heaven that bends above you,
How oft! I bless the lot that made me love you.

An Angel Visitant

Within these circling hollies woodbine-clad—
Beneath this small blue roof of vernal sky—
How warm, how still! Tho' tears should dim mine eye,
Yet will my heart for days continue glad,
For here, my love, thou art, and here am I!   5

Recollections of Love

I

How warm this woodland wild Recess!
  Love surely hath been breathing here;
  And this sweet bed of heath, my dear!
Swells up, then sinks with faint caress,
  As if to have you yet more near.   5

II

Eight springs have flown, since last I lay
  On sea-ward Quantock's heathy hills,
  Where quiet sounds from hidden rills
Float here and there, like things astray,
  And high o'er head the sky-lark shrills.   10

III

No voice as yet had made the air
  Be music with your name; yet why
  That asking look? that yearning sigh?
That sense of promise every where?
  Belovéd! flew your spirit by?   15

IV

As when a mother doth explore
  The rose-mark on her long-lost child,
  I met, I loved you, maiden mild!
As whom I long had loved before—
  So deeply had I been beguiled.   20

You stood before me like a thought,
  A dream remembered in a dream.
  But when those meek eyes first did seem
To tell me, Love within you wrought—
  O Greta, dear domestic stream!   25

Has not, since then, Love's prompture deep,
  Has not Love's whisper evermore
  Been ceaseless, as thy gentle roar?
Sole voice, when other voices sleep,
  Dear under-song in clamor's hour.   30

Constancy to an Ideal Object

Since all that beat about in Nature's range,
Or veer or vanish; why should'st thou remain
The only constant in a world of change,
O yearning Thought! that liv'st but in the brain?
Call to the Hours, that in the distance play, 5
The faery people of the future day—
Fond Thought! not one of all that shining swarm
Will breathe on thee with life-enkindling breath,
Till when, like strangers shelt'ring from a storm,
Hope and Despair meet in the porch of Death! 10
Yet still thou haunt'st me; and though well I see,
She is not thou, and only thou art she,
Still, still as though some dear embodied Good,
Some living Love before my eyes there stood
With answering look a ready ear to lend, 15
I mourn to thee and say – "Ah! loveliest friend!
That this the meed of all my toils might be,
To have a home, an English home, and thee!"
Vain repetition! Home and Thou are one.
The peacefull'st cot, the moon shall shine upon, 20
Lulled by the thrush and wakened by the lark,
Without thee were but a becalméd bark,
Whose Helmsman on an ocean waste and wide
Sits mute and pale his mouldering helm beside.

And art thou nothing? Such thou art, as when 25
The woodman winding westward up the glen
At wintry dawn, where o'er the sheep-track's maze
The viewless snow-mist weaves a glist'ning haze,
Sees full before him, gliding without tread,
An image with a glory round its head; 30
The enamoured rustic worships its fair hues,
Nor knows he makes the shadow, he pursues!

VI

CONFESSIONAL
POEMS

Confessional Poems

PREFACE

FROM EARLY MIDDLE AGE, Coleridge slowly began to produce a new poetry of confession and "allegoric" revelation quite unlike anything he had previously written. It could be called the poetry of his "darker self", with an inward, metaphysical quality that is wholly new. All sorts of personal anxieties and spiritual doubts, previously unsuspected (although going right back to childhood) begin to surface in its strange and difficult imagery (see "Limbo", No. 68).

This is probably the least known, and certainly the least appreciated, part of Coleridge's work. It is ignored by almost all modern criticism, by most contemporary anthologies, and also perhaps by many young readers who do not like the idea of the Romantic poet growing old. But the troubling visitations of the young self upon the old self are one of Coleridge's most piercing and repeated motifs (see "Phantom or Fact", No. 71).

Even though these fifteen poems are scattered over more than thirty years, between 1802 and Coleridge's death in 1834, they form as distinctive a group as the Conversation Poems, and have a similar autobiographical thread. Two of the families who supported Coleridge in the "dark years", after the break up of the Lake District household, are significant if shadowy presences: the Morgans (see "To Two Sisters", No. 61) and the Gillmans of Highgate (see "The Garden of Boccaccio", No. 70). The difference is that the autobiography is now introverted and lacks a familiar external landscape. Instead, the new psychological inwardness is expressed in the repeated use of "allegories": projected scenes of self-confrontation or self-discovery, which Coleridge describes as "moving Masquerades" or "emblems" (see "Hope and Time", No. 64). Images of reflection – moons, mirrors, shadows, doubles, dreams – are frequent. Coleridge's conversations are held with himself, or between versions of himself (see the doubled titles, "Hope and Time", "Youth and

Age", "Phantom or Fact"), and so the new confessional form emerges.

Collected here as a sequence, there are no unfinished fragments and several sustained poems of considerable length (see "The Garden of Boccaccio", No. 70). Many of the poems were evidently worked on and returned to over more than a decade (see "The Pang More Sharp Than All", No. 63), and show Coleridge's consistent and painstaking workmanship. (A touching emblem of this can be found elsewhere in the little fragment, "The Yellow Hammer", No. 83.) Altogether they form a "confession" of more than five hundred lines of verse, which is almost as long as "The Rime of the Ancient Mariner" (No. 32) and in its way no less dramatic.

It could be argued that the real subject of Coleridge's confession is his prolonged and self-destructive opium addiction. This addiction was well-established by the winter of 1802 (see "The Pains of Sleep", No. 60); by 1811 it had brought him to professional breakdown and personal despair (see "The Suicide's Argument", No. 65). Despite repeated attempts to break its hold, his unhappy personal life always drove him back to it (see "The Visionary Hope", No. 66). It was only partly brought under control, after 1816, by his confidante and friend, the surgeon James Gillman, at Highgate (see "Limbo", No. 68) though the threat of a relapse into severe addiction remained with him as late as 1828 (see "The Garden of Boccaccio", No. 70).

But what unifies these poems at a far deeper level is Coleridge's long struggle with mental depression. The experience of depression is itself an almost defining characteristic of the Romantic mind, closely connected with an increase in solitary self-awareness and a decrease in religious faith. The language to describe it actually changed at this period, from the antique "hypochondria" and "melancholy" (used by Boswell and Keats), to the modern "dejection" and "depressed spirits" (used by Coleridge and Shelley).

Coleridge had identified a large theme. Depression of some kind is now a common experience for most people at some point in their lives, and not necessarily in old age. Psychologists also presume to say that it is almost universal for creative artists. Coleridge's Confessional Poems examine depression in many ways, describing it variously as the loss of spiritual "Hope" (Nos. 64, 66), the loss of human "Love" (Nos. 63, 72) and the loss of inner creative power (Nos. 62, 70). In one of his most subtle, allegoric pieces, he describes it memorably as the loss of the "magic Child" within the adult's "secret heart" (see No. 63).

It is this terrible sense of dissolving identity, of powerlessness, of dispersing energy and joy, which seems to lie at the heart of the Confessional Poems. (The concept of "negative" energy, and "negation" is also recurrent.) Against it, Coleridge invokes an elusive but persistent metaphysic of "Hope", as a fundamental force in both the natural and moral universe (see No. 66). The theme clearly grows out of "Dejection: An Ode" (No. 50), but it is pursued much further and, significantly, with greater courage. Though there are often strong elements of self-pity, the prevailing tone is one of bleak and bitter realism, frequently touched with a certain self-mockery.

On the whole these are poems of doubt and dark reflection: mature, sombre, and self-questioning. They include some of Coleridge's most dense, speculative metaphysical poetry, such as the double-sonnet "Human Life" (No. 67), and his most desperate religious poems such as "Epitaph" (No. 73). But there is also a thin, persistent silvery thread of light-verse, which produces odd atonal effects, like "An Ode to the Rain" (No. 59), and "A Tombless Epitaph" (No. 62). It also produces, towards the end, a playful bitter-sweet masterpiece like "Youth and Age" (No. 69). It would be quite wrong to think that, as a poet, Coleridge never escaped from his depression. (On the theme of joyful escape, see "The Delinquent Travellers", No. 101.)

An Ode to the Rain

I

I know it is dark; and though I have lain,
Awake, as I guess, an hour or twain,
I have not once opened the lids of my eyes,
But I lie in the dark, as a blind man lies.
O Rain! that I lie listening to,   5
You're but a doleful sound at best:
I owe you little thanks, 'tis true,
For breaking thus my needful rest!
Yet if, as soon as it is light,
O Rain! you will but take your flight,   10
I'll neither rail, nor malice keep,
Though sick and sore for want of sleep.
But only now, for this one day,
Do go, dear Rain! do go away!

II

O Rain! with your dull two-fold sound,   15
The clash hard by, and the murmur all round!
You know, if you know aught, that we,
Both night and day, but ill agree:
For days and months, and almost years,
Have limped on through this vale of tears,   20
Since body of mine, and rainy weather,
Have lived on easy terms together.
Yet if, as soon as it is light,
O Rain! you will but take your flight,
Though you should come again to-morrow,   25
And bring with you both pain and sorrow;
Though stomach should sicken and knees should swell –

I'll nothing speak of you but well.
But only now for this one day,
Do go, dear Rain! do go away!   30

III

Dear Rain! I ne'er refused to say
You're a good creature in your way;
Nay, I could write a book myself,
Would fit a parson's lower shelf,
Showing how very good you are. –   35
What then? sometimes it must be fair
And if sometimes, why not to-day?
Do go, dear Rain! do go away!

IV

Dear Rain! if I've been cold and shy,
Take no offence! I'll tell you why.   40
A dear old Friend e'en now is here,
And with him came my sister dear;
After long absence now first met,
Long months by pain and grief beset –
We three dear friends! in truth, we groan   45
Impatiently to be alone.
We three, you mark! and not one more!
The strong wish makes my spirit sore.
We have so much to talk about,
So many sad things to let out;   50
So many tears in our eye-corners,
Sitting like little Jacky Horners –
In short, as soon as it is day,
Do go, dear Rain! do go away.

V

And this I'll swear to you, dear Rain!   55
Whenever you shall come again,
Be you as dull as e'er you could
(And by the bye 'tis understood,
You're not so pleasant as you're good),

200

Yet, knowing well your worth and place, 60
I'll welcome you with cheerful face;
And though you stayed a week or more,
Were ten times duller than before;
Yet with kind heart, and right good will,
I'll sit and listen to you still; 65
Nor should you go away, dear Rain!
Uninvited to remain.
But only now, for this one day,
Do go, dear Rain! do go away.

The Pains of Sleep

Ere on my bed my limbs I lay,
It hath not been my use to pray
With moving lips or bended knees;
But silently, by slow degrees,
My spirit I to Love compose,   5
In humble trust mine eye-lids close,
With reverential resignation,
No wish conceived, no thought exprest,
Only a sense of supplication;
A sense o'er all my soul imprest   10
That I am weak, yet not unblest,
Since in me, round me, every where
Eternal Strength and Wisdom are.

But yester-night I prayed aloud
In anguish and in agony,   15
Up-starting from the fiendish crowd
Of shapes and thoughts that tortured me:
A lurid light, a trampling throng,
Sense of intolerable wrong,
And whom I scorned, those only strong!   20
Thirst of revenge, the powerless will
Still baffled, and yet burning still!
Desire with loathing strangely mixed
On wild or hateful objects fixed.
Fantastic passions! maddening brawl!   25
And shame and terror over all!
Deeds to be hid which were not hid,
Which all confused I could not know
Whether I suffered, or I did:
For all seemed guilt, remorse or woe,   30
My own or others still the same
Life-stifling fear, soul-stifling shame.

So two nights passed: the night's dismay
Saddened and stunned the coming day.
Sleep, the wide blessing, seemed to me   35
Distemper's worst calamity.
The third night, when my own loud scream
Had waked me from the fiendish dream,
O'ercome with sufferings strange and wild,
I wept as I had been a child;   40
And having thus by tears subdued
My anguish to a milder mood,
Such punishments, I said, were due
To natures deepliest stained with sin, –
For aye entempesting anew   45
The unfathomable hell within,
The horror of their deeds to view,
To know and loathe, yet wish and do!
Such griefs with such men well agree,
But wherefore, wherefore fall on me?   50
To be beloved is all I need,
And whom I love, I love indeed.

To Two Sisters

To know, to esteem, to love, – and then to part –
Makes up life's tale to many a feeling heart;
Alas for some abiding-place of love,
O'er which my spirit, like the mother dove,
Might brood with warming wings!
                                        O fair! O kind!   5
Sisters in blood, yet each with each intwined
More close by sisterhood of heart and mind!
Me disinherited in form and face
By nature, and mishap of outward grace;
Who, soul and body, through one guiltless fault   10
Waste daily with the poison of sad thought,
Me did you soothe, when solace hoped I none!
And as on unthaw'd ice the winter sun,
Though stern the frost, though brief the genial day,
You bless my heart with many a cheerful ray;   15
For gratitude suspends the heart's despair,
Reflecting bright though cold your image there.
Nay more! its music by some sweeter strain
Makes us live o'er our happiest hours again,
Hope re-appearing dim in memory's guise –   20
Even thus did you call up before mine eyes
Two dear, dear Sisters, prized all price above,
Sisters, like you, with more than sisters' love;
So like you *they*, and so in *you* were seen
Their relative statures, tempers, looks, and mien,   25
That oft, dear ladies! you have been to me
At once a vision and reality.
Sight seem'd a sort of memory, and amaze
Mingled a trouble with affection's gaze.

Oft to my eager soul I whisper blame,   30
A Stranger bid it feel the Stranger's shame –
My eager soul, impatient of the name,

No strangeness owns, no Stranger's form descries:
The chidden heart spreads trembling on the eyes.
First-seen I gazed, as I would look you thro'!   35
My best-beloved regain'd their youth in you, –
And still I ask, though now familiar grown,
Are you for *their* sakes dear, or for your own?
O doubly dear! may Quiet with you dwell!

In Grief I love you, yet I love you well!   40
Hope long is dead to me! an orphan's tear
Love wept despairing o'er his nurse's bier.
Yet still she flutters o'er her grave's green slope:
For Love's despair is but the ghost of Hope!

Sweet Sisters! were you placed around one hearth   45
With those, your other selves in shape and worth,
Far rather would I sit in solitude,
Fond recollections all my fond heart's food,
And dream of *you*, sweet Sisters! (ah! not mine!)
And only *dream* of you (ah! dream and pine!)   50
Than boast the presence and partake the pride,
And shine in the eye, of all the world beside.

A Tombless Epitaph

'Tis true, Idoloclastes Satyrane!
(So call him, for so mingling blame with praise,
And smiles with anxious looks, his earliest friends,
Masking his birth-name, wont to character
His wild-wood fancy and impetuous zeal,)   5
'Tis true that, passionate for ancient truths,
And honouring with religious love the Great
Of elder times, he hated to excess,
With an unquiet and intolerant scorn,
The hollow Puppets of a hollow Age,   10
Ever idolatrous, and changing ever
Its worthless Idols! Learning, Power, and Time,
(Too much of all) thus wasting in vain war
Of fervid colloquy. Sickness, 'tis true,
Whole years of weary days, besieged him close,   15
Even to the gates and inlets of his life!
But it is true, no less, that strenuous, firm,
And with a natural gladness, he maintained
The citadel unconquered, and in joy
Was strong to follow the delightful Muse.   20
For not a hidden path, that to the shades
Of the beloved Parnassian forest leads,
Lurked undiscovered by him; not a rill
There issues from the fount of Hippocrene,
But he had traced it upward to its source,   25
Through open glade, dark glen, and secret dell,
Knew the gay wild flowers on its banks, and culled
Its med'cinable herbs. Yea, oft alone,
Piercing the long-neglected holy cave,
The haunt obscure of old Philosophy,   30
He bade with lifted torch its starry walls
Sparkle, as erst they sparkled to the flame
Of odorous lamps tended by Saint and Sage.
O framed for calmer times and nobler hearts!

O studious Poet, eloquent for truth! 35
Philosopher! contemning wealth and death,
Yet docile, childlike, full of Life and Love!
Here, rather than on monumental stone,
This record of thy worth thy Friend inscribes,
Thoughtful, with quiet tears upon his cheek. 40

The Pang More Sharp Than All

AN ALLEGORY

I

He too has flitted from his secret nest,
Hope's last and dearest child without a name! –
Has flitted from me, like the warmthless flame,
That makes false promise of a place of rest
To the tired Pilgrim's still believing mind; –   5
Or like some Elfin Knight in kingly court,
Who having won all guerdons in his sport,
Glides out of view, and whither none can find!

II

Yes! he hath flitted from me – with what aim,
Or why, I know not! 'Twas a home of bliss,   10
And he was innocent, as the pretty shame
Of babe, that tempts and shuns the menaced kiss,
From its twy-cluster'd hiding place of snow!
Pure as the babe, I ween, and all aglow
As the dear hopes, that swell the mother's breast –   15
Her eyes down gazing o'er her claspéd charge; –
Yet gay as that twice happy father's kiss,
That well might glance aside, yet never miss,
Where the sweet mark emboss'd so sweet a targe –
Twice wretched he who hath been doubly blest!   20

III

Like a loose blossom on a gusty night
He flitted from me – and has left behind
(As if to them his faith he ne'er did plight)
Of either sex and answerable mind
Two playmates, twin-births of his foster-dame: –   25
The one a steady lad (Esteem he hight)
And Kindness is the gentler sister's name.
Dim likeness now, though fair she be and good,

Of that bright Boy who hath us all forsook; –
But in his full-eyed aspect when she stood,   30
And while her face reflected every look,
And in reflection kindled – she became
So like Him, that almost she seem'd the same!

IV

Ah! he is gone, and yet will not depart! –
Is with me still, yet I from him exiled!   35
For still there lives within my secret heart
The magic image of the magic Child,
Which there he made up-grow by his strong art,
As in that crystal orb – wise Merlin's feat, –
The wondrous "World of Glass," wherein inisled   40
All long'd-for things their beings did repeat; –
And there he left it, like a Sylph beguiled,
To live and yearn and languish incomplete!

V

Can wit of man a heavier grief reveal?
Can sharper pang from hate or scorn arise? –   45
Yes! one more sharp there is that deeper lies,
Which fond Esteem but mocks when he would heal.
Yet neither scorn nor hate did it devise,
But sad compassion and atoning zeal!
One pang more blighting-keen than hope betray'd!   50
And this it is my woeful hap to feel,
When, at her Brother's hest, the twin-born Maid
With face averted and unsteady eyes,
Her truant playmate's faded robe puts on;
And inly shrinking from her own disguise   55
Enacts the faery Boy that's lost and gone.
O worse than all! O pang all pangs above
Is Kindness counterfeiting absent Love!

Hope and Time

In the great City rear'd, my fancy rude
By natural Forms unnurs'd and unsubdued
An Alien from the Rivers and the Fields
And all the Charms, that Hill or Woodland yields,
It was the pride and passion of my Youth   5
T' impersonate and color moral Truth:
Rare Allegories in those Days I spun,
That oft had mystic senses oft'ner none.
Of all Resemblances however faint,
So dear a Lover was I, that with quaint   10
Figures fantastically grouped I made
Of commonest Thoughts a moving Masquerade.
'Twas then I fram'd this obscure uncouth Rhyme,
A sort of Emblem 'tis of HOPE and TIME.

In ancient Days, but when I have not read,   15
Nor know I, where – but 'twas some elfish Place—
Their pennons, ostrich-like for Sails outspread,
Two wingéd Children run an endless Race—
    A Sister and a Brother!
    But HOPE outruns the other—   20
Yet ever flies she with reverted Face,
And looks and listens for the Boy behind:
Time is his Name – and he, alas! is blind,
With regular Step o'er rough and smooth he passed,
And knows not whether he is first or last.   25

The Suicide's Argument

Ere the birth of my life, if I wished it or no,
No question was asked me – it could not be so!
If the life was the question, a thing sent to try,
And to live on be Yes; what can No be? to die.

NATURE'S ANSWER

Is't returned, as 'twas sent? Is't no worse for the wear?   5
Think first, what you are! Call to mind what you were!
I gave you innocence, I gave you hope,
Gave health, and genius, and an ample scope.
Return you me guilt, lethargy, despair?
Make out the invent'ry; inspect, compare!   10
Then die – if die you dare!

The Visionary Hope

Sad lot, to have no Hope! Though lowly kneeling
He fain would frame a prayer within his breast,
Would fain entreat for some sweet breath of healing,
That his sick body might have ease and rest;
He strove in vain! the dull sighs from his chest   5
Against his will the stifling load revealing,
Though Nature forced; though like some captive guest,
Some royal prisoner at his conqueror's feast,
An alien's restless mood but half concealing,
The sternness on his gentle brow confessed,   10
Sickness within and miserable feeling:
Though obscure pangs made curses of his dreams,
And dreaded sleep, each night repelled in vain,
Each night was scattered by its own loud screams:
Yet never could his heart command, though fain,   15
One deep full wish to be no more in pain.

   That Hope, which was his inward bliss and boast,
Which waned and died, yet ever near him stood,
Though changed in nature, wander where he would –
For Love's Despair is but Hope's pining Ghost!   20
For this one hope he makes his hourly moan,
He wishes and can wish for this alone!
Pierced, as with light from Heaven, before its gleams
(So the love-stricken visionary deems)
Disease would vanish, like a summer shower,   25
Whose dews fling sunshine from the noon-tide bower!
Or let it stay! yet this one Hope should give
Such strength that he would bless his pains and live.

Human Life

ON THE DENIAL OF IMMORTALITY

If dead, we cease to be; if total gloom
  Swallow up life's brief flash for aye, we fare
As summer-gusts, of sudden birth and doom,
  Whose sound and motion not alone declare,
But are their whole of being! If the breath   5
  Be Life itself, and not its task and tent,
If even a soul like Milton's can know death;
  O Man! thou vessel purposeless, unmeant,
Yet drone-hive strange of phantom purposes!
  Surplus of Nature's dread activity,   10
Which, as she gazed on some nigh-finished vase,
Retreating slow, with meditative pause,
  She formed with restless hands unconsciously.
Blank accident! nothing's anomaly!

If rootless thus, thus substanceless thy state,   15
Go, weigh thy dreams, and be thy hopes, thy fears,
The counter-weights! – Thy laughter and thy tears
  Mean but themselves, each fittest to create
And to repay the other! Why rejoices
  Thy heart with hollow joy for hollow good?   20
Why cowl thy face beneath the mourner's hood?
Why waste thy sighs, and thy lamenting voices,
  Image of Image, Ghost of Ghostly Elf,
That such a thing as thou feel'st warm or cold?
Yet what and whence thy gain, if thou withhold   25
  These costless shadows of thy shadowy self?
Be sad! be glad! be neither! seek, or shun!
Thou hast no reason why! Thou canst have none;
Thy being's being is contradiction.

Limbo

'Tis a strange place, this Limbo! – not a Place,
Yet name it so; – where Time and weary Space
Fettered from flight, with night-mare sense of fleeing,
Strive for their last crepuscular half-being, –
Lank Space, and scytheless Time with branny hands   5
Barren and soundless as the measuring sands,
Not mark'd by flit of Shades, – unmeaning they
As moonlight on the dial of the day!

But that is lovely – looks like human Time, –
An Old Man with a steady look sublime,   10
That stops his earthly task to watch the skies;
But he is blind – a statue hath such eyes; –
Yet having moonward turn'd his face by chance,
Gazes the orb with moon-like countenance,
With scant white hairs, with foretop bald and high,   15
He gazes still, – his eyeless face all eye; –
As 'twere an organ full of silent sight,
His whole face seemeth to rejoice in light! –
Lip touching lip, all moveless, bust and limb –
He seems to gaze at that which seems to gaze on him!   20

No such sweet sights doth Limbo den immure,
Wall'd round, and made a spirit-jail secure,
By the mere horror of blank Naught-at-all,
Whose circumambience doth these ghosts enthrall.
A lurid thought is growthless, dull Privation,   25
Yet that is but a Purgatory curse;
Hell knows a fear far worse,
A fear – a future state; – 'tis positive Negation!

Youth and Age

Verse, a breeze mid blossoms straying,
Where Hope clung feeding, like a bee –
Both were mine! Life went a-maying
      With Nature, Hope, and Poesy,
            When I was young!   5
When I was young? – Ah, woful When!
Ah! for the change 'twixt Now and Then!
This breathing house not built with hands,
This body that does me grievous wrong,
O'er aery cliffs and glittering sands,   10
How lightly then it flashed along: –
Like those trim skiffs, unknown of yore,
On winding lakes and rivers wide,
That ask no aid of sail or oar,
That fear no spite of wind or tide!   15
Nought cared this body for wind or weather
When Youth and I lived in't together.

Flowers are lovely; Love is flower-like;
Friendship is a sheltering tree;
O! the joys, that came down shower-like,   20
Of Friendship, Love, and Liberty,
            Ere I was old!
Ere I was old? Ah woful Ere,
Which tells me, Youth's no longer here!
O Youth! for years so many and sweet,   25
'Tis known, that Thou and I were one,
I'll think it but a fond conceit –
It cannot be that Thou art gone!
Thy vesper-bell hath not yet toll'd: –
And thou wert aye a masker bold!   30
What strange disguise hast now put on,
To make believe, that thou art gone?
I see these locks in silvery slips,

This drooping gait, this altered size:
But Spring-tide blossoms on thy lips,   35
And tears take sunshine from thine eyes!
Life is but thought: so think I will
That Youth and I are house-mates still.

Dew-drops are the gems of morning,
But the tears of mournful eve!   40
Where no Hope is, life's a warning
That only serves to make us grieve,
                    When we are old:
That only serves to make us grieve
With oft and tedious taking-leave,   45
Like some poor nigh-related guest,
That may not rudely be dismist;
Yet hath outstay'd his welcome while,
And tells the jest without the smile.

The Garden of Boccaccio

Of late, in one of those most weary hours,
When life seems emptied of all genial powers,
A dreary mood, which he who ne'er has known
May bless his happy lot, I sate alone;
And, from the numbing spell to win relief,   5
Call'd on the Past for thought of glee or grief.
In vain! bereft alike of grief and glee,
I sate and cow'r'd o'er my own vacancy!
And as I watch'd the dull continuous ache,
Which, all else slumb'ring, seem'd alone to wake;   10
O Friend! long wont to notice yet conceal,
And soothe by silence what words cannot heal,
I but half saw that quiet hand of thine
Place on my desk this exquisite design.
Boccaccio's Garden and its faery,   15
The love, the joyaunce, and the gallantry!
An Idyll, with Boccaccio's spirit warm,
Framed in the silent poesy of form.

Like flocks adown a newly-bathéd steep
Emerging from a mist: or like a stream   20
Of music soft that not dispels the sleep,
But casts in happier moulds the slumberer's dream,
Gazed by an idle eye with silent might
The picture stole upon my inward sight.
A tremulous warmth crept gradual o'er my chest,   25
As though an infant's finger touch'd my breast.
And one by one (I know not whence) were brought
All spirits of power that most had stirr'd my thought
In selfless boyhood, on a new world tost
Of wonder, and in its own fancies lost;   30
Or charm'd my youth, that, kindled from above,
Loved ere it loved, and sought a form for love;
Or lent a lustre to the earnest scan

Of manhood, musing what and whence is man!
Wild strain of Scalds, that in the sea-worn caves   35
Rehearsed their war-spell to the winds and waves;
Or fateful hymn of those prophetic maids,
That call'd on Hertha in deep forest glades;
Or minstrel lay, that cheer'd the baron's feast;
Or rhyme of city pomp, of monk and priest,   40
Judge, mayor, and many a guild in long array,
To high-church pacing on the great saint's day:
And many a verse which to myself I sang,
That woke the tear, yet stole away the pang
Of hopes, which in lamenting I renew'd: 45
And last, a matron now, of sober mien,
Yet radiant still and with no earthly sheen,
Whom as a faery child my childhood woo'd
Even in my dawn of thought – Philosophy;
Though then unconscious of herself, pardie,   50
She bore no other name than Poesy;
And, like a gift from heaven, in lifeful glee,
That had but newly left a mother's knee,
Prattled and play'd with bird and flower, and stone,
As if with elfin playfellows well known,   55
And life reveal'd to innocence alone.

Thanks, gentle artist! now I can descry
Thy fair creation with a mastering eye,
And all awake! And now in fix'd gaze stand,
Now wander through the Eden of thy hand;   60
Praise the green arches, on the fountain clear
See fragment shadows of the crossing deer;
And with that serviceable nymph I stoop,
The crystal, from its restless pool, to scoop.
I see no longer! I myself am there,   65
Sit on the ground-sward, and the banquet share.
'Tis I, that sweep that lute's love-echoing strings,
And gaze upon the maid who gazing sings:
Or pause and listen to the tinkling bells
From the high tower, and think that there she dwells.   70
With old Boccaccio's soul I stand possest,
And breathe an air like life, that swells my chest.
The brightness of the world, O thou once free,

And always fair, rare land of courtesy!
O Florence! with the Tuscan fields and hills   75
And famous Arno, fed with all their rills;
Thou brightest star of star-bright Italy!
Rich, ornate, populous, – all treasures thine,
The golden corn, the olive, and the vine.
Fair cities, gallant mansions, castles old,   80
And forests, where beside his leafy hold
The sullen boar hath heard the distant horn,
And whets his tusks against the gnarléd thorn;
Palladian palace with its storied halls;
Fountains, where Love lies listening to their falls;   85
Gardens, where flings the bridge its airy span,
And Nature makes her happy home with man;
Where many a gorgeous flower is duly fed
With its own rill, on its own spangled bed,
And wreathes the marble urn, or leans its head,   90
A mimic mourner, that with veil withdrawn
Weeps liquid gems, the presents of the dawn; –
Thine all delights, and every muse is thine;
And more than all, the embrace and intertwine
Of all with all in gay and twinkling dance!   95
Mid gods of Greece and warriors of romance,
See! Boccace sits, unfolding on his knees
The new-found roll of old Maeonides;
But from his mantle's fold, and near the heart,
Peers Ovid's Holy Book of Love's sweet smart!   100
O all-enjoying and all-blending sage,
Long be it mine to con thy mazy page,
Where, half conceal'd, the eye of fancy views
Fauns, nymphs, and wingéd saints, all gracious to thy muse!

Still in thy garden let me watch their pranks,   105
And see in Dian's vest between the ranks
Of the trim vines, some maid that half believes
The vestal fires, of which her lover grieves,
With that sly satyr peeping through the leaves!

Phantom or Fact

A DIALOGUE IN VERSE

AUTHOR

A lovely form there sate beside my bed,
And such a feeding calm its presence shed,
A tender love so pure from earthly leaven,
That I unnethe the fancy might control,
'Twas my own spirit newly come from heaven,   5
Wooing its gentle way into my soul!
But ah! the change – It had not stirr'd, and yet –
Alas! that change how fain would I forget!
That shrinking back, like one that had mistook!
That weary, wandering, disavowing look!   10
'Twas all another, feature, look, and frame,
And still, methought, I knew, it was the same!

FRIEND

This riddling tale, to what does it belong?
Is't history? vision? or an idle song?
Or rather say at once, within what space   15
Of time this wild disastrous change took place?

AUTHOR

Call it a moment's work (and such it seems)
This tale's a fragment from the life of dreams;
But say, that years matur'd the silent strife,
And 'tis a record from the dream of life.   20

Love's Apparition and Evanishment

AN ALLEGORIC ROMANCE

Like a lone Arab, old and blind,
Some caravan had left behind,
Who sits beside a ruin'd well,
Where the shy sand-asps bask and swell;
And now he hangs his agéd head aslant, 5
And listens for a human sound – in vain!
And now the aid, which Heaven alone can grant,
Upturns his eyeless face from Heaven to gain; –
Even thus, in vacant mood, one sultry hour,
Resting my eye upon a drooping plant, 10
With brow low bent, within my garden-bower,
I sate upon the couch of camomile;
And – whether 'twas a transient sleep, perchance,
Flitted across the idle brain, the while
I watch'd the sickly calm with aimless scope, 15
In my own heart; or that, indeed a trance,
Turn'd my eye inward – thee, O genial Hope,
Love's elder sister! thee did I behold,
Drest as a bridesmaid, but all pale and cold,
With roseless cheek, all pale and cold and dim, 20
 Lie lifeless at my feet!
And then came Love, a sylph in bridal trim,
 And stood beside my seat;
She bent, and kissed her sister's lips,
 As she was wont to do; – 25
Alas! 'twas but a chilling breath
Woke just enough of life in death
 To make Hope die anew.

Epitaph

Stop, Christian passer-by! – Stop, child of God,
And read with gentle breast. Beneath this sod
A poet lies, or that which once seem'd he.
O, lift one thought in prayer for S. T. C.;
That he who many a year with toil of breath   5
Found death in life, may here find life in death!
Mercy for praise – to be forgiven for fame
He ask'd, and hoped, through Christ. Do thou the same!

VII

VISIONARY
FRAGMENTS

Visionary Fragments

PREFACE

COLERIDGE IS THE GREAT master of the creative fragment. He can almost be said to have turned it into a literary form of its own, with as much authenticity as the conversation poem or the ballad. A great deal of his criticism, too, is most powerful in the fragmentary state: the marginal note in his essays, the sudden detached image in the *Biographia Literaria* or *The Friend*, the many volumes of "Marginalia" themselves, or the sudden aside in his Shakespearean Lectures (as the famous remark on Hamlet's silence, "Suppression prepares for overflow", which could be said to contain all Freud).

But what exactly is a Coleridgean fragment? It might be simply a small and haphazard piece of unfinished work, like the jotting from an artist's sketchbook, and several of these are contained in this group, such as "The Knight's Tomb" (No. 85) or "The Netherlands" (No. 92). They have their own particular interest, giving us a sense of Coleridge's "workshop", the way he played with the sound of language, or caught at particular atmospheres in a landscape. The connection between musicality, mood and emotion emerges as unusually important to him, as shown in the two contrasted "Songs" (Nos. 87, 88), and the "Four Metrical Experiments" (No. 86).

But the Coleridgean fragment more often contains the idea or seed for some much larger construction. This is what is implied by "visionary". It is the small unfinished piece, which somehow implies a huge completed opus. Like the carefully designed "ruin" in an eighteenth-century park, it is a powerfully Romantic form of architectural suggestion or evocation, in which the visible part suggests the invisible whole. The finest example of this is "Kubla Khan" (No. 74), which Coleridge explicitly says was originally "not less than from two to three hundred lines": he cannot recall the whole, but we are magically led to believe that it is there.

Coleridge became fascinated in later life with the psychology of creativity, and the mechanism of inspiration. He added prose prefaces to previously abandoned poems, and published them as specimens of this kind of creative fragment (see Nos. 74, 75, 77, 90). Like "Kubla Khan", they are presented as "psychological curiosities".

Coleridge is fascinated by the way that the creative powers work, but also how they fail to work. His Notebooks show that he had a strikingly modern idea of creativity coming from an "unconscious" part of the mind, and once described consciousness as the "narrow neck" of a vast bottle in which memory and imagination floated. In the preface to "Kubla Khan" he describes this poetic unconscious as being accessible in a "state of reverie", and capable of composing a long poem without conscious effort or control. But it can also be closed off from the powers of recollection, like a ruffled pool of water losing an image from its surface.

Similar problems of conscious recollection, and lost inspiration, are described in the preface to "The Wanderings of Cain" (No. 75). And in the preface to "The Blossoming of the Solitary Date-Tree" (No. 77), Coleridge wistfully asks for some younger poet to recover his inspiration for him, and turn the prose notes back into poetry. Another, light-hearted account of a poem's inspiration appears in "Aria Spontanea" (No. 90), where Coleridge merely gives a fragment of "the music", and then vividly describes how it first came to him, like a bumble bee whirling over the top of Quantock. "Ars Poetica" (No. 89) gives a more analytical account of the conscious, shaping imagination at work, by "transforming" a piece of flat, descriptive verse into an emotive image.

In this way Coleridge's fragments bring us as close as we can get to the threshold of the creative process itself. Coleridge tended to associate it, at least metaphorically, with the action of flowing water or with the free flight of birds. Throughout his letters and Notebooks he also compared it to the mental patterns revealed in dreams, where the mind spontaneously dramatizes and visualizes a large series of symbolic events without conscious control or censorship. He spoke of the "streamy" nature of these sequences and likened poetry to a "waking dream". But the inability to recover or reconstruct these patterns at will, except in fragments, seemed to him an inherent problem for all creative artists.

All his life he was visited by such dreams or reveries (as well as nightmares), but he remained doubtful of his powers to present them more than fleetingly in poetry or make sense of them philosophically. The dream that produced "Kubla Khan" in 1797 remains the most famous of these mysterious visitations, but as late as 1827 Coleridge could record similar experiences:

> . . . I awoke last night, or rather with the poor relic of Volition breaking the Enchanter's Talisman, succeeded at length in awakening myself out of a terrific fantastic Dream, which would have required tenfold the imagination of a Dante to have constructed in the waking state . . . After many years' watchful notice of the phenomena of the somnial state, and an elaborate classification of its *characteristic* distinctions, I remain incapable of explaining any one Figure of all the numberless Personages of this shadowy world."
>
> (*Letter*, 28 November 1827.)

Yet despite this disclaimer, few poets have given us a more vivid sense of the creative unconscious in its dream-like state of flow or fugue.

Some of his most powerful and disturbing fragments are "emblem" poems, where there is a strong sense of menacing or forbidden meanings. Here again the small or tell-tale image mysteriously implies some much larger concept. The fragment "A Sunset" (No. 78) seems almost to suggest that the Divine Creator is retreating from his Universe; and this is echoed by "A Dark Sky" (No. 79) though such an idea was abhorrent to Coleridge's conscious Christian faith. While "The Tropic Tree" (No. 80) suggests some monstrous shape haunting Coleridge's most personal relationships. These can be compared with the "allegoric" revelations of the Confessional Poems. Other emblems are clearer, but none the less suggest some large, unconscious anxiety: in "Psyche" (No. 81) it is the ravenous, caterpillar hunger of the unhappy soul; and in "The World That Spidery Witch" (No. 91), it is the claustrophobic weavings of old age.

Above all, the fragments give us a unique sense of Coleridge actually at work as a poet. They show him sketching out one idea in a few amazing moments; or developing another over several years. But always he is experimenting, rejecting, forgetting and recovering. Perhaps one sees two sides to him as a creative artist: the one "drifting and wailing", like "The Sea Mew" (No. 82); the other carefully "filing" a piece of shining metal, like "The Yellow Hammer" (No. 83). He is simultaneously the passive, astonished dreamer and the active, meticulous craftsman.

74

Kubla Khan:

OR, A VISION IN A DREAM. A FRAGMENT

The following fragment is here published at the request of a
poet of great and deserved celebrity [Lord Byron], and, as
far as the Author's own opinions are concerned, rather as a
psychological curiosity, than on the ground of any supposed
poetic merits.

    In the summer of the year 1797, the Author, then in ill   5
health, had retired to a lonely farm-house between Porlock
and Linton, on the Exmoor confines of Somerset and Devon-
shire. In consequence of a slight indisposition, an anodyne had
been prescribed, from the effects of which he fell asleep in
his chair at the moment that he was reading the following
sentence, or words of the same substance, in "Purchas's   10
Pilgrimage": "Here the Khan Kubla commanded a palace to
be built, and a stately garden thereunto. And thus ten miles of
fertile ground were inclosed with a wall." The Author con-
tinued for about three hours in a profound sleep, at least of the
external senses, during which time he has the most vivid   15
confidence, that he could not have composed less than from
two to three hundred lines; if that indeed can be called compo-
sition in which all the images rose up before him as *things*, with
a parallel production of the correspondent expressions, with-
out any sensation or consciousness of effort. On awaking he   20
appeared to himself to have a distinct recollection of the whole,
and taking his pen, ink, and paper, instantly and eagerly wrote
down the lines that are here preserved. At this moment he was
unfortunately called out by a person on business from Porlock,
and detained by him above an hour, and on his return to his   25
room, found, to his no small surprise and mortification, that
though he still retained some vague and dim recollection of
the general purport of the vision, yet, with the exception
of some eight or ten scattered lines and images, all the rest
had passed away like the images on the surface of a stream   30
into which a stone has been cast, but, alas! without the after
restoration of the latter!

Then all the charm

Is broken — all that phantom-world so fair
Vanishes, and a thousand circlets spread,   35

And each mis-shape the other. Stay awhile,
Poor youth! who scarcely dar'st lift up thine eyes —
The stream will soon renew its smoothness, soon
The visions will return! And lo, he stays,
And soon the fragments dim of lovely forms   40
Come trembling back, unite, and now once more
The pool becomes a mirror.

Yet from the still surviving recollections in his mind, the Author has frequently purposed to finish for himself what had been originally, as it were, given to him. Αὔριον ἄδιον ἄσω: 20 [tomorrow I shall sing a sweeter song]: but the to-morrow is yet to come.

In Xanadu did Kubla Khan
A stately pleasure-dome decree:
Where Alph, the sacred river, ran
Through caverns measureless to man
  Down to a sunless sea.   5
So twice five miles of fertile ground
With walls and towers were girdled round:
And there were gardens bright with sinuous rills,
Where blossomed many an incense-bearing tree;
And here were forests ancient as the hills,   10
Enfolding sunny spots of greenery.

But oh! that deep romantic chasm which slanted
Down the green hill athwart a cedarn cover!
A savage place! as holy and enchanted
As e'er beneath a waning moon was haunted   15
By woman wailing for her demon-lover!
And from this chasm, with ceaseless turmoil seething,
As if this earth in fast thick pants were breathing,
A mighty fountain momently was forced:
Amid whose swift half-intermitted burst   20

Huge fragments vaulted like rebounding hail,
Or chaffy grain beneath the thresher's flail:
And 'mid these dancing rocks at once and ever
It flung up momently the sacred river.
Five miles meandering with a mazy motion   25
Through wood and dale the sacred river ran,
Then reached the caverns measureless to man,
And sank in tumult to a lifeless ocean:
And 'mid this tumult Kubla heard from far
Ancestral voices prophesying war!   30
    The shadow of the dome of pleasure
    Floated midway on the waves;
    Where was heard the mingled measure
    From the fountain and the caves.
It was a miracle of rare device,   35
A sunny pleasure-dome with caves of ice!

    A damsel with a dulcimer
    In a vision once I saw:
    It was an Abyssinian maid,
    And on her dulcimer she played,   40
    Singing of Mount Abora.
    Could I revive within me
    Her symphony and song,
    To such a deep delight 'twould win me,
That with music loud and long,   45
I would build that dome in air,
That sunny dome! those caves of ice!
And all who heard should see them there,
And all should cry, Beware! Beware!
His flashing eyes, his floating hair!   50
Weave a circle round him thrice,
And close your eyes with holy dread,
For he on honey-dew hath fed,
And drunk the milk of Paradise.

75

The Wanderings of Cain

A prose composition, one not in metre at least, seems *prima facie* to require explanation or apology. It was written in the year 1798, near Nether Stowey, in Somersetshire, at which place (*sanctum et amabile nomen!* rich by so many associations and recollections) the author had taken up his residence in order to enjoy the society and close neighbourhood of a dear and honoured friend, T. Poole, Esq. The work was to have been written in concert with another [Wordsworth], whose name is too venerable within the precincts of genius to be unnecessarily brought into connection with such a trifle, and who was then residing at a small distance from Nether Stowey. The title and subject were suggested by myself, who likewise drew out the scheme and the contents for each of the three books or cantos, of which the work was to consist, and which, the reader is to be informed, was to have been finished in one night! My partner undertook the first canto: I the second: and which ever had *done first*, was to set about the third. Almost thirty years have passed by; yet at this moment I cannot without something more than a smile moot the question which of the two things was the more impracticable, for a mind so eminently original to compose another man's thoughts and fancies, or for a taste so austerely pure and simple to imitate the Death of Abel? Methinks I see his grand and noble countenance as at the moment when having despatched my own portion of the task at full finger-speed, I hastened to him with my manuscript – that look of humourous despondency fixed on his almost blank sheet of paper, and then its silent mock-piteous admission of failure struggling with the sense of the exceeding ridiculousness of the whole scheme – which broke up in a laugh: and the Ancient Mariner was written instead.

Years afterward, however, the draft of the plan and proposed incidents, and the portion executed, obtained favour in the eyes of more than one person, whose judgment on a poetic work could not but have weighed with me, even though no parental partiality had been thrown into the same scale, as a make-weight: and I determined on commencing anew, and composing the whole in stanzas, and made some progress in realising this intention, when adverse gales drove my bark off the "Fortunate Isles" of the Muses: and then other and more momentous interests prompted a different voyage, to firmer anchorage and a securer port. I have in vain tried to recover the lines from the palimpsest tablet of my memory: and I can only offer the introductory stanza, which had been committed to writing for the purpose of procuring a friend's judgment on the metre, as a specimen: –

> Encinctured with a twine of leaves,
> That leafy twine his only dress!
> A lovely Boy was plucking fruits,
> By moonlight, in a wilderness.
> The moon was bright, the air was free,
> And fruits and flowers together grew
> On many a shrub and many a tree:
> And all put on a gentle hue,
> Hanging in the shadowy air
> Like a picture rich and rare.
> It was a climate where, they say,
> The night is more belov'd than day.
> But who that beauteous Boy beguil'd,
> That beauteous Boy to linger here?
> Alone, by night, a little child,
> In place so silent and so wild –
> Has he no friend, no loving mother near?

I have here given the birth, parentage, and premature decease of the "Wanderings of Cain, a poem", – intreating, however, my Readers, not to think so meanly of my judgment as to suppose that I either regard or offer it as any excuse for the publication of the following fragment (and I may add, of one or two others in its neighbourhood) in its primitive crudity. But I should find still greater difficulty in forgiving myself were I to record pro *taedio* publico a set of petty mishaps and annoyances which I myself wish to forget. I must be content therefore with assuring the friendly Reader, that the less he attributes its appearance to the Author's will, choice, or judgment, the nearer to the truth he will be.

233

"A little further, O my father, yet a little further, and we shall come into the open moonlight." Their road was through a forest of fir-trees; at its entrance the trees stood at distances from each other, and the path was broad, and the moonlight and the moonlight shadows reposed upon it, and appeared quietly to inhabit that solitude. But soon the path winded and became narrow; the sun at high noon sometimes speckled, but never illumined it, and now it was dark as a cavern.

"It is dark, O my father!" said Enos, "but the path under our feet is smooth and soft, and we shall soon come out into the open moonlight."

"Lead on, my child!" said Cain; "guide me, little child!" And the innocent little child clasped a finger of the hand which had murdered the righteous Abel, and he guided his father. "The fir branches drip upon thee, my son." "Yea, pleasantly, father, for I ran fast and eagerly to bring thee the pitcher and the cake, and my body is not yet cool. How happy the squirrels are that feed on these fir-trees! they leap from bough to bough, and the old squirrels play round their young ones in the nest. I clomb a tree yesterday at noon, O my father, that I might play with them, but they leaped away from the branches, even to the slender twigs did they leap, and in a moment I beheld them on another tree. Why, O my father, would they not play with me? I would be good to them as thou art good to me: and I groaned to them even as thou groanest when thou givest me to eat, and when thou coverest me at evening, and as often as I stand at thy knee and thine eyes look at me?" Then Cain stopped, and stifling his groans he sank to the earth, and the child Enos stood in the darkness beside him.

And Cain lifted up his voice and cried bitterly, and said, "The Mighty One that persecuteth me is on this side and on that; he pursueth my soul like the wind, like the sand-blast he passeth through me; he is around me even as the air! O that I might be utterly no more! I desire to die – yea, the things that never had life, neither move they upon the earth – behold! they seem precious to mine eyes. O that a man might live without the breath of his nostrils. So I might abide in darkness, and blackness, and an empty space! Yea, I would lie down, I would not rise, neither would I stir my limbs till I became as

the rock in the den of the lion, on which the young lion resteth   40
his head whilst he sleepeth. For the torrent that roareth far off
hath a voice: and the clouds in heaven look terribly on me;
the Mighty One who is against me speaketh in the wind of the
cedar grove; and in silence am I dried up." Then Enos spake
to his father, "Arise, my father, arise, we are but a little way   45
from the place where I found the cake and the pitcher." And
Cain said, "How knowest thou!" and the child answered –
"Behold the bare rocks are a few of thy strides distant from the
forest; and while even now thou wert lifting up thy voice, I
heard the echo." Then the child took hold of his father, as if   50
he would raise him: and Cain being faint and feeble rose slowly
on his knees and pressed himself against the trunk of a fir, and
stood upright and followed the child.

The path was dark till within three strides' length of its
termination, when it turned suddenly; the thick black trees   55
formed a low arch, and the moonlight appeared for a moment
like a dazzling portal. Enos ran before and stood in the open
air; and when Cain, his father, emerged from the darkness, the
child was affrighted. For the mighty limbs of Cain were wasted
as by fire; his hair was as the matted curls on the bison's fore-   60
head, and so glared his fierce and sullen eye beneath: and the
black abundant locks on either side, a rank and tangled mass,
were stained and scorched, as though the grasp of a burning
iron hand had striven to rend them; and his countenance told
in a strange and terrible language of agonies that had been, and   65
were, and were still to continue to be.

The scene around was desolate; as far as the eye could reach
it was desolate: the bare rocks faced each other, and left a long
and wide interval of thin white sand. You might wander on
and look round and round, and peep into the crevices of the   70
rocks and discover nothing that acknowledged the influence
of the seasons. There was no spring, no summer, no autumn:
and the winter's snow, that would have been lovely, fell not
on these hot rocks and scorching sands. Never morning lark
had poised himself over this desert; but the huge serpent often   75
hissed there beneath the talons of the vulture, and the vulture
screamed, his wings imprisoned within the coils of the serpent.
The pointed and shattered summits of the ridges of the rocks
made a rude mimicry of human concerns, and seemed to
prophecy mutely of things that then were not; steeples, and   80

battlements, and ships with naked masts. As far from the wood as a boy might sling a pebble of the brook, there was one rock by itself at a small distance from the main ridge. It had been precipitated there perhaps by the groan which the Earth uttered when our first father fell. Before you approached, it appeared to lie flat on the ground, but its base slanted from its point, and between its point and the sands a tall man might stand upright. It was here that Enos had found the pitcher and cake, and to this place he led his father. But ere they had reached the rock they beheld a human shape: his back was towards them, and they were advancing unperceived, when they heard him smite his breast and cry aloud, "Woe is me! woe is me! I must never die again, and yet I am perishing with thirst and hunger."

Pallid, as the reflection of the sheeted lightning on the heavy-sailing night-cloud, became the face of Cain; but the child Enos took hold of the shaggy skin, his father's robe, and raised his eyes to his father, and listening whispered, "Ere yet I could speak, I am sure, O my father, that I heard that voice. Have not I often said that I remembered a sweet voice? O my father! this is it": and Cain trembled exceedingly. The voice was sweet indeed, but it was thin and querulous, like that of a feeble slave in misery, who despairs altogether, yet can not refrain himself from weeping and lamentation. And, behold! Enos glided forward, and creeping softly round the base of the rock, stood before the stranger, and looked up into his face. And the Shape shrieked, and turned round, and Cain beheld him, that his limbs and his face were those of his brother Abel whom he had killed! And Cain stood like one who struggles in his sleep because of the exceeding terribleness of a dream.

Thus as he stood in silence and darkness of soul, the Shape fell at his feet, and embraced his knees, and cried out with a bitter outcry, "Thou eldest born of Adam, whom Eve, my mother, brought forth, cease to torment me! I was feeding my flocks in green pastures by the side of quiet rivers, and thou killedst me; and now I am in misery." Then Cain closed his eyes, and hid them with his hands; and again he opened his eyes, and looked around him, and said to Enos, "What beholdest thou? Didst thou hear a voice, my son?" "Yes, my father, I beheld a man in unclean garments, and he uttered a sweet voice, full of lamentation." Then Cain raised up the Shape that was like Abel, and said: – "The Creator of our father, who had

respect unto thee, and unto thy offering, wherefore hath he
forsaken thee?" Then the Shape shrieked a second time, and
rent his garment, and his naked skin was like the white sands
beneath their feet; and he shrieked yet a third time, and threw 125
himself on his face upon the sand that was black with the
shadow of the rock, and Cain and Enos sate beside him; the
child by his right hand, and Cain by his left. They were all
three under the rock, and within the shadow. The Shape that
was like Abel raised himself up, and spake to the child, "I know 130
where the cold waters are, but I may not drink, wherefore didst
thou then take away my pitcher?" But Cain said, "Didst thou
not find favour in the sight of the Lord thy God?" The Shape
answered, "The Lord is God of the living only, the dead have
another God." Then the child Enos lifted up his eyes and 135
prayed; but Cain rejoiced secretly in his heart. "Wretched shall
they be all the days of their mortal life," exclaimed the Shape,
"who sacrifice worthy and acceptable sacrifices to the God of
the dead; but after death their toil ceaseth. Woe is me, for I
was well beloved by the God of the living, and cruel wert thou, 140
O my brother, who didst snatch me away from his power and
his dominion." Having uttered these words, he rose suddenly,
and fled over the sands: and Cain said in his heart, "The curse
of the Lord is on me; but who is the God of the dead?" and
he ran after the Shape, and the Shape fled shrieking over the 145
sands, and the sands rose like white mists behind the steps of
Cain, but the feet of him that was like Abel disturbed not the
sands. He greatly outrun Cain, and turning short, he wheeled
round, and came again to the rock where they had been sitting,
and where Enos still stood; and the child caught hold of his 150
garment as he passed by, and he fell upon the ground. And
Cain stopped, and beholding him not, said, "he has passed into
the dark woods," and he walked slowly back to the rocks; and
when he reached it the child told him that he had caught hold
of his garment as he passed by, and that the man had fallen 155
upon the ground: and Cain once more sate beside him, and
said, "Abel, my brother, I would lament for thee, but that the
spirit within me is withered, and burnt up with extreme agony.
Now, I pray thee, by thy flocks, and by thy pastures, and by
the quiet rivers which thou lovedst, that thou tell me all that 160
thou knowest. Who is the God of the dead? where doth he
make his dwelling? what sacrifices are acceptable unto him? for

I have offered, but have not been received; I have prayed, and have not been heard; and how can I be afflicted more than I already am?" The Shape arose and answered, "O that thou 165 hadst had pity on me as I will have pity on thee. Follow me, Son of Adam! and bring thy child with thee!"

And they three passed over the white sands between the rocks, silent as the shadows.

The Mad Monk

I heard a voice from Etna's side;
  Where o'er a cavern's mouth
  That fronted to the south
A chestnut spread its umbrage wide:
A hermit or a monk the man might be;   5
  But him I could not see:
And thus the music flow'd along,
In melody most like to old Sicilian song:

"There was a time when earth, and sea, and skies,
  The bright green vale, and forest's dark recess,   10
With all things, lay before mine eyes
  In steady loveliness:
But now I feel, on earth's uneasy scene,
  Such sorrows as will never cease; –
  I only ask for peace;   15
If I must live to know that such a time has been!"
A silence then ensued:
    Till from the cavern came
    A voice; – it was the same!
And thus, in mournful tone, its dreary plaint renew'd: 20

"Last night, as o'er the sloping turf I trod,
  The smooth green turf, to me a vision gave
Beneath mine eyes, the sod –
  The roof of Rosa's grave!

"My heart has need with dreams like these to strive,   25
  For, when I woke, beneath mine eyes I found
  The plot of mossy ground,
On which we oft have sat when Rosa was alive. –
Why must the rock, and margin of the flood,
  Why must the hills so many flow'rets bear,   30
Whose colours to a *murder'd* maiden's blood,
  Such sad resemblance wear? –

"*I struck the wound*, – this hand of mine!
For Oh, thou maid divine,
   I lov'd to agony!   35
The youth whom thou call'd'st thine
   Did never love like me!

"Is it the stormy clouds above
   That flash'd so red a gleam?
   On yonder downward trickling stream? –   40
'Tis not the blood of her I love. –
The sun torments me from his western bed,
   Oh, let him cease for ever to diffuse
   Those crimson spectre hues!
Oh, let me lie in peace, and be for ever dead!"   45

Here ceas'd the voice. In deep dismay,
Down thro' the forest I pursu'd my way.

The Blossoming of
the Solitary Date-Tree

A LAMENT

I seem to have an indistinct recollection of having read either
in one of the ponderous tomes of George of Venice, or in
some other compilation from the uninspired Hebrew writers,
an apologue or Rabbinical tradition to the following purpose:

> While our first parents stood before their offended Maker,   5
> and the last words of the sentence were yet sounding in
> Adam's ear, the guileful false serpent, a counterfeit and a
> usurper from the beginning, presumptuously took on him-
> self the character of advocate or mediator, and pretending
> to intercede for Adam, exclaimed: "Nay, Lord, in thy justice,   10
> not so! for the man was the least in fault. Rather let the
> Woman return at once to the dust, and let Adam remain in
> this thy Paradise." And the word of the Most High answered
> Satan: "*The tender mercies of the wicked are cruel.* Treacherous
> Fiend! if with guilt like thine, it had been possible for thee   15
> to have the heart of a Man, and to feel the yearning of a
> human soul for its counterpart, the sentence, which thou
> now counsellest, should have been inflicted on thyself."

The title of the following poem was suggested by a fact men-
tioned by Linnaeus, of a date-tree in a nobleman's garden which   20
year after year had put forth a full show of blossoms, but never
produced fruit, till a branch from another date-tree had been
conveyed from a distance of some hundred leagues. The first
leaf of the MS. from which the poem has been transcribed, and
which contained the two or three introductory stanzas, is   25
wanting: and the author has in vain taxed his memory to repair
the loss. But a rude draught of the poem contains the substance
of the stanzas, and the reader is requested to receive it as the
substitute. It is not impossible, that some congenial spirit, whose
years do not exceed those of the Author at the time the poem   30
was written, may find a pleasure in restoring the Lament to its
original integrity by a reduction of the thoughts to the requisite
metre.   S. T. C.

I

Beneath the blaze of a tropical sun the mountain peaks are the Thrones of Frost, through the absence of objects to reflect the rays. "What no one with us shares, seems scarce our own." The presence of a ONE,

The best belov'd, who loveth me the best,   5

is for the heart, what the supporting air from within is for the hollow globe with its suspended car. Deprive it of this, and all without, that would have buoyed it aloft even to the seat of the gods, becomes a burthen and crushes it into flatness.

2

The finer the sense for the beautiful and the lovely, and the   10 fairer and lovelier the object presented to the sense; the more exquisite the individual's capacity of joy, and the more ample his means and opportunities of enjoyment, the more heavily will he feel the ache of solitariness, the more unsubstantial becomes the feast spread around him. What matters it, whether   15 in fact the viands and the ministering graces are shadowy or real, to him who has not hand to grasp nor arms to embrace them?

3

Imagination; honourable aims;
Free commune with the choir that cannot die;   20
Science and song; delight in little things,
The buoyant child surviving in the man;
Fields, forests, ancient mountains, ocean, sky,
With all their voices – O dare I accuse
My earthly lot as guilty of my spleen,   25
Or call my destiny niggard! O no! no!
It is her largeness, and her overflow,
Which being incomplete, disquieteth me so!

4

For never touch of gladness stirs my heart,
But tim'rously beginning to rejoice   30
Like a blind Arab, that from sleep doth start
In lonesome tent, I listen for thy voice.
Belovéd! 'tis not thine; thou art not there!
Then melts the bubble into idle air,
And wishing without hope I restlessly despair.   35

5

The mother with anticipated glee
Smiles o'er the child, that, standing by her chair
And flatt'ning its round cheek upon her knee,
Looks up, and doth its rosy lips prepare
To mock the coming sounds. At that sweet sight   40
She hears her own voice with a new delight;
And if the babe perchance should lisp the notes aright,

6

Then is she tenfold gladder than before!
But should disease or chance the darling take,
What then avail those songs, which sweet of yore   45
Were only sweet for their sweet echo's sake?
Dear maid! no prattler at a mother's knee
Was e'er so dearly prized as I prize thee:
Why was I made for Love and Love denied to me?

A Sunset

Upon the mountain's edge with light touch resting,
There a brief while the globe of splendour sits
    And seems a creature of the earth; but soon
      More changeful than the Moon,
To wane fantastic his great orb submits,   5
Or cone or mow of fire: till sinking slowly
Even to a star at length he lessens wholly.

Abrupt, as Spirits vanish, he is sunk!
A soul-like breeze possesses all the wood.
    The boughs, the sprays have stood   10
As motionless as stands the ancient trunk!
But every leaf through all the forest flutters,
And deep the cavern of the fountain mutters.

· A Dark Sky

COELI ENARRANT

The stars that wont to start, as on a chase,
Mid twinkling insult on Heaven's darken'd face,
Like a conven'd conspiracy of spies
Wink at each other with confiding eyes!
Turn from the portent – all is blank on high,   5
No constellations alphabet the sky:
The Heavens one large Black Letter only shew,
And as a child beneath its master's blow
Shrills out at once its task and its affright –
The groaning world now learns to read aright, 10
And with its Voice of Voices cries out, O!

The Tropic Tree

As some vast Tropic tree, itself a wood,
That crests its head with clouds, beneath the flood
Feeds its deep roots, and with the bulging flank
Of its wide base controls the fronting bank –
(By the slant current's pressure scoop'd away   5
The fronting bank becomes a foam-piled bay)
High in the Fork the uncouth Idol knits
His channel'd brow; low murmurs stir by fits
And dark below the horrid Faquir sits –
An Horror from its broad Head's branching wreath   10
Broods o'er the rude Idolatry beneath –

Psyche

The butterfly the ancient Grecians made
The soul's fair emblem, and its only name—
But of the soul, escaped the slavish trade
Of mortal life! – For in this earthly frame
Ours is the reptile's lot, much toil, much blame,   5
Manifold motions making little speed,
And to deform and kill the things whereon we feed.

The Sea Mew

Sea-ward, white gleaming thro' the busy scud
With arching Wings, the sea-mew o'er my head
Posts on, as bent on speed, now passaging
Edges the stiffer Breeze, now, yielding, drifts,
Now floats upon the air, and sends from far   5
A wildly-wailing Note.

The Yellow Hammer

The spruce and limber yellow-hammer
In the dawn of spring and sultry summer,
In hedge or tree the hours beguiling
With notes as of one who brass is filing.

On Donne's Poetry

With Donne, whose muse on dromedary trots,
Wreathe iron pokers into true-love knots;
Rhyme's sturdy cripple, fancy's maze and clue,
Wit's forge and fire-blast, meaning's press and screw.

The Knight's Tomb

Where is the grave of Sir Arthur O'Kellyn?
Where may the grave of that good man be? –
By the side of a spring, on the breast of Helvellyn,
Under the twigs of a young birch tree!
The oak that in summer was sweet to hear,   5
And rustled its leaves in the fall of the year,
And whistled and roared in the winter alone,
Is gone, – and the birch in its stead is grown. –
The Knight's bones are dust,
And his good sword rust; –   10
His soul is with the saints, I trust.

Four Metrical Experiments

1

IAMBICS

No cold shall thee benumb,
Nor darkness stain thy sight;
To thee new Heat, new Light
Shall from this object come,
Whose Praises if thou now wilt sound aright,
My Pen shall give thee leave hereafter to be dumb.

2

TROCHAICS

Thus she said, and, all around,
Her diviner spirit, gan to borrow;
Earthly Hearings hear unearthly sound,
Hearts heroic faint, and sink aswound.
Welcome, welcome, spite of pain and sorrow.
    Love to-day, and Thought to-morrow.

3

A PLAINTIVE MOVEMENT

Go little Pipe! for ever I must leave thee,
            Ah, vainly true!
Never, ah never! must I more receive thee?
            Adieu! adieu!
Well, thou art gone! and what remains behind,
            Soothing the soul to Hope?
            The moaning Wind —
Hide with sere leaves my Grave's undaisied Slope.

PINDARIC

Once again, sweet Willow, wave thee!
   Why stays my Love?
Bend, and in yon streamlet – lave thee!
   Why stays my Love?
Oft have I at evening straying,
Stood, thy branches long surveying,
 Graceful in the light breeze playing, –
   Why stays my Love?

Song from *Remorse*

Hear, sweet Spirit, hear the spell,
Lest a blacker charm compel!
So shall the midnight breezes swell
With thy deep long-lingering knell.

And at evening evermore,   5
In a chapel on the shore,
Shall the chaunter, sad and saintly,
Yellow tapers burning faintly,
Doleful masses chaunt for thee,
    Miserere Domine!   10

Hush! the cadence dies away
  On the quiet moonlight sea:
The boatmen rest their oars and say,
    Miserere Domine!

Song from *Zapolya*

A sunny shaft did I behold,
  From sky to earth it slanted:
And poised therein a bird so bold –
  Sweet bird, thou wert enchanted!

He sank, he rose, he twinkled, he trolled   5
  Within that shaft of sunny mist;
His eyes of fire, his beak of gold,
  All else of amethyst!

And thus he sang: "Adieu! adieu!
Love's dreams prove seldom true.   10
The blossoms they make no delay:
The sparkling dew-drops will not stay.
  Sweet month of May,
    We must away;
      Far, far away!   15
        To-day! to-day!"

Ars Poetica

It has been before observed that images, however beautiful, though faithfully copied from nature, and accurately represented in words, do not of themselves characterize the poet. They become proofs of original genius only as far as they are modified by a predominant passion; or by associated thoughts or images awakened by that passion; or when they have the effect of reducing multitude to unity, or succession to an instant; or lastly, when a human and intellectual life is transferred to them from the poet's own spirit,

"Which shoots its being through earth, sea and air".

In the two following lines, for instance, there is nothing objectionable, nothing which would preclude them from forming, in their proper place, part of a descriptive poem: –

"Behold yon row of pines, that shorn and bow'd
Bend from the sea-blast, seen at twilight eve."

But with the small alteration of rhythm, the same words would be equally in their place in a book of topography, or in a descriptive tour. The same image will rise into a semblance of poetry if thus conveyed: –

"Yon row of bleak and visionary pines,
By twilight-glimpse discerned, mark! how they flee
From the fierce sea-blast, all their tresses wild
Streaming before them."

Aria Spontanea

10 SEPT 1823. WEDNESDAY MORNING, 10 O'CLOCK

On the tenth day of September, –
Eighteen hundred Twenty Three,
Wednesday morn, and I remember
Ten on the *Clock* the Hour to be
[*The Watch and Clock do both agree*]   5

An *Air* that whizzed διὰ ἐγκεφάλου (right across the diameter of
my Brain) exactly like a Hummel Bee, *alias* Dumbeldore, the gentle-
man with Rappee Spenser (*sic*), with bands of Red, and Orange Plush
Breeches, close by my ear, at once sharp and burry, right over the
summit of Quantock at earliest Dawn just between the Nightingale
that I stopt to hear in the Copse at the Foot of Quantock, and the
first Sky-Lark that was a Song-Fountain, dashing up and sparkling
to the Ear's eye, in full column, or ornamented Shaft of sound in
the order of Gothic Extravaganza, out of Sight, over the Cornfields
on the Descent of the Mountain on the other side – out of sight,
tho' twice I beheld its *mute* shoot downward in the sunshine like a
falling star of silver: –

ARIA SPONTANEA

Flowers are lovely, Love is flower-like,
Friendship is a shelt'ring tree –   20
O the Joys, that came down shower-like,
Of Beauty, Truth, and Liberty,
When I was young, ere I was old!

The World That Spidery Witch

MY DEAR FRIEND

I have often amused myself with the thought of a self-conscious Looking-glass, and the various metaphorical applications of such a fancy – and this morning it struck across the Eolian Harp of my Brain that there was something pleasing and emblematic (of what I did not distinctly make out) in two such Looking-glasses fronting, each seeing the other in itself, and itself in the other. Have you ever noticed the Vault or snug little Apartment which the Spider spins and weaves for itself, by spiral threads round and round, and sometimes with strait lines, so that its lurking parlour or withdrawing-room is an oblong square? This too connected itself in my mind with the melancholy truth, that as we grow older, the World (alas! how often it happens that the less we love it, the more we care for it, the less reason we have to value its Shews, the more anxious are we about them – alas! how often do we become more and more loveless, as Love which can outlive all change save a change with regard to itself, and all loss save the loss of its *Reflex*, is more needed to sooth us and alone is able so to do!) What was I saying? O, I was adverting to the fact that as we advance in years, the World, that spidery Witch, spins its threads narrower and narrower, still closing on us, till at last it shuts us up within four walls, walls of flues and films, windowless – and well if there be sky-lights, and a small opening left for the Light from above.

I speak in figures, inward thoughts and woes
Interpreting by Shapes and outward shews:
Where daily nearer me with magic Ties,
What time and where, (wove close with magic Ties
Line over line, and thickning as they rise)   5
The World her spidery threads on all sides spin
Side answ'ring side with narrow interspace,
My Faith (say I; I and my Faith are one)
Hung, as a Mirror, there! And face to face
(For nothing else there was between or near)   10
One Sister Mirror hid the dreary Wall,
But *that* is broke! And with that bright compeer
I lost my object and my inmost All –
Faith *in* the Faith of THE ALONE MOST DEAR!
Ah! me!!   15
Call the World spider: and at fancy's touch
Thought becomes image and I see it such.
With viscous masonry of films and threads
Tough as the nets in Indian Forests found
It blends the Waller's and the Weaver's trades   20
And soon the tent-like Hangings touch the ground
A dusky chamber that excludes the day
But cease the prelude and resume the lay.

The Netherlands

Water and windmills, greenness, Islets green; —
Willows whose Trunks beside the shadows stood
Of their own higher half, and willowy swamp: —
Farmhouses that at anchor seem'd — in the inland sky
The fog-transfixing Spires —   5

VIII

POLITICAL,
IDEOLOGICAL AND
TOPICAL POEMS

Political, Ideological and Topical Poems

PREFACE

THE POEMS IN THIS final section really form an appendix, and are included more for their historical interest, than their intrinsic poetic merit. They show a preliminary background of revolutionary ideas, loosely expressed in verse, but not yet fully absorbed into Coleridge's poetry. They form a scrapbook of Coleridge's early thoughts on public affairs, and his later changing sense of the poet's function in society. The high political passions of his youth gradually give way to a more sceptical comedy, which still retains remarkable energy and conviction.

The group is dominated by Coleridge's excited response to events in France, beginning with the fall of the Bastille in 1789, when he was sixteen (No. 93). Wild millennial hopes for some apocalyptic change in society fill his mind in "Religious Musings" (No. 95), though the exaggerated rhetoric of this is already disclaimed elsewhere in the first of the Conversation Poems, which also belongs to 1794 (see No. 22). Over the next five years, French military ambitions, the invasion of Switzerland, and the advent of Napoleon, move Coleridge to a liberal position opposed to Jacobin revolutionary violence, but committed to a concept of political freedom (see "France: An Ode", No. 98). Coleridge's reading in philosophy, science and travel literature meanwhile produces a new line of mythological thought about the "Invisible Powers" in the universe (No. 96). This will lead directly to the ballads, with their interest in primitive forces and psychological archetypes, and the virtual abandonment of political poetry after 1799.

Coleridge develops surprisingly early the use of light and comic verse, which seems to allow him to say what would otherwise be unacceptable or indecorous. Pathos and humour are effectively combined in "To a Young Ass" (No. 94), which is not only an authentic expression of Pantisocratic brio, but also perhaps the first recorded Animal Rights poem in English. The popular broad-sheet comic ballad, "The Devil's Thoughts" (No. 99) turned out to be the most successful poem Coleridge ever published in a newspaper. Over twenty years later, he again uses a punchy, short comic verse-line (this time a form of Skeltonics) to defend himself in "A Character" (No. 100) from the charge of political apostasy (levelled by Hazlitt and other radicals) and the grossly unfair suggestion that he has been feathering his own nest with state grants.

Perhaps Coleridge's most unexpected late success in this comic mode is "The Delinquent Travellers" (No. 101), which might claim to be a Romantic comic version of the "The Rime of the Ancient Mariner", in the new age of the steamship. It records the first great craze for "tourism", after the Napoleonic War had finally ended in Europe. Coleridge envisages himself departing once more to the southern oceans, but this time for Australia, an utopian land where a new generation of Pantisocrats might still flourish.

The emergence of this benign comedic vision of the public world, during the late 1820s, is hardly recognized by modern criticism, though it is foretold in the many humorous cadenzas of Coleridge's private letters, his lifelong love of puns, and his relentless exchange of absurdities with Charles Lamb. While serious thoughts about social issues continued to pour out in his prose – the *Lay Sermons*, *The Friend*, *On the Constitution of Church and State* – to the very end of his life (see Chronology), Coleridge's poetry could still sometimes lift him into a lighter and brighter dimension, where the distant peaks of Xanadu were yet remotely visible from the upper windows of Highgate Hill.

An Ode on the Destruction
of the Bastille

I

Heard'st thou yon universal cry,
  And dost thou linger still on Gallia's shore?
Go, Tyranny! beneath some barbarous sky
  Thy terrors lost and ruin'd power deplore!
    What tho' through many a groaning age   5
    Was felt thy keen suspicious rage,
    Yet Freedom rous'd by fierce Disdain
    Has wildly broke thy triple chain,
And like the storm which Earth's deep entrails hide,
At length has burst its way and spread the ruins wide.   10

*   *   *

IV

In sighs their sickly breath was spent; each gleam
  Of Hope had ceas'd the long long day to cheer;
Or if delusive, in some flitting dream,
  It gave them to their friends and children dear –
    Awaked by lordly Insult's sound   15
    To all the doubled horrors round,
    Oft shrunk they from Oppression's band
    While Anguish rais'd the desperate hand
For silent death; or lost the mind's controll,
Thro' every burning vein would tides of Frenzy roll.   20

V

But cease, ye pitying bosoms, cease to bleed!
  Such scenes no more demand the tear humane;
I see, I see! glad Liberty succeed
  With every patriot virtue in her train!

And mark yon peasant's raptur'd eyes;   25
   Secure he views his harvests rise;
   No fetter vile the mind shall know,
   And Eloquence shall fearless glow.
Yes! Liberty the soul of Life shall reign,
Shall throb in every pulse, shall flow thro' every vein!   30

VI

Shall France alone a Despot spurn?
   Shall she alone, O Freedom, boast thy care?
Lo, round thy standard Belgia's heroes burn,
   Tho' Power's blood-stain'd streamers fire the air,
      And wider yet thy influence spread,   35
      Nor e'er recline thy weary head,
      Till every land from pole to pole
      Shall boast one independent soul!
And still, as erst, let favour'd Britain be
First ever of the first and freest of the free!   40

To a Young Ass

ITS MOTHER BEING TETHERED NEAR IT

Poor little Foal of an oppresséd race!
I love the languid patience of thy face:
And oft with gentle hand I give thee bread,
And clap thy ragged coat, and pat thy head.
But what thy dulled spirits hath dismay'd,　　　　　5
That never thou dost sport along the glade?
And (most unlike the nature of things young)
That earthward still thy moveless head is hung?
Do thy prophetic fears anticipate,
Meek Child of Misery! thy future fate?　　　　　10
The starving meal, and all the thousand aches
"Which patient Merit of the Unworthy takes"?
Or is thy sad heart thrill'd with filial pain
To see thy wretched mother's shorten'd chain?
And truly, very piteous is *her* lot—　　　　　15
Chain'd to a log within a narrow spot,
Where the close-eaten grass is scarcely seen,
While sweet around her waves the tempting green!

Poor Ass! thy master should have learnt to show
Pity – best taught by fellowship of Woe!　　　　　20
For much I fear me that *He* lives like thee,
Half famish'd in a land of Luxury!
How *askingly* its footsteps hither bend?
It seems to say, "And have I then *one* friend?"
Innocent foal! thou poor despis'd forlorn!　　　　　25
I hail thee *Brother* – spite of the fool's scorn!
And fain would take thee with me, in the Dell
Of Peace and mild Equality to dwell,
Where Toil shall call the charmer Health his bride,
And Laughter tickle Plenty's ribless side!　　　　　30
How thou wouldst toss thy heels in gamesome play,

And frisk about, as lamb or kitten gay!
Yea! and more musically sweet to me
Thy dissonant harsh bray of joy would be,
Than warbled melodies that soothe to rest   35
The aching of pale Fashion's vacant breast!

The Present State of Society

EXTRACT FROM "RELIGIOUS MUSINGS"

Ah! far removed from all that glads the sense,
From all that softens or ennobles Man,
The wretched Many! Bent beneath their loads
They gape at pageant Power, nor recognise
Their cots' transmuted plunder! From the tree   5
Of Knowledge, ere the vernal sap had risen
Rudely disbranchéd! Blessed Society!
Fitliest depictured by some sun-scorched waste,
Where oft majestic through the tainted noon
The Simoom sails, before whose purple pomp*   10
Who falls not prostrate dies! And where by night,
Fast by each precious fountain on green herbs
The lion couches: or hyaena dips
Deep in the lucid stream his bloody jaws;
Or serpent plants his vast moon-glittering bulk,   15
Caught in whose monstrous twine Behemoth† yells,
His bones loud-crashing!

                    O ye numberless,
Whom foul Oppression's ruffian gluttony
Drives from Life's plenteous feast! O thou poor Wretch
Who nursed in darkness and made wild by want,   20
Roamest for prey, yea thy unnatural hand

---

* At eleven o'clock, while we contemplated with great pleasure the rugged top of Chiggre, to which we were fast approaching, and where we were to solace ourselves with plenty of good water, IDRIS cried out with a loud voice, 'Fall upon your faces, for here is the Simoom'. I saw from the S.E. an haze come on, in colour like the purple part of the rainbow, but not so compresssed or thick. It did not occupy twenty yards in breadth, and was about twelve feet high from the ground. – We all lay flat on the ground, as if dead, till IDRIS told us it was blown over. The meteor, or purple haze, which I saw, was indeed passed; but the light air that still blew was of heat to threaten suffocation. Bruce's *Travels*, vol. 4, p. 557.

† Behemoth, in Hebrew, signifies wild beasts in general. Some believe it is the Elephant, some the Hippopotamus; some affirm it is the Wild Bull. Poetically, it designates any large Quadruped.

Dost lift to deeds of blood! O pale-eyed form,
The victim of seduction, doomed to know
Polluted nights and days of blasphemy;
Who in loathed orgies with lewd wassailers   25
Must gaily laugh, while thy remembered Home
Gnaws like a viper at thy secret heart!
O agéd Women! ye who weekly catch
The morsel tossed by law-forced charity,
And die so slowly, that none call it murder!   30
O loathly suppliants! ye, that unreceived
Totter heart-broken from the closing gates
Of the full Lazar-house; or, gazing, stand,
Sick with despair! O ye to Glory's field
Forced or ensnared, who, as ye gasp in death,   35
Bleed with new wounds beneath the vulture's beak!
O thou poor widow, who in dreams dost view
Thy husband's mangled corse, and from short doze
Start'st with a shriek; or in thy half-thatched cot
Waked by the wintry night-storm, wet and cold   40
Cow'rst o'er thy screaming baby! Rest awhile
Children of Wretchedness! More groans must rise,
More blood must stream, or ere your wrongs be full.
Yet is the day of Retribution nigh:
The Lamb of God hath opened the fifth seal:*   45
And upward rush on swiftest wing of fire
The innumerable multitude of wrongs
By man on man inflicted! Rest awhile,
Children of Wretchedness! The hour is nigh
And lo! the Great, the Rich, the Mighty Men,   50
The Kings and the Chief Captains of the World,

---

* See the sixth chapter of the Revelation of St. John the Divine. – And I looked
and beheld a pale horse; and his name that sat on him was Death, and Hell followed
with him. And power was given unto them over the FOURTH part of the Earth to
kill with sword, and with hunger, and with pestilence, and with the beasts of the
Earth. – And when he had opened the fifth seal, I saw under the altar the souls of them
that were slain for the word of God, and for the testimony which they held; and white
robes were given unto every one of them; and it was said unto them, that they
should rest yet for a little season, until their fellow servants also, and their brethren
that should be killed as they were should be fulfilled. And I beheld when he had
opened the sixth seal, the stars of Heaven fell unto the Earth, even as a fig-tree
casteth her untimely figs when she is shaken of a mighty wind: And the kings of
the earth, and the great men, and the rich men, and the chief captains, &c.

With all that fixed on high like stars of Heaven
Shot baleful influence, shall be cast to earth,
Vile and down-trodden, as the untimely fruit
Shook from the fig-tree by a sudden storm.   55
Even now the storm begins:* each gentle name.
Faith and meek Piety, with fearful joy
Tremble far-off – for lo! the Giant Frenzy
Uprooting empires with his whirlwind arm
Mocketh high Heaven; burst hideous from the cell   60
Where the old Hag, unconquerable, huge,
Creation's eyeless drudge, black Ruin, sits
Nursing the impatient earthquake.

                         O return!
Pure Faith! meek Piety! The abhorréd Form†
Whose scarlet robe was stiff with earthly pomp,   65

Who drank iniquity in cups of gold,
Whose names were many and all blasphemous,
Hath met the horrible judgment! Whence that cry?
The mighty army of foul Spirits shrieked
Disherited of earth! For she hath fallen   70
On whose black front was written Mystery;
She that reeled heavily, whose wine was blood;
She that worked whoredom with the Daemon Power,
And from the dark embrace all evil things
Brought forth and nurtured: mitred Atheism!   75
And patient Folly who on bended knee
Gives back the steel that stabbed him; and pale Fear
Haunted by ghastlier shapings than surround
Moon-blasted Madness when he yells at midnight!
Return pure Faith! return meek Piety!   80
The kingdoms of the world are your's: each heart
Self-governed, the vast family of Love
Raised from the common earth by common toil
Enjoy the equal produce. Such delights

---

* Alluding to the French Revolution.
  † And there came one of the seven Angels which had the seven vials, and talked with me, saying unto me, come hither! I will show unto thee the judgment of the great Whore, that sitteth upon many waters: with whom the kings of the earth have committed fornication, &c. Revelation of St. John the Divine, chapter the seventeenth.

As float to earth, permitted visitants! 85
When in some hour of solemn jubilee
The massy gates of Paradise are thrown
Wide open, and forth come in fragments wild
Sweet echoes of unearthly melodies,
And odours snatched from beds of Amaranth, 90
And they, that from the crystal river of life
Spring up on freshened wing, ambrosial gales!
The favoured good man in his lonely walk
Perceives them, and his silent spirit drinks
Strange bliss which he shall recognise in heaven. 95
And such delights, such strange beatitudes
Seize on my young anticipating heart
When that blest future rushes on my view!
For in his own and in his Father's might
The Saviour comes! While as the Thousand Years* 100
Lead up their mystic dance, the Desert shouts!
Old Ocean claps his hands! The mighty Dead
Rise to new life, whoe'er from earliest time
With conscious zeal had urged Love's wondrous plan,
Coadjutors of God. To Milton's trump 105
The high groves of the renovated Earth
Unbosom their glad echoes: inly hushed,
Adoring Newton his serener eye
Raises to heaven: and he of mortal kind
Wisest, he† first who marked the ideal tribes 110
Up the fine fibres through the sentient brain.
Lo! Priestley there, patriot, and saint, and sage,
Him, full of years, from his loved native land
Statesmen blood-stained and priests idolatrous
By dark lies maddening the blind multitude 115
Drove with vain hate. Calm, pitying he retired,
And mused expectant on these promised years.

* The Millenium: – in which I suppose, that Man will continue to enjoy the highest glory, of which his human nature is capable. – That all who in past ages have endeavoured to ameliorate the state of man will rise and enjoy the fruits and flowers, the imperceptible seeds of which they had sown in their former Life: and that the wicked will during the same period, be suffering the remedies adapted to their several bad habits. I suppose that this period will be followed by the passing away of this Earth and by our entering the state of pure intellect; when all Creation shall rest from its labours.

† David Hartley.

96

Invisible Powers

EXTRACT FROM "THE DESTINY OF NATIONS"

For what is Freedom, but the unfettered use
Of all the powers which God for use had given?
But chiefly this, him First, him Last to view
Through meaner powers and secondary things
Effulgent, as through clouds that veil his blaze.   5
For all that meets the bodily sense I deem
Symbolical, one mighty alphabet
For infant minds; and we in this low world
Placed with our backs to bright Reality,
That we may learn with young unwounded ken   10
The substance from its shadow. Infinite Love,
Whose latence is the plenitude of All,
Thou with retracted beams, and self-eclipse
Veiling, revealest thine eternal Sun.

But some there are who deem themselves most free   15
When they within this gross and visible sphere
Chain down the wingèd thought, scoffing ascent,
Proud in their meanness: and themselves they cheat
With noisy emptiness of learnèd phrase,
Their subtle fluids, impacts, essences,   20
Self-working tools, uncaused effects, and all
Those blind Omniscients, those Almighty Slaves,
Untenanting creation of its God.

But Properties are God: the naked mass
(If mass there be, fantastic guess or ghost)   25
Acts only by its inactivity.
Here we pause humbly. Others boldlier think
That as one body seems the aggregate
Of atoms numberless, each organized;
So by a strange and dim similitude   30
Infinite myriads of self-conscious minds
Are one all-conscious Spirit, which informs

With absolute ubiquity of thought
(His one eternal self-affirming act!)
All his involvéd Monads, that yet seem   35
With various province and apt agency
Each to pursue its own self-centering end.
Some nurse the infant diamond in the mine;
Some roll the genial juices through the oak;
Some drive the mutinous clouds to clash in air,   40
And rushing on the storm with whirlwind speed,
Yoke the red lightnings to their volleying car.
Thus these pursue their never-varying course,
No eddy in their stream. Others, more wild,
With complex interests weaving human fates,   45
Duteous or proud, alike obedient all,
Evolve the process of eternal good.

    And what if some rebellious, o'er dark realms
Arrogate power? yet these train up to God,
And on the rude eye, unconfirmed for day,   50
Flash meteor-lights better than total gloom.
As ere from Lieule-Oaive's vapoury head
The Laplander beholds the far-off Sun
Dart his slant beam on unobeying snows,
While yet the stern and solitary Night   55
Brooks no alternate sway, the Boreal Morn
With mimic lustre substitutes its gleam,
Guiding his course or by Niemi lake
Or Balda Zhiok,* or the mossy stone
Of Solfar-kapper, while the snowy blast   60
Drifts arrowy by, or eddies round his sledge,
Making the poor babe at its mother's back†
Scream in its scanty cradle: he the while
Wins gentle solace as with upward eye
He marks the streamy banners of the North,   65
Thinking himself those happy spirits shall join
Who there in floating robes of rosy light

---

* Balda-Zhiok, i.e. mons altitudinis, the highest mountain in Lapland.
† The Lapland women carry their infants at their backs in a piece of excavated wood which serves them for a cradle: opposite to the infant's mouth there is a hole for it to breathe through.

Dance sportively. For Fancy is the power
That first unsensualises the dark mind,
Giving it new delights; and bids it swell   70
With wild activity; and peopling air,
By obscure fears of Beings invisible,
Emancipates it from the grosser thrall
Of the present impulse, teaching Self-control,
Till Superstition with unconscious hand   75
Seat Reason on her throne. Wherefore not vain,
Nor yet without permitted power impressed,
I deem those legends terrible, with which
The polar ancient thrills his uncouth throng:
Whether of pitying Spirits that make their moan   80
O'er slaughter'd infants, or that Giant Bird
Vuokho, of whose rushing wings the noise
Is Tempest, when the unutterable Shape
Speeds from the mother of Death, and utters once
That shriek, which never murderer heard, and lived.   85

    Or if the Greenland Wizard in strange trance
Pierces the untravelled realms of Ocean's bed
Over the abysm, even to that uttermost cave
By mis-shaped prodigies beleaguered, such
As Earth ne'er bred, nor Air, nor the upper Sea: 90
Where dwells the Fury Form, whose unheard name
With eager eye, pale cheek, suspended breath,
And lips half-opening with the dread of sound,
Unsleeping Silence guards, worn out with fear
Lest haply 'scaping on some treacherous blast   95
The fateful word let slip the Elements
And frenzy Nature. Yet the wizard her,
Arm'd with Torngarsuck's power, the Spirit of Good,*
Forces to unchain the foodful progeny
Of the Ocean stream; – thence thro' the realm of Souls,   100

---

* They call the Good Spirit, Torngarsuck. The other great but malignant spirit
a nameless female; she dwells under the sea in a great house where she can detain
in captivity all the animals of the ocean by her magic power. When a dearth befalls
the Greenlanders, an Angekok or magician must undertake a journey thither: he
passes through the kingdom of souls, over an horrible abyss into the palace of this
phantom, and by his enchantments causes the captive creatures to ascend directly
to the surface of the ocean. See Crantz, *History of Greenland*, vol. i. 206.

Where live the Innocent, as far from cares
As from the storms and overwhelming waves
That tumble on the surface of the Deep,
Returns with far-heard pant, hotly pursued
By the fierce Warders of the Sea, once more,   105
Ere by the frost foreclosed, to repossess
His fleshly mansion, that had staid the while
In the dark tent within a cow'ring group
Untenanted. – Wild phantasies! yet wise,
On the victorious goodness of high God   110
Teaching reliance, and medicinal hope,
Till from Bethabra northward, heavenly Truth
With gradual steps, winning her difficult way,
Transfer their rude Faith perfected and pure.

97

Fire, Famine, and Slaughter

A WAR ECLOGUE

The Scene a desolated Tract in La Vendée. FAMINE *is discovered lying on the ground; to her enter* FIRE *and* SLAUGHTER.

> *Fam.* Sisters! sisters! who sent you here?
> *Slau.* [*to Fire*]. I will whisper it in her ear.
>   *Fire.* No! no! no!
> Spirits hear what spirits tell:
> 'Twill make a holiday in Hell.   5
>   No! no! no!
> Myself, I named him once below,
> And all the souls, that damnéd be,
> Leaped up at once in anarchy,
> Clapped their hands and danced for glee.   10
> They no longer heeded me;
> But laughed to hear Hell's burning rafters
> Unwillingly re-echo laughters!
>   No! no! no!
> Spirits hear what spirits tell: 15
> 'Twill make a holiday in Hell!
>   *Fam.* Whisper it, sister! so and so!
> In a dark hint, soft and slow.
>   *Slau.* Letters four do form his name –
> And who sent you?
>   *Both.*   The same! the same!   20
>   *Slau.* He came by stealth, and unlocked my den,
> And I have drunk the blood since then
> Of thrice three hundred thousand men.
>   *Both.* Who bade you do 't?
>   *Slau.*   The same! the same!
> Letters four do form his name.   25
> He let me loose, and cried Halloo!
> To him alone the praise is due.
>   *Fam.* Thanks, sister, thanks! the men have bled,
> Their wives and their children faint for bread.

I stood in a swampy field of battle; 30
With bones and skulls I made a rattle,
To frighten the wolf and carrion-crow
And the homeless dog – but they would not go.
So off I flew: for how could I bear
To see them gorge their dainty fare? 35
I heard a groan and a peevish squall,
And through the chink of a cottage-wall –
Can you guess what I saw there?
   Both. Whisper it, sister! in our ear.
   Fam. A baby beat its dying mother: 40
I had starved the one and was starving the other!
   Both. Who bade you do 't?
   Fam.   The same! the same!
Letters four do form his name.
He let me loose, and cried, Halloo!
To him alone the praise is due. 45
   Fire. Sisters! I from Ireland came!
Hedge and corn-fields all on flame,
I triumph'd o'er the setting sun!
And all the while the work was done,
On as I strode with my huge strides, 50
I flung back my head and I held my sides,
It was so rare a piece of fun
To see the sweltered cattle run
With uncouth gallop through the night,
Scared by the red and noisy light! 55
By the light of his own blazing cot
Was many a naked Rebel shot:
The house-stream met the flame and hissed,
While crash! fell in the roof, I wist,
On some of those old bed-rid nurses, 60
That deal in discontent and curses.
   Both. Who bade you do 't?
   Fire.   The same! the same!
Letters four do form his name.
He let me loose, and cried Halloo!
To him alone the praise is due. 65
   All. He let us loose, and cried Halloo!
How shall we yield him honour due?
   Fam. Wisdom comes with lack of food.

I'll gnaw, I'll gnaw the multitude,
Till the cup of rage o'erbrim: 70
They shall seize him and his brood –
  Slau. They shall tear him limb from limb!
  Fire. O thankless beldames and untrue!
And is this all that you can do
For him, who did so much for you?   75
Ninety months he, by my troth!
Hath richly catered for you both;
And in an hour would you repay
An eight years' work? – Away! away!
I alone am faithful! I   80
Cling to him everlastingly.

98

France: An Ode

ARGUMENT

"*First Stanza*. An invocation to those objects in Nature the contemplation of which had inspired the Poet with a devotional love of Liberty. *Second Stanza*. The exultation of the Poet at the commencement of the French Revolution, and his unqualified abhorrence of the Alliance against the Republic. *Third Stanza*. The blasphemies and horrors during the domination of the Terrorists regarded by the Poet as a transient storm, and as the natural consequence of the former despotism and of the foul superstition of Popery. Reason, indeed, began to suggest many apprehensions; yet still the Poet struggled to retain the hope that France would make conquests by no other means than by presenting to the observation of Europe a people more happy and better instructed than under other forms of Government. *Fourth Stanza*. Switzerland, and the Poet's recantation. *Fifth Stanza*. An address to Liberty, in which the Poet expresses his conviction that those feelings and that grand *ideal* of Freedom which the mind attains by its contemplation of its individual nature, and of the sublime surrounding objects (see Stanza the First) do not belong to men, as a society, nor can possibly be either gratified or realised, under any form of human government; but belong to the individual man, so far as he is pure, and inflamed with the love and adoration of God in Nature."

I

Ye Clouds! that far above me float and pause,
    Whose pathless march no mortal may controul!
    Ye Ocean-Waves! that, wheresoe'er ye roll,
Yield homage only to eternal laws!
Ye Woods! that listen to the night-birds singing,   5
    Midway the smooth and perilous slope reclined,
Save when your own imperious branches swinging,
    Have made a solemn music of the wind!

Where, like a man beloved of God,
Through glooms, which never woodman trod,   10
    How oft, pursuing fancies holy,
My moonlight way o'er flowering weeds I wound,
    Inspired, beyond the guess of folly,
By each rude shape and wild unconquerable sound!
O ye loud Waves! and O ye Forests high!   15
    And O ye Clouds that far above me soared!
Thou rising Sun! thou blue rejoicing Sky!
    Yea, every thing that is and will be free!
    Bear witness for me, wheresoe'er ye be,
    With what deep worship I have still adored   20
        The spirit of divinest Liberty.

II

When France in wrath her giant-limbs upreared,
    And with that oath, which smote air, earth, and sea,
    Stamped her strong foot and said she would be free,
Bear witness for me, how I hoped and feared!   25
With what a joy my lofty gratulation
    Unawed I sang, amid a slavish band:
And when to whelm the disenchanted nation,
    Like fiends embattled by a wizard's wand,
        The Monarchs marched in evil day,   30
        And Britain joined the dire array;
    Though dear her shores and circling ocean,
Though many friendships, many youthful loves
    Had swoln the patriot emotion
And flung a magic light o'er all her hills and groves;   35
Yet still my voice, unaltered, sang defeat
    To all that braved the tyrant-quelling lance,
And shame too long delayed and vain retreat!
For ne'er, O Liberty! with partial aim
I dimmed thy light or damped thy holy flame;   40
    But blessed the paeans of delivered France,
And hung my head and wept at Britain's name.

"And what," I said, "though Blasphemy's loud scream
   With that sweet music of deliverance strove!
   Though all the fierce and drunken passions wove   45
A dance more wild than e'er was maniac's dream!
   Ye storms, that round the dawning East assembled,
The Sun was rising, though ye hid his light!"
   And when, to soothe my soul, that hoped and trembled,
The dissonance ceased, and all seemed calm and bright;   50
   When France her front deep-scarr'd and gory
   Concealed with clustering wreaths of glory;
   When, insupportably advancing,
   Her arm made mockery of the warrior's ramp;
   While timid looks of fury glancing,   55
   Domestic treason, crushed beneath her fatal stamp,
Writhed like a wounded dragon in his gore;
   Then I reproached my fears that would not flee;
"And soon," I said, "shall Wisdom teach her lore.
In the low huts of them that toil and groan!   60
And, conquering by her happiness alone,
   Shall France compel the nations to be free,
Till Love and Joy look round, and call the Earth their own."

Forgive me, Freedom! O forgive those dreams!
   I hear thy voice, I hear thy loud lament,   65
   From bleak Helvetia's icy caverns sent –
I hear thy groans upon her blood-stained streams!
   Heroes, that for your peaceful country perished,
And ye that, fleeing, spot your mountain-snows
   With bleeding wounds; forgive me, that I cherished   70
One thought that ever blessed your cruel foes!
   To scatter rage, and traitorous guilt,
   Where Peace her jealous home had built;
     A patriot-race to disinherit
Of all that made their stormy wilds so dear;   75
     And with inexpiable spirit
To taint the bloodless freedom of the mountaineer –
O France, that mockest Heaven, adulterous, blind,

And patriot only in pernicious toils!
Are these thy boasts, Champion of human kind?   80
    To mix with Kings in the low lust of sway,
Yell in the hunt, and share the murderous prey;
To insult the shrine of Liberty with spoils
    From freemen torn; to tempt and to betray?

                                    v

    The Sensual and the Dark rebel in vain,   85
    Slaves by their own compulsion! In mad game
    They burst their manacles and wear the name
        Of Freedom, graven on a heavier chain!
    O Liberty! with profitless endeavour
Have I pursued thee, many a weary hour;   90
    But thou nor swell'st the victor's strain, nor ever
Didst breathe thy soul in forms of human power.
    Alike from all, howe'er they praise thee,
        (Nor prayer, nor boastful name delays thee)
        Alike from Priestcraft's harpy minions,   95
    And factious Blasphemy's obscener slaves,
        Thou speedest on thy subtle pinions,
The guide of homeless winds, and playmate of the waves!
And there I felt thee! – on that sea-cliff's verge,
    Whose pines, scarce travelled by the breeze above,   100
Had made one murmur with the distant surge!
Yes, while I stood and gazed, my temples bare,
And shot my being through earth, sea, and air,
    Possessing all things with intensest love,
        O Liberty! my spirit felt thee there.   105

99

The Devil's Thoughts

I

From his brimstone bed at break of day
A walking the Devil is gone,
To visit his snug little farm the earth,
And see how his stock goes on.

II

Over the hill and over the dale,   5
And he went over the plain,
And backward and forward he switched his long tail
As a gentleman switches his cane.

III

And how then was the Devil drest?
Oh! he was in his Sunday's best: 10
His jacket was red and his breeches were blue,
And there was a hole where the tail came through.

IV

He saw a Lawyer killing a Viper
On a dunghill hard by his own stable;
And the Devil smiled, for it put him in mind   15
Of Cain and his brother, Abel.

V

He saw an Apothecary on a white horse
      Ride by on his vocations,
And the Devil thought of his old Friend
      Death in the Revelations.   20

He saw a cottage with a double coach-house,
  A cottage of gentility;
And the Devil did grin, for his darling sin
  Is pride that apes humility.

He peep'd into a rich bookseller's shop,   25
  Quoth he! we are both of one college!
For I sate myself, like a cormorant, once
  Hard by the tree of knowledge.

Down the river did glide, with wind and tide,
  A pig with vast celerity;   30
And the Devil look'd wise as he saw how the while,
It cut its own throat. "There!" quoth he with a smile,
  "Goes 'England's commercial prosperity.'"

As he went through Cold-Bath Fields he saw
  A solitary cell;   35
And the Devil was pleased, for it gave him a hint
  For improving his prisons in Hell.

He saw a Turnkey in a trice
  Fetter a troublesome blade;
"Nimbly," quoth he, "do the fingers move   40
  If a man be but used to his trade."

He saw the same Turnkey unfetter a man,
  With but little expedition,
Which put him in mind of the long debate
  On the Slave-trade abolition.   45

XII

He saw an old acquaintance
  As he passed by a Methodist meeting; –
She holds a consecrated key,
  And the devil nods her a greeting.

XIII

She turned up her nose, and said,   50
  "Avaunt! my name's Religion,"
And she looked to Mr——
  And leered like a love-sick pigeon.

XIV

He saw a certain minister
  (A minister to his mind)   55
Go up into a certain House,
  With a majority behind.

XV

The Devil quoted Genesis
  Like a very learnèd clerk,
How "Noah and his creeping things   60
  Went up into the Ark."

XVI

He took from the poor,
  And he gave to the rich,
And he shook hands with a Scotchman,
  For he was not afraid of the—   65

XVII

General ———'s burning face
  He saw with consternation,
And back to hell his way did he take,
For the Devil thought by a slight mistake
  It was general conflagration.   70

100

A Character

A bird, who for his other sins –
Had liv'd amongst the Jacobins;
Though like a kitten amid rats,
Or callow tit in nest of bats,
He much abhorr'd all democrats;   5
Yet nathless stood in ill report
Of wishing ill to Church and Court,
Tho' he'd nor claw, nor tooth, nor sting,
And learnt to pipe God save the King;
Tho' each day did new feathers bring,   10
All swore he had a leathern wing;
Nor polish'd wing, nor feather'd tail,
Nor down-clad thigh would aught avail;
And tho' – his tongue devoid of gall –
He civilly assur'd them all: –   15
"A bird am I of Phoebus' breed,
And on the sunflower cling and feed;
My name, good Sirs, is Thomas Tit!"
The bats would hail him Brother Cit,
Or, at the furthest, cousin-german.   20
At length the matter to determine,
He publicly denounced the vermin;
He spared the mouse, he praised the owl;
But bats were neither flesh nor fowl.
Blood-sucker, vampire, harpy, goul,   25
Came in full clatter from his throat,
Till his old nest-mates chang'd their note
To hireling, traitor, and turncoat, –
A base apostate who had sold
His very teeth and claws for gold; –   30
And then his feathers! – sharp the jest –
No doubt he feather'd well his nest!
"A Tit indeed! aye, tit for tat –
With place and title, brother Bat,

We soon shall see how well he'll play   35
Count Goldfinch, or Sir Joseph Jay!"
    Alas, poor Bird! and ill-bestarr'd –
Or rather let us say, poor Bard!
And henceforth quit the allegoric,
With metaphor and simile,   40
For simple facts and style historic: –
Alas, poor Bard! no gold had he;
Behind another's team he stept,
And plough'd and sow'd, while others reapt;
The work was his, but theirs the glory,   45
Sic vos non vobis, his whole story.
Besides, whate'er he wrote or said
Came from his heart as well as head;
And though he never left in lurch
His king, his country, or his church,   50
'Twas but to humour his own cynical
Contempt of doctrines Jacobinical;
To his own conscience only hearty,
'Twas but by chance he serv'd the party; –
The self-same things had said and writ,   55
Had Pitt been Fox, and Fox been Pitt;
Content his own applause to win,
Would never dash thro' thick and thin,
And he can make, so say the wise,
No claim who makes no sacrifice; –   60
And bard still less: – what claim had he,
Who swore it vex'd his soul to see
So grand a cause, so proud a realm,
With Goose and Goody at the helm;
Who long ago had fall'n asunder   65
But for their rivals' baser blunder,
The coward whine and Frenchified
Slaver and slang of the other side? –

    Thus, his own whim his only bribe,
Our Bard pursued his old A. B. C.   70
Contented if he could subscribe
In fullest sense his name "Εστησε;
('Tis Punic Greek for "he hath stood!")
Whate'er the men, the cause was good;

And therefore with a right good will,   75
Poor fool, he fights their battles still.
Tush! squeak'd the Bats; – a mere bravado
To whitewash that base renegado;
'Tis plain unless you're blind or mad,
His conscience for the bays he barters; –   80
And true it is – as true as sad –
These circlets of green baize he had –
But then, alas! they were his garters!
   Ah! silly Bard, unfed, untended,
His lamp but glimmer'd in its socket;   85
He lived unhonour'd and unfriended
With scarce a penny in his pocket; –
Nay – tho' he hid it from the many –
With scarce a pocket for his penny!

101

The Delinquent Travellers

Some are home-sick – some two or three,
Their third year on the Arctic Sea –
Brave Captain Lyon tells us so –
Spite of those charming Esquimaux.
But O, what scores are sick of Home,   5
Agog for Paris or for Rome!
Nay! tho' contented to abide,
You should prefer your own fireside;
Yet since grim War has ceas'd its madding,
And Peace has set John Bull agadding,   10
'Twould such a vulgar taste betray,
For very shame you must away!
"What? not yet seen the coast of France!
The folks will swear, for lack of bail,
You've spent your last five years in jail!"   15

Keep moving! Steam, or Gas, or Stage,
Hold, cabin, steerage, hencoop's cage –
Tour, Journey, Voyage, Lounge, Ride, Walk,
Skim, Sketch, Excursion, Travel-talk –
For move you must! 'Tis now the rage,   20
The law and fashion of the Age.
If you but perch, where Dover tallies,
So strangely with the coast of Calais,
With a good glass and knowing look,
You'll soon get matter for a book!   25
Or else, in Gas-car, take your chance
Like that adventurous king of France,
Who, once, with twenty thousand men
Went up – and then came down again;
At least, he moved if nothing more: 30
And if there's nought left to explore,
Yet while your well-greased wheels keep spinning,
The traveller's honoured name you're winning,

And, snug as Jonas in the Whale,
You may loll back and dream a tale.   35
Move, or be moved – there's no protection,
Our Mother Earth has ta'en the infection –
(That rogue Copernicus, 'tis said
First put the whirring in her head,)
A planet She, and can't endure   40
T'exist without her annual Tour:
The *name* were else a mere misnomer,
Since Planet is but Greek for *Roamer*.
The atmosphere, too, can do no less
Than ventilate her emptiness,   45
Bilks turn-pike gates, for no one cares,
And gives herself a thousand airs –
While streams and shopkeepers, we see,
Will have their run toward the sea –
And if, meantime, like old King Log,   50
Or ass with tether and a clog,
Must graze at home! to yawn and bray
"I guess we shall have rain to-day!"
Nor clog nor tether can be worse
Than the dead palsy of the purse.   55
Money, I've heard a wise man say,
Makes herself wings and flys away:
Ah! would She take it in her head
To make a pair for me instead!
At all events, the Fancy's free,   60
No traveller so bold as she.
From Fear and Poverty released
I'll saddle Pegasus, at least,
And when she's seated to her mind,
I within I can mount behind: 65
And since this outward I, you know,
Must stay because he cannot go,
My fellow-travellers shall be they
Who go because they cannot stay –
Rogues, rascals, sharpers, blanks and prizes,   70
Delinquents of all sorts and sizes,
Fraudulent bankrupts, Knights burglarious,
And demireps of means precarious –
All whom Law thwarted, Arms or Arts,

Compel to visit foreign parts, 75
All hail! No compliments, I pray,
I'll follow where you lead the way!
But ere we cross the main once more,
Methinks, along my native shore,
Dismounting from my steed I'll stray 80
Beneath the cliffs of Dumpton Bay,
Where, Ramsgate and Broadstairs between,
Rude caves and grated doors are seen:
And here I'll watch till break of day,
(For Fancy in her magic might 85
Can turn broad noon to starless night!)
When lo! methinks a sudden band
Of smock-clad smugglers round me stand.
Denials, oaths, in vain I try,
At once they gag me for a spy, 90
And stow me in the boat hard by.
Suppose us fairly now afloat,
Till Boulogne mouth receives our Boat.
But, bless us! what a numerous band
Of cockneys anglicise the strand! 95
Delinquent bankrupts, leg-bail'd debtors,
Some for the news, and some for letters –
With hungry look and tarnished dress,
French shrugs and British surliness.
Sick of the country for their sake 100
Of them and France *French leave* I take –
And lo! a transport comes in view
I hear the merry motley crew,
Well skill'd in pocket to make entry,
Of Dieman's Land the elected Gentry, 105
And founders of Australian Races. –
The Rogues! I see it in their faces!
Receive me, Lads! I'll go with you,
Hunt the black swan and kangaroo,
And that New Holland we'll presume 110
Old England with some elbow-room.
Across the mountains we will roam,
And each man make himself a home:
Or, if old habits ne'er forsaking,
Like clock-work of the Devil's making, 115

Ourselves inveterate rogues should be,
We'll have a virtuous progeny;
And on the dunghill of our vices
Raise human pine-apples and spices.
Of all the children of John Bull   120
With empty heads and bellies full,
Who ramble East, West, North and South,
With leaky purse and open mouth,
In search of varieties exotic
The usefullest and most patriotic,   125
And merriest, too, believe me, Sirs!
Are your Delinquent Travellers!

NOTES

Notes to the Sonnets

1. "TO THE AUTUMNAL MOON"

One of Coleridge's earliest known poems, written at the age of sixteen; first published in *Poems* 1796. He later recalled how he spent many homesick hours star-gazing from the "leads", or flat roof, of Christ's Hospital in London, and how the moon appeared as a messenger from his lost country home at Ottery St Mary, far in the west. The mid-eighteenth-century sub-Miltonic style of invocations, personifications, exclamations, and double-epithets ("wildly-working", "sorrow-clouded") show Coleridge's adolescent influences, together with a touch of the fashionably Gothic ("dragon-wing'd Despair"). The symbol of the Moon, and the figures of Hope and Despair, appear frequently in the mature poetry.

2. "LIFE"

"Sonnet written just after the author left the Country in September 1789" (Coleridge's MS. note); not published until *Poetical Works* 1834. Coleridge spent the school summer holiday of 1789 at Ottery St Mary and Exeter, visiting his beloved elder sister Anne (3) who was gravely ill. Coleridge's delight in the magic landscape of the river valley, where he had grown up until the age of nine, suggests his future interest in symbolic topographies.

3. "ON RECEIVING AN ACCOUNT THAT HIS ONLY DEATH WAS INEVITABLE"

Written at Christ's Hospital School in early 1791; not published until *Poetical Works* 1834. Coleridge's sense that he was an "orphan" cast out from his home (see No. 25) was increased by the many early deaths in his family (11). His father, the Reverend John Coleridge, had died in 1782; his elder brother Luke in 1790; and finally his sister Anne (4) in March 1791. Two other brothers, Frank and James, later died in India. Coleridge mentions Anne's death again in the first Conversation Poem (No. 22).

4. "ON QUITTING SCHOOL FOR COLLEGE"

First published in *Poetical Works* 1834. Coleridge left Christ's Hospital in summer 1791, as a "Grecian" or Classics scholar with an Exhibition to

Jesus College, Cambridge. Charles Lamb later recalled in his *Essays of Elia* how Coleridge had held his fellow schoolboys spellbound with his brilliant talk in the school cloisters (**5**); but there is evidence from Coleridge's letters that he was deeply unhappy during much of his schooldays. The tone of pathos and nostalgia shows the new influence of William Bowles (1762–1850), and partly imitates the latter's poem "On Quitting Winchester College".

5. "TO THE RIVER OTTER"

First published as part of a longer poem, "The Recollection", in Coleridge's journal *The Watchman*, 1796; and then as a sonnet in *Poems* 1797. Possibly composed as early as 1793, during Coleridge's summer vacation at Ottery, when he was depressed by debts and failure to win an academic prize at Cambridge, and influenced by Bowles's "Sonnet to the River Itchin". One of Coleridge's finest early poems, it suggests many characteristic themes: the symbolism of a magic river, the romantic innocence of childhood, the "bright transparence" of memory (**11**) and the longing for home. The movement of the poet's mind as he recollects and re-creates (a subject of great psychological interest to Coleridge) is subtly compared to the leaps of a stone skimmed across water, as in the schoolboys' game of "ducks and drakes" (**4–5**).

TO THE
RIVER ITCHIN, NEAR WINTON.

by William Bowles

Itchin, when I behold thy banks again,
 Thy crumbling margin, and thy silver breast,
On which the self-same tints still seem'd to rest,
Why feels my heart the shiv'ring sense of pain?
Is it – that many a summer's day has past
 Since, in life's morn, I caroll'd on thy side?
 Is it – that oft, since then, my heart has sigh'd,
As Youth, and Hope's delusive gleams, flew fast?
 Is it – that those, who circled on thy shore,
 Companions of my youth, now meet no more?
Whate'er the cause, upon thy banks I bend,
 Sorrowing, yet feel such solace at my heart,
As at the meeting of some long-lost friend,
 From whom, in happier hours, we wept to part.

6. "TO THE AUTHOR OF *THE ROBBERS*"

Composed at Jesus College, Cambridge in November 1794; first published *Poems* 1797. Friedrich von Schiller (1759–1805), dramatist and lyric poet in the "*sturm und drang*" (storm and stress) style, was Professor of History at the University of Jena, and friend of Goethe with whom he collaborated on a collection of ballads (like Coleridge and Wordsworth). This sonnet marks Coleridge's rapturous discovery of German Gothic literature. He wrote in a letter: "Tis past one o'clock in the morning – I sate down at twelve o'clock to read the "Robbers" of Schiller – I had read chill and trembling until I came to the part where the Moor fires a pistol over the Robbers who are asleep – I could read no more – My God! Southey! Who is this Schiller? This Convulser of the Heart? Did he write his Tragedy amid the yelling of Fiends? . . . Why have we ever called Milton sublime?" (3 November 1794).

7. "TO THE REV. W.L. BOWLES"

First published as part of a series of twelve "Sonnets on Eminent Characters" in the *Morning Chronicle*, December 1794; and then in an adapted version in *Poems* 1796. Bowles's own collection of *Sonnets written chiefly on Picturesque Spots, during a Tour* (1789), the "kindred Lays" (**8**), had a powerful effect on Coleridge, who made no less than forty copies by hand to give to friends. They made his own poetic style more personal and emotional. Lamb called Bowles "the Genius of the Sacred Fountain of Tears". The other "Eminent Characters", who made up Coleridge's intellectual pantheon at this period, included Edmund Burke, Joseph Priestley, William Godwin, his friend Robert Southey, and the actress Sarah Siddons. These sonnets mark Coleridge's first appearance in print, after he had abandoned Cambridge and moved to London in preparation for Pantisocracy.

8. "PANTISOCRACY"

First sent by Coleridge in a letter to Southey of September 1794; then published as Southey's in 1849; finally restored to Coleridge in *Poetical Works* 1893. Coleridge adds that the second and third lines were contributed by Robert Favell. The confusion over authorship is typical of the first excitement of the Pantisocratic scheme, when private property was to be abolished, and even the ownership of a poem was communal. Twelve couples were due to sail to America in March 1795, to start an ideal farming community (**4–6**) on the banks of the Susquehannah river, in upstate Pennsylvania. Here "all would govern equally", and there would be dancing and sexual magic (**7–8**). But there is also a surprising early reference to Coleridge's nightmares (**11**).

9. "PITY"

Written late 1794, and published in *Poems* 1796. A product of Coleridge's most radical Christian phase, emphasizing the Unitarian view of Jesus, the "Galilaean" (**12**), as a social revolutionary. The naïve philanthropy of the poem should not hide its technical skill, with free-running lines, and new conversational ease. It has the first reference to Coleridge's fiancée, Sara Fricker (**9**), whom he had met with his fellow Pantisocrats in Bristol, and who initially shared his missionary zeal. (See No. 24). Coleridge could not decide the title of the poem – calling it "Mercy", then "Charity" – and finally told his Jacobin friend Thelwall that the whole morality of the sonnet was "detestable" because so patronizing.

10. "ON RECEIVING A LETTER INFORMING ME OF THE BIRTH OF A SON"

This and the next two sonnets were composed after the birth of Hartley Coleridge at Bristol, on 19 September 1796. This first sonnet was not published until the 1847 Supplement to the *Biographia Literaria*. Coleridge was away in Birmingham, collecting subscribers for his journal the *Watchman*, and wrote the poems as he hurried home. He later sent all three to his friend Tom Poole in a letter of 1 November 1796. "This sonnet puts in no claim to poetry (indeed as a composition I think so little of them that I neglected to repeat [*ie. recite*] them to you) but it is a most faithful picture of my feelings on a very interesting event. When I was with you they were, indeed, excepting the first, in a rude and undrest state." The strong religious tone of the first sonnet becomes more philosophical in the second, and finally intimate and domestic in the third. Thus according to Coleridge's theory on the sonnet form (see Preface), the "lonely feeling" of paternity becomes grounded in the common experience of family love.

11. "COMPOSED ON A JOURNEY HOMEWARD; THE AUTHOR HAVING RECEIVED INTELLIGENCE OF THE BIRTH OF A SON"

First published in *Poems* 1797 (see previous note). The sonnet explores two characteristic metaphysical speculations: the Pythagorean idea of pre-existence, as if little Hartley had existed in some spiritual sphere before birth (**1–6**); and Coleridge's fear that in his absence the baby might hasten to return to that "sphere", as if he had already served his "sentence" on a wicked earth (**10–12**). Explaining the former to Poole, Coleridge wrote of line **6**: "Almost all the followers of Fenelon believe that men are degraded Intelligences who had all once existed together in a paradisiacal or perhaps heavenly state. The first four lines express a feeling which I have often had – the present has appeared like a vivid dream or exact similitude of some past circumstance." Twenty years later in Chapter 22 of the *Biographia Literaria*, Coleridge re-examined this idea, in his analysis of Wordsworth's "Ode: Intimations of Immortality in Early Childhood".

12. "TO A FRIEND WHO ASKED, HOW I FELT WHEN THE NURSE FIRST PRESENTED MY INFANT TO ME

First published *Poems* 1797 (see previous two notes). The "friend" may have been Charles Lloyd, who was staying with Coleridge, or Charles Lamb in London. The last and finest of Coleridge's sonnets about the experience of fatherhood, now expanding to a new conception of married love. Sara's maternal presence is richly acknowledged (**11–14**), and points to her important role in the Conversation poems. Lamb wrote to Coleridge: "I love you for those simple, tender, heart-flowing lines with which you conclude your last, and in my eyes, best 'sonnet' (as you call 'em) . . . Cultivate simplicity, Coleridge; or rather, I should say, banish elaborateness." But the erotic image of the child at the breast (**6**) had complex overtones for Coleridge (see the Asra poems).

13. "ON A RUINED HOUSE IN A ROMANTIC COUNTRY"

Third in a series of three comic sonnets, first published in the *Monthly Magazine*, November 1797; then in *Biographia Literaria*, 1817. Coleridge's aim was to parody the worst excesses of the early "Romantic" style (already a significant term) as used by Lamb, Lloyd, himself and others. He wrote afterwards: "Under the name of Nehemiah Higginbottom I contributed three sonnets, the first of which had for its object to excite a good-natured laugh at the spirit of doleful egotism and the recurrence of favourite phrases. . . . The second was on low creeping language and thoughts under the pretence of *simplicity* . . . The third, the phrases of which were borrowed entirely from my own poems, on the indiscriminate use of elaborate and swelling language and imagery. . . ." (Compare No. 22.) The sonnet is a vamped version of the well-known children's nursery rhyme, "The House that Jack Built", adapted to stock "Romantic" figures such as the guilty father, the forlorn maiden, the amorous knight, and the harvest moon (considered *a posteriori*).

14. "TO ASRA"

Original draft prefixed to a MS copy of "Christabel", given to Sara Hutchinson on Coleridge's departure for Malta in 1804; first published in *Poetical Works* 1893. "Asra" was Coleridge's private anagram and romantic name for Sara Hutchinson, with whom he had fallen in love in 1799. (See Preface to the Asra Poems.) The image of love as a fountain (**5–6**) springing up spontaneously in the human heart (and therefore mysterious in its origins) appears frequently in Coleridge's poetry and prose: see for example "The Rime of The Ancient Mariner", part 4 (No. 32); "Inscription for a Fountain on a Heath" (No. 55); and the essay "On the Communication of Truth", (*The Friend*, I, p. 65).

Drafts of this sonnet appear in Coleridge's Malta Notebooks (1804–6); first published in *Poetical Works* 1893. Except for one line it is a close translation of the Italian original, "Alla Sua Amico", by Giambattista Marino, in which Coleridge saw parallels with his own unrequited love. Marino (1569–1625) was a Neapolitan-born poet whose rakish life included two spells of imprisonment, an assassination attempt by a rival poet, Murtola, and numerous love-affairs. He revolutionized the courtly Petrarchism of the *cinquecento* (which Coleridge described as "all one cold glitter of heavy conceits") with a flamboyant, bizarre style of lurid emotions, much in evidence here. To this torrid, southern Mediterranean love poem of fire and hell, Coleridge added the striking image of the "Adder's eye" (**5**). The idea of the beloved woman as a poisonous serpent, evidently relates to Geraldine's sexual transformation into a snake-like or "lamia" creature in "Christabel" (No. 33).

16. "FAREWELL TO LOVE"

Written in the margin of Lamb's copy of *The Elegant Works of Fulke Greville* (1633), on Coleridge's return from Italy in 1806; published in *the Courier*, 27 September 1806; and collected in *Literary Remains*, 1836. The poem is a skilful revision of Greville's "Sonnet 74 to Coelica", which opens "Farewell, sweet Boy, complain not of my truth. . . . " Coleridge uses Greville's rhyme-scheme, but subtly adapts each line to apply to his own impossible love for Asra. He pictures himself, in the Jacobean courtly manner, as wholly dedicated to Love's service (**5–8**), and retains the traditional trope of Cupid as the blind god (**12**). The quality of Coleridge's revision of Greville's stumbling and mechanical sonnet can be suggested by his re-handling of line 12 alone. Greville had written: "The spectacles to my life was thy blindness". Coleridge revised this to: "*Your* dreams alone I dreamt, and caught your blindness". Coleridge renews the formal conventions of Greville's work with the intensity of personal experience, emphasized by the stressed pronouns, the whispered aliteration (eg. **4, 8**) and the sense of poignant confidentiality.

17. "FANCY IN NUBIBUS: OR THE POET IN THE CLOUDS"

First published in *Felix Farley's Bristol Journal*, 7 February 1818; then collected in *Poetical Works* 1828. An early MS. has the note, "A Sonnet composed by the Seaside, October 1817" – probably at Little Hampton in Sussex. Coleridge had now settled in Highgate (1816) after his years of wandering, and spent regular autumn holidays at the newly-fashionable seaside resorts, especially after 1820 at Ramsgate in Kent (see No. 69). Here he walked, bathed, met literary friends and meditated on clouds and seascapes. The easy, playful, holiday manner perhaps disguises the skill of the single, perambulating sentence with its references to Shakespeare (*Hamlet*,

4−6) and Homer (11−14), and its painterly sense of limitless horizons.

There is an intriguing echo (6−11) of Keats's sonnet "On First Looking into Chapman's Homer" (published in the *Examiner*, 1 December 1816). While Stolberg's lyric "An das Meer" ("At the Sea") probably suggested the final image of the "blind bard" seeing his epic poems rise out of the sea. The marine view from the promenade is made in the evening, not the daylight (2), so perhaps this is an after-dinner sonnet, more genial and expansive than entirely original.

18. "TO NATURE"

First published by Thomas Allsop in *Letters, Conversations, and Recollections of S. T. Coleridge*, 1836; collected in *Poems* 1863. Allsop, who was Coleridge's young protégé and sometime amanuensis in the Highgate years, found the sonnet "on a detached sheet of paper, without note or observation", and had "some faint impression" that he took it down from Coleridge's dictation in about 1820. The poem is a defiant late reflection of Coleridge's early Pantheism, now seen in conventional and even sentimental terms. The circumstance that Coleridge was addressing such a sympathetic and admiring friend as Allsop (to whom he wrote many confessional letters), perhaps accounts for the tone of "earnest piety" (5) and pathos. The touching idea of the fifty-year-old Coleridge building his "altar in the fields", and living outdoors under the "fretted dome" of the sky (9−10), can be taken as a genial "phantasy" of the old Pantheist of Stowey days (see No. 8). In fact this was a period in which Coleridge was much worried by unorthodox religious doubts, and was publicly persecuted for his "mysticism" by sceptical critics like Hazlitt (see Confessional Poems). Perhaps the poem is more defensive and anxious than it sounds.

19. "WORK WITHOUT HOPE"

Originally composed as part of a much longer poem in a Notebook entry dated 21 February, 1825 (see No. 91); published in the *Bijou* magazine, 1828; collected in *Poetical Works* 1828. One of Coleridge's best known later poems: the sense of personal despair is subtly offset by the images of natural energy and busy springtime re-birth. The "emblematic" suggestion of these images − the bees, the fount, the sieve − were compared by Coleridge to the religious poems of George Herbert. The self-disgust implicit in "slugs" (1) so shocked the editor of the *Bijou*, that he printed it as "stags". "Amaranths" (9) are the eternal flowers of the classical Elysian Fields, symbols of artistic achievement. The "spells that drowse my soul" (12) is a possible reference to Coleridge's opium addiction. The sonnet may have been inspired by a hostile article by William Hazlitt of 1825, reprinted as "Mr Coleridge" in *The Spirit of the Age*, which cruelly referred to Coleridge's failure to gather "fruits and flowers, immortal fruits and amaranthine flowers" in a wasted artistic career. The violent contrast to the tone of the previous sonnet (No. 18) gives some indication of Coleridge's intense swings of mood in later life, when periods of tranquillity were interrupted by renewed guilt over his addiction, anxiety about his son Hartley, and the nagging failure to complete his great philosophical work, the *Opus Maximum* (see Chronology).

20. "DUTY SURVIVING SELF-LOVE"

Composed at Highgate, September 1826; first published in *Poetical Works* 1828. One of Coleridge's most powerful late poems, calm but grimly self-justifying in tone. He subtitled it: "The only sure Friend of Declining Life. A Soliloquy." The image of friendship as failing light is steadily developed: from the early "wanings" of affection (3), through the distinction between the type of friends who radiate or absorb light (9–10), to the final quenching of friends like oil-lamps burning dim in "noisome" or polluted air (12). Coleridge's sense of isolation is made harsher by his own conviction that he is "unchanged within" (1), and that he stands unshaken by "feeble yearnings" for love (7). Many of Coleridge's old friends had indeed fallen away by this date – Southey, Hazlitt, Wordsworth – though they would have given very different accounts of the reasons for this. In fact Coleridge craved friendship more than ever, and found it at Highgate with the Gillmans, J. H. Green, Thomas Allsop, Charles Tulk MP, and his nephew H. N. Coleridge (see Chronology). In a MS. version Coleridge says the poem arose from a question that Ann Gillman ("Alia") once put to him: whether his Philosophy had made him "happier" in life? Coleridge replied: "calmer at least and the less unhappy". He then described how the sonnet followed when "Alia" left the room. "The grey-haired philosopher, left to his own musings, continued playing with the thoughts that Alia's question had excited, till he murmured them to himself in half audible words, which at first casually, and then for the amusement of his ear, he *punctuated* with rhymes, without conceiting that he had by these means changed them into poetry."

21. "TO THE YOUNG ARTIST"

Composed in November 1833, some eight months before Coleridge died at Highgate, and one of his last known poems; first published in *Poetical Works* 1834. The handsome young German portrait painter, Johann Kayser, had charmed the old, sick poet during a visit to Highgate. Coleridge's florid complimentary verses become, unexpectedly, a touching farewell and handing on of the creative torch from one generation to the next. Kayser's pencil drawing of Coleridge has survived, showing a stout, shrunken invalid, who appears breathless and in pain. Coleridge remarked that "the unhappy Density of the Nose and idiotic Drooping of the Lip" was no great flattery. But he was always appalled by his portraits in old age: "a glow-worm with a pin thro it, as seen in broad daylight." The reference to the "blank scroll" turning to a "magic glass" (5) makes one wonder if Kayser had tried to take a daguerreotype photograph of Coleridge; if so, alas, none is known.

Notes to the Conversation Poems

22. "TO A FRIEND" [CHARLES LAMB]

Given to Lamb in London in December 1794, with an unfinished draft of "Religious Musings" (see No. 95); first published in *Poems* 1796. The "dear-lov'd Sister" (8) was Mary Lamb, who suffered periods of insanity; while Coleridge's own sister Anne (12) had died in 1792 (see No. 3). The "lambent glories" (24) is a pun on his friend's name. This first Conversation Poem begins with rejection of the epic mode, "the rhyme/Elaborate and swelling", for a more familiar poetic style of sentimental reminiscence and religious consolation, very close to an actual letter which Coleridge wrote in September 1794: "I *had* a Sister – an only Sister. Most tenderly did I love her. . . ." (Compare 12–13.) The idea of love and friendship cherished (20) among an intimate group, the "tenderest tones medicinal of love" (11), is a central theme.

23. "THE EOLIAN HARP" [TO SARA COLERIDGE]

First published in *Poems* 1796 as "Effusion XXV", where it is dated 20 August 1795; the beautiful "one Life" passage (26–33) was added in *Sibylline Leaves* 1817. Coleridge rented the cottage (3) at Clevedon, overlooking the Bristol Channel (11), in the summer before his marriage to Sara Fricker on 4 October 1795. This is partly a poem of courtship, in which tender sexual feelings are set within a pastoral landscape of hill and coast. The Eolian harp (12) was a rectangular novelty instrument, much in vogue at the end of the eighteenth century, consisting of eight gut strings stretched over a decorated wooden soundbox, which was usually placed on an outside windowsill or table. The wind passing freely over the strings produced a haunting, longdrawn chord, rising and falling, in a manner suggestive of physical longing or excitement. Coleridge uses it first as an image of his love-making with Sara (14–17); then as an extended simile for the poet's transforming imagination playing on a visionary landscape (17–33); and finally as a metaphor for his philosophic speculations about "animated nature" being played on by an "intellectual breeze", which is God (44–48). Sara reproves him for taking liberties both physical and metaphysical (49–64), but the "one Life" passage of 1817 seems to confirm the notion of a harmonious world tuned like a harp to "joyance everywhere" (29).

First published in the *Monthly Magazine*, October 1796, with the title "Reflections on entering into active life. A Poem which affects not to be poetry"; then in *Poems* 1797. The motto from Horace was translated by Lamb as "properer for a Sermon". Coleridge regretfully left the Clevedon cottage (see No. 23) to launch his radical Christian newspaper the *Watchman* in Bristol in December 1795. The poem contrasts his longings for domestic happiness with his sense of public and religious duty (**41–62**). Despite these rival demands, it is the pastoral landscape of the north Somersetshire hills which most affects Coleridge and dominates the poem (**27–42**). The familiar style is increasingly adapted to this landscape, with vivid topographical images, and the natural repetitions and exclamations of speech, as in Coleridge's description of the Bristol businessman weekending in the countryside, who so admires his bucolic existence with Sara (**9–26**). "Howard" (**49**) was the philanthropist and prison reformer John Howard (1726–90), who died in Russia while tending the sick.

First published as the Dedication to *Poems* 1797, where it is dated "Nether Stowey, Somerset, May 26, 1797". George was Coleridge's elder brother, who had encouraged him with his early poetry, and helped him through many adolescent crises (**39–68**). The epigraph from Horace reads: "remarkable for his fatherly spirit towards his brothers".

Coleridge moved to Stowey at the end of 1796 (**33–5**), where he began a series of autobiographical letters to his "one Friend" Tom Poole (**32**), reflecting on his unhappy childhood and restless upbringing. This theme now enters the Conversation Poems (**15–39**). Though "too soon transplanted" (**18**) from his birthplace at Ottery St Mary on the death of his father, Coleridge was watched over by George, who encouraged his writing at Christ's Hospital, paid off his debts at Cambridge, and even bailed him out of the Army: acts of paternal care and kindness that form the backgound to this poem. However, George did not approve of Coleridge's radical journalism or impetuous marriage to Sara, and hence the requests for forgiveness of "discordant" themes in the poetry (**69–74**). He also did not accept Coleridge's central myth of childhood, that he was "most a stranger" in his own home (**41–2**); or that he had begun to glimpse a new pastoral paradise at Stowey (**52–61**). Coleridge wrote in a copy of *Poems* 1797: "If this volume should ever be delivered according to its direction, i.e. to Posterity, let it be known that the Reverend George Coleridge was displeased and thought his character endangered by the Dedication".

The "Manchineel" (**26**) was a fabled Caribbean tree with luscious fruit and foliage, said to poison with its finely defused sap, or even with its shade.

Written at Stowey, July 1797; first published in the *Annual Anthology* 1800; and then in *Sibylline Leaves* 1817. Coleridge gives a revealing account of the poem's inception in a letter to Southey: "The second day after Wordsworth came to me, dear Sara accidently emptied a skillet of boiling milk on my foot, which confined me during the whole times of C. Lamb's stay & still prevents me from all *walks* longer than a furlong. – While Wordsworth, his Sister, & C. Lamb were out one evening; sitting in the arbour of T. Poole's garden, which communicates with mine, I wrote these lines, with which I am pleased:

> Well – they are gone: and here I must remain,
> Lam'd by the scathe of fire, lonely & faint,
> This lime-tree bower my prison! . . ."

The 1800 text is addressed "To Charles Lamb, of the India House, London." But an earlier MS. version twice substitutes Sara Coleridge's name for Lamb's (**68**, "My Sara and my Friends"; **75**, "For You my Sara and my Friends").
 The poem follows the course of their imagined walk over the top of Quantock (**7**), down to Holford Combe (**11–20**), and back up to Alfoxden at sunset overlooking the Bristol Channel (**20–37**), while Coleridge waits in his bower for their return (**45–67**). It ends on a sacred note of evensong and homecoming (**68–76**), which becomes characteristic of the Conversation Poems. "In the great City pent" (**30**): Lamb worked as a clerk in India House. "On the wide landscape, gaze till all doth seem/Less gross than bodily" (**40–1**): Coleridge remarked of these lines, "You remember I am a Berkeleyan", which suggests the reading: "till all seems less a material substance (the earth), than a single living entity (the one Life of nature)." Bishop George Berkeley (1685–1753) was the idealist philosopher, after whom Coleridge named his second child. Berkeley argued that existence depended on perception, and that God "spoke" to man through the ordered and unified "language" of the natural world (see Nos. 27 and 96).

27. "FROST AT MIDNIGHT"

Set in the parlour of Coleridge's Stowey cottage, in the freezing February of 1798. First published in a quarto pamphlet (J. Johnson, St Paul's Churchyard, 1798); and then in *Sibylline Leaves* 1817, after many changes. Perhaps the most perfect of Coleridge's Conversation Poems, addressed to his sixteen-month-old baby son Hartley. The poem spools back through memories of Coleridge's own childhood at Ottery St Mary and Christ's Hospital (**23–43**) and then moves forward to a vision of Hartley's idealized upbringing in the country (**44–64**), ending with a beautiful passage of pastoral "blessing" (**65–74**). Coleridge originally added a further verse paragraph, which also included Sara (MS. **74–80**):

> . . . Quietly shining to the quiet Moon,
> Like those, my babe! which ere tomorrow's warmth
> Have capp'd their sharp keen points with pendulous drops,
> Will catch thine eye, and with their novelty
> Suspend thy little soul; then make thee shout,
> And stretch and flutter from thy mother's arms
> As thou would fly for very eagerness.

But later Coleridge removed this because it destroyed "the rondo, and return upon itself of the Poem", with the shaping idea of the "secret ministry" (**1** and **72**), the mysterious priest-like powers of Nature. "Only that film . . ." (**15**): the transparent heat-tremour above a firegrate, which in Devonshire folklore was known as a "stranger" (**26, 41**) and promised "the arrival of some absent friend" at the door. But also an image of Coleridge's "fluttering" imagination playing above his sleeping child, and contrasting with the various images of sacred "quietness" throughout the poem.

28. "FEARS IN SOLITUDE"

Dated by Coleridge "Nether Stowey, April 20, 1798", at the height of a French invasion scare, after landings in Ireland. Published in the quarto pamphlet (J. Johnson, 1798) together with No. 27 and No. 98 ("France: An Ode"). Republished with No. 98 in the *Morning Post*, 14 October 1802; and in *Sibylline Leaves* 1817. Though structured as an interior monologue during the course of a daylong walk, the poem arose from Coleridge's political conversations with friends at Stowey about the war with France, and their avid reading of the newspaper reports together. It is an important statement of Coleridge's political reflections on such contemporary issues as British colonialism (**41 ff**), parliamentary corruption (**53 ff**), discredited State religion (**63 ff**), and popular warmongering (**88 ff**). Coleridge calls for a sober resolution against any invader (**129 ff**), and an end to factional strife between the "radical" and "patriot" parties (**154 ff**). Coleridge wrote on one MS.: "NB. The above is perhaps not Poetry, – but rather a sort of middle thing between Poetry and Oratory – *sermoni propriora*. Some parts are, I am conscious, too tame even for animated prose." However, the poem rises to a passionate expression of Coleridge's own love for Britain (**174 ff**), and concludes with one of his finest evocations of home-coming (**203 ff**), a slumbering twilit vision of Stowey (the church, Poole's house, the elms, his own cottage with Sara and little Hartley) seen from the "green sheep-track" winding down from the Quantock hills, where Coleridge has spent the day in solitary meditation. This final note of sacred pastoral has been compared to paintings by Samuel Palmer.

First published in the *Lyrical Ballads* 1798, with the subtitle "A Conversational Poem" (Coleridge's first use of the term); and then in *Sibylline Leaves* 1817, as "A Conversation Poem. Written in April 1798." Coleridge celebrates and explores the meaning of the nightingale's song, often heard in the holly groves between Stowey and Alfoxden in the spring of 1798. Far from being the solitary and "most melancholy bird" of Milton's poem "Il Penseroso" (13), the nightingale represents an active principle of joy in the natural universe (40–49) and crowded together they "answer and provoke" (58) each other like a harmonious circle of friends. The poem is addressed to William and Dorothy Wordsworth (40), and also perhaps to young William Hazlitt who took part in these expeditions, as he later recalled in *My First Acquaintance with Poets* (1821): "Returning that same evening, I got into a metaphysical argument with Wordsworth, while Coleridge was explaining the different notes of the nightingale to his sister. . . ." The "gentle Maid" (69) living near the castle is perhaps a premonition of Christabel, another night-walker in the woods. The climactic incident under the moonlight (90 ff), one of Nature's mysterious "ministrations" (see No. 27) was originally recorded in prose in one of Coleridge's notebooks: "Hartley fell down and hurt himself – I caught him up crying & screaming & ran out of doors with him. The Moon caught his eye – he ceased crying immediately – & his eyes & the tears in them, how they glittered in the Moonlight!" (CNB I, 219). Coleridge sent the original MS. draft of the poem up to Wordsworth at Alfoxden, with a humorous doggerel note, beginning:

> In stale blank verse a subject stale
> I send *per post* my *Nightingale*;
> And like an honest bard, dear Wordsworth,
> You'll tell me what you think my Bird's worth. . . .

30. "TO WILLIAM WORDSWORTH"

First published *Sibylline Leaves* 1817. A MS. version dated January 1807 was published in Campbell's edition of the *Poetical Works* 1893. Coleridge's MS. title reads: "To W. Wordsworth. Lines Composed, for the greater part on the Night, on which he finished the recitation of his Poem (in thirteen Books) concerning the growth and history of his own Mind, Jan. 7, 1807, Coleorton, near Ashby de la Zouche." Wordsworth read the unpublished *Prelude* over several nights to Coleridge on his return from Malta, and this last Conversation Poem is Coleridge's response, first giving an account of its themes: Wordsworth's childhood in the Lakes (11–26); his experiences in revolutionary France (27–38); his return to England and self-dedication to poetry (39–47). Coleridge's overwhelming sense of Wordsworth's genius, and his own comparative failure to fulfil the creative promise of the Quantock days follows (**47–75**). Coleridge compares his own states of feeling successively to the condition of a drowning man, a crying baby, a corpse in a coffin, and "the constellated foam" of the sea. The poem ends with a final healing version of the homecoming motif. (**107**, MS. version: "All whom I deepliest love – in one room all!". This refers to the other listeners, including Dorothy, Asra, and Mary Wordsworth.) Wordsworth did not wish Coleridge to publish this poem, because of the intensity of emotion it revealed between the two friends, who later quarrelled in 1810. This led Coleridge to suppress a remarkable passage from the MS. version, which expressed his feelings for Wordsworth:

> Dear shall it be to every human heart
> To me how more than dearest! me, on whom
> Comfort from thee, and utterance of thy love,
> Came with such heights and depths of harmony,
> Such sense of wings uplifting, that the storm
> Scatter'd and whirl'd me, till my thoughts became
> A bodily tumult; and thy faithful hopes,
> Thy hopes of me, dear Friend! by me unfelt!
> Were troublous to me, almost as a voice,
> Familiar once, and more than musical;
> To one cast forth, whose hope had seem'd to die
> A wanderer with a worn-out heart
> Mid strangers pining with untended wounds.
> O Friend, too well thou know'st, of what sad years
> The long suppression had benumb'd my soul,
> That even as life returns upon the drown'd,
> The unusual joy awoke a throng of pains –
> Keen pangs of Love, awakening as a babe . . .

In the published version this was starkly replaced by **61–5**.

Notes to the Ballads

31. "THE THREE GRAVES"

First published in this fragmentary form in *The Friend*, September 1809; and then in *Sibylline Leaves* 1817. This was Coleridge's first unfinished experiment with the ballad form, composed at Stowey in summer 1797. It was a continuation of a poem begun by Wordsworth at Racedown (MS. Parts I and II, not printed here), the story of which Coleridge summarizes in his prose Preface.

Based on a folktale of rural witchcraft, it is set in an English country village recognizable as belonging to the Quantock region in the early eighteenth century. Coleridge uses the narrative voice of an "old country Sexton", deliberately naïve, to tell the tale of a mother's supernatural curse against her daughter. The style and theme (the curse) bear an evident relation to "The Rime of the Ancient Mariner" (No. 32), begun some months later; while the vivid woodland settings amidst the changing seasons suggest the haunted world of "Christabel" (No. 33). Coleridge emphasizes his "exclusively psychological" interest in the pathology of fear and superstition, and the way "an idea violently and suddenly impressed" on the imagination, can gradually possess it. "I have endeavoured to trace the progress to madness, step by step." The curse arises out of the mother's extreme sexual jealousy, and moves irresistibly from her daughter Mary, to Mary's friend Ellen, and finally to Mary's young husband Edward. Coleridge relates this pattern to recent anthropological studies of native witchcraft in the West Indies, such as Bryan Edwards's *History of the British Colonies* (1793). He later explained his fascination with such material in chapter 14 of the *Biographia Literaria*, arguing that psychic or supernatural "delusion" could still reveal the "dramatic truth" of extreme human emotions, which are "real in this sense" and therefore of universal interest and valid for poetry, rather than merely picturesque fictions.

32. "THE RIME OF THE ANCIENT MARINER"

First version composed November 1797–March 1798, published in *Lyrical Ballads*, 1798; alterations made in *Lyrical Ballads*, 1800; further alterations and prose gloss added *Sibylline Leaves* 1817; final text in *Poetical Works* 1834.

Coleridge's most famous poem was begun during a long winter walk over Quantockshead to the harbour of Watchet, and down through Exmoor, with Wordsworth and Dorothy. His sources included the voyages of Captain Shelvocke (who mentions the albatross) and Captain Cook (who describes the southern ocean); the dream of a "spectre ship" told by his Stowey neighbour George Cruikshank; plot suggestions by Wordsworth; and his own experience of nursing a fellow dragoon through the hallucinations of a smallpox fever in 1794 (see Chronology).

The fast, flexible stanza (four to nine lines), the weird sea-shanty music of the rhymes, the haunting imagery of sun, moon and stars, are all notable developments which Coleridge continued to refine over twenty years. The ballad has been variously interpreted as a Christian allegory of fall and redemption; a moral study of the origins of Evil; a symbolic account of the *poète maudit* figure; an autobiographical vision of opium addiction; a "Green parable" of man's destruction of nature and Nature's revenge; and a psychological investigation into post-traumatic stress syndrome with its well-established features of obsessive recall and compulsive guilt. Coleridge insisted in his *Table Talk* that it was a poem of "pure imagination".

First published in *Christabel; Kubla Khan, A Vision; The Pains of Sleep* (John Murray, 1816); then collected in *Poetical Works* 1828. Originally intended for the second edition of the *Lyrical Ballads* 1800, but rejected by Wordsworth as unfinished and discordant with the rest of the collection. Coleridge once described it as "a Legend in five Acts", and told the whole plot to James Gillman as late as 1820, but was never able to complete it. The "celebrated poets" who had previously heard recitations of "Christabel", and imitated its archaic phrasing, were Byron and Walter Scott.

The story draws on various folktales of demon lovers, vampires and lamias (women who are really serpents, see **583–96**) such as C. M. Wieland's *Oberon* (1780). Geraldine's seduction of the teenage Christabel in the mysterious, twinkling night-scene of Part I; and her enthralment of Christabel's father, Sir Leoline, in the lavish, "daylight witchery", court-scene of Part II, suggest she is some kind of preternatural spirit, lawless rather than evil. She belongs to the wild wood (**31–70**) outside the symbolic castle of domestic civilization (**123–34**). Christabel's innocence, and Geraldine's sexual power, are central to the psychological drama of enchantment, initiation and spell-binding which follows (**245–78**). This is emphasized by the snake and the dove of Bracey's allegoric dream (**523–82**). Coleridge chose a courtly, medieval period setting, with the kind of antiquarian interest in dress, architecture, and ritual gesture that later fascinated the Pre-Raphaelite painters. This in itself may have made the ballad difficult to continue, because of its complex "machinery" and fragile, trance-like atmosphere. Coleridge later compared Christabel's trial to the spiritual "martyrdom" of the Spanish mystic St Teresa of Avila, as described by the seventeenth-century poet Richard Crashaw, "A Hymn to Saint Teresa" (1652). The Conclusion to Part II is traditionally taken as a portrait of Hartley Coleridge, and highlights the impossibility of guarding innocence.

The genius of the ballad lies in its subtle combination of decorative, occult and erotic elements, which continually hint at some appalling act of daemonic possession without ever being quite explicit. (Hazlitt remarked that there was "something disgusting at the bottom . . . like moon-beams playing on a charnel-house.") As with "The Rime of the Ancient Mariner", Coleridge later began to write an explanatory prose gloss, but decided not to use it. The most revealing paragraph (alongside **451–56**) reads in the MS.: "Christabel then recollects the whole, and knows that it was not a Dream; but yet cannot disclose the fact, that the strange Lady is a supernatural Being with the stamp of the Evil Ones on her." (Princeton MS.)

34. "THE BALLAD OF THE DARK LADIÉ"

First published in this fragmentary form, *Poetical Works* 1834. Very little is known of this ballad, except that it was begun at Stowey in spring 1798, for the *Lyrical Ballads*. Coleridge's undated MS. list of his unpublished poems before 1817 includes "The Black Ladié, 190 lines" – so much has been lost. The woodland setting, the medieval figures, and the suggestion that the Dark Ladie has been seduced (**29–32**), and will soon be betrayed, by her knight (**41–8**), obviously links it to the world of "Christabel". The wedding feast with its "nodding minstrels" (**53**) also recalls the opening of "The Rime of The Ancient Mariner". Describing his collaboration with Wordsworth, in Chapter 14 of the *Biographia Literaria*, Coleridge later wrote: "It was agreed that my endeavours should be directed to persons and characters supernatural, or at least romantic; yet so as to transfer from our inward nature a human interest and a semblance of truth sufficient to procure for these shadows of imagination that willing suspension of disbelief for the moment, which constitutes poetic faith. . . . With this in view I wrote the 'Ancient Mariner', and was preparing, among other poems, the 'Dark Ladié', and the 'Christabel', in which I should have more nearly realised my ideal than I had done in my first attempt."

35. "LOVE"

First version published in *The Morning Post*, 21 December 1799; revised for *Lyrical Ballads*, 1800; collected in *Sibylline Leaves* 1817. Composed after Coleridge's return from Germany, when he went to visit Wordsworth at Sockburn, Lancashire, in November 1799. Here Coleridge first met Mary and Sara Hutchinson, at their brother's farm on the banks of the river Tees. (See Asra Poems.) The ballad is set in the Sockburn landscape, and the early version makes mention of a local "greystone" in the fields, and the Conyers family tomb in Sockburn church (**13–16**).

Its simplicity is deceptive. The poem is constructed as one ballad containing another, with two time-scales, and two sets of medieval lovers; the fate of the first pair decides the fate of the second. The speaker is a lovelorn minstrel (his harp with "a Cypress and a Myrtle" bound, also appears in the early version) who is courting the lovely Lady Genevieve. (These are the first, or foreground, pair of lovers.) The minstrel tells the story of the Knight of the Burning Brand and his beloved, the Lady of the Land (**29–36**). (These are the second, or mythical, pair of lovers.) The Knight has been "crazed" by the vision of an "angel beautiful and bright" (**49–52**): a *femme fatale* who is really a "Fiend". She eventually drives the Knight to his death, despite all the ministrations of his own devoted Lady, who nurses him in a cave amidst the "yellow forest-leaves". The Lady Genevieve is so moved by this tale, that she apparently surrenders to the minstrel's wooing (**65ff**). But in the tell-tale phrase of the last line, Coleridge leaves open the possibility that Genevieve is herself a reincarnation of the "Fiend", and the fatality will be repeated. Keats brilliantly developed the autumnal atmosphere of the Knight's story in "La Belle Dame sans Merci" (1820).

First published in *Poetical Works* 1834. Composed at Highgate as late as 1827–8, it represents a remarkable return to Coleridge's ballad experiments of the early years. The reference to "Dan Ovid's mazy tales of love" (**37**) connects it to "The Garden of Boccaccio" (No. 70), and the inspiration of Ann Gillman at this time. (See Notes to No. 70 and No. 91.)

The beautiful young Alice Du Clos is betrothed to the handsome, but hot-headed Lord Julian. One spring morning Julian sends her a message inviting her to join him on a hunting expedition in the green wood. This message is carried by the lecherous vassal knight, Sir Hugh, and his provocative speech to Alice opens the poem (**1–24**). Alice blithely rejects his treacherous advances, and unhurriedly rides with her young page Florian to join Lord Julian in the wood. But Sir Hugh gets there first, and with Iago-like insinuations, convinces Lord Julian that Alice has been unfaithful with Florian (**126–69**). When Alice rides up through the trees, Julian instantly kills her with a hunting spear.

The heraldic settings, the stylized violence, and the worldly mixture of chivalry and jealousy, are reminiscent of Coleridge's favourite Elizabethan poet Edmund Spenser. But the ballad remains remarkably innovative for its skilful psychological shifts in points of view – between Hugh, Alice, Florian and Julian; for the way spoken language, "the forked tongue", is constantly used to dissemble or falsify real feelings; and for the extreme, dream-like speed of the action. Almost entirely ignored by modern criticism, there is no more striking proof of Coleridge's continuing interest in methods of poetic narrative. Though obviously lacking the symbolic power of previous work, the poem combines the formal intricacy of a medieval tapestry, with the lethal rapidity of a modern film sequence. Though presented as a "moral" tale, there is something terrifying in the inconsequentiality of Alice's death, which shows Coleridge's undiminished grasp of the irrational universe.

Notes to the Hill Walking Poems

37. "LINES COMPOSED WHILE CLIMBING THE LEFT ASCENT OF BROCKLEY COOMB, SOMERSETSHIRE, MAY 1795"

First published in *Poems* 1796. Composed during Coleridge's early Bristol period, while lecturing and walking with Southey. Coleridge made several springtime expeditions to the hill country south of the city: along the Mendips, the Quantocks, the edge of Exmoor, or simply out to the coastal hills bordering the Bristol Channel. Brockley Coomb, now a local beauty spot, lies here just inland from Clevedon at Wrington Hill (sometimes known as Goblin Coomb) with a fine view of the "prospect-bounding

Sea" (**14**). The generalized eighteenth-century topographical style of James Thomson ("sweet songsters" with their "wild-wood melody") is giving way to accurate observations of startled sheep, muscular yew trees, and vivid may-thorn blossom, which are valued for themselves. The pattern of the steep, laboured climb, followed by the sudden expansion of physical vision and moral feeling at the summit, provides the basic structure for many of the Hill Walking Poems. The sheer effort and exhilaration of climbing, the "outdoor" spirit with its touch of professionalism ("the Left Ascent"), is new to the genre. Coleridge also adds the sudden, direct emotional revelation of the last lines: he is missing Sara Fricker, to whom he is engaged.

38. "TO A YOUNG FRIEND ON HIS PROPOSING TO DOMESTICATE
    WITH THE AUTHOR"

First published in *Poems* 1797. The friend was the twenty-one-year-old poet Charles Lloyd, talented but unstable heir to the rich Birmingham banking family, who came to stay with Coleridge and Sara at the Clevedon cottage in autumn 1796, when this poem was composed. Lloyd (who suffered from epilepsy) was to be Coleridge's paying guest and pupil, while Coleridge was to be his mentor, tutor, and one-man university. Coleridge's pastoral care was to include the type of vigorous, open-air excursion to which he invites Lloyd here (**16–19**), improving him with physical exertion, close observation of the natural world, and intimate talk on uplifting subjects. The daylong climb would end back at the cottage, in "Domestic Bliss", with Sara (**45–8**). The expedition, whose upward stages are marked by various trees – the mountain ash, the yew, the pine – is also a Baconian allegory of climbing the "Hill of Knowledge" (**50**) together in "loveliest sympathy" (**20**). Up-lifted from the mundane care of the world, Nature will pour through their eyes "all its healthful greenness on the soul" (**68**). The pupilage of Charles Lloyd was not a success, and Coleridge soon came to reject this direct moralizing of Nature. But the Conversation Poems grew from this kind of landscaped narrative.

39. "LINES WRITTEN IN THE ALBUM AT ELBINGERODE,
    IN THE HARTZ FOREST"

First published in the *Morning Post* on 17 September 1799; then collected in *Sibylline Leaves* 1817. Home thoughts from abroad. Original draft sent by Coleridge in a letter to Sara dated 17 May 1799, from Gottingen in Germany, where he was studying at the university.

Coleridge made several expeditions through the Hartz mountains in the spring of 1799, particularly to see the legendary "Brocken spectre" (see note to No. 58) and explore the countryside associated with Goethe's *Faust I*. The inns of the Hartz region kept *stammbuchs*, or visitors' albums, for the poetical comments of Romantic tourists. But Coleridge's poem, with its strong underlying melancholy, becomes a meditation on homesickness and patriotism. First describing his laborious descent down the heavily wooded hillside of the Brocken, it returns in imagination to the summit, from where his thoughts fly westwards towards "dear England" (26). The philosophic reflection on the power of "outward forms" (15−19) was not added until 1817, and closely relates to a passage in "Dejection: An Ode" (No. 50, Stanza IV).

40. "A THOUGHT SUGGESTED BY A VIEW OF SADDLEBACK IN CUMBERLAND"

First published in the *Amulet*, 1833; first collected in *Poems and Dramatic Works* 1877. Composed in autumn 1800, during Coleridge's first year in the Lake District, when he did much solitary fell-climbing. The range of hills containing Skiddaw, Carrock and Saddleback (Blencartha) stretches north and east of Keswick, above Threkeld, and is notable for its bleak beauty and many streams. Coleridge gives a vivid account of being caught in a storm on Carrock in a letter to Humphry Davy of 18 October 1800, shortly after Wordsworth had rejected "Christabel" for the *Lyrical Ballads*. Coleridge constantly found a mirror for his moods and inner feelings in the Cumberland landscape, and in the poem the "things that seek the earth" include his own tempestuous emotions. His Notebooks of this period are full of similar prose studies of Nature's transcendent "energy", bodied forth in water, wind, or cloud.

41. "INSCRIPTION FOR A FOUNTAIN ON A HEATH"

First published in the *Morning Post* on 24 September 1802; then in *Sibylline Leaves* 1817. Coleridge uses the classical form of the "lapidary verse" − the stone-carved inscription above a tomb or a drinking fountain − to address the traveller coming down from the hills. The idea of physical refreshment is gradually transformed into that of spiritual replenishment, the combined objects of the traditional pilgrimage (16). The beautiful, solemn movement of the blank verse combines the biblical image of the resting Patriachs, with the Theocritan blessing of the peaceful bees. Coleridge frequently observed the "tiny cone of sand" (9) dancing in the natural springs of the Lake District fells, a pulsation which he associated with the movement of love in the human heart. (Compare No. 14, and No. 32, lines 282−7.) The repeated reference to children and innocence, associated with water, subtly evokes the idea of Christian baptism into the waters of Eternal Life.

42. "A STRANGER MINSTREL"

First published in a section of memorial verses in the posthumous *Memoirs of Mrs Robinson, Written by Herself*, 1801; finally collected in *Poems and*

Dramatic Works 1877. The poem was sent to Mrs Robinson, an enthusiast of the Lake District, during a severe arthritic illness which resulted in her death at the age of forty-two. It is written in a mood of "sad and humorous thought" (**9**). Lying halfway up the great fell above Keswick, which she had often climbed herself, Coleridge conducts an imaginary conversation about her with the mountain, "old Skiddaw": they sigh amorously, and wish she would return in better health.

Coleridge had first met Mary "Perdita" Robinson (1758–1800) in London: actress, novelist and poet, she had been the mistress of the young George III (a scandal delicately alluded to at **45**). She had taken opium, and one of her poems quotes from "Kubla Khan"; Coleridge returns the compliment with quotations from her own poems "The Haunted Beach" (**55**), and "Jasper" (**58**). The dialogue between man and mountain is a curious mixture of comedy and elegy, which makes delicate fun of Mrs Robinson's poetic powers of "divinest melody" (**51**), and yet genuinely celebrates a shared enthusiasm for the fells. Many of the natural observations, such as the "helm of cloud" (**12**) above Skiddaw will be familiar to modern fell-walkers.

43. "HYMN BEFORE SUN-RISE, IN THE VALE OF CHAMOUNI"

First published, with a long preface describing the Swiss Alps, in the *Morning Post*, on 11 September 1802; collected in *Sibylline Leaves* 1817.

The alpine setting is entirely fictitious. Coleridge had never been to Switzerland, and this "Hymn in the manner of the Psalms" was actually inspired by climbing Scafell in August 1802, during the course of a solitary eight-day climbing tour across the central Lake District fells as far as St Bees. The tour is vividly recorded in a long, serial letter to Sara Hutchinson (Asra), partly written on the summit of Scafell. Coleridge also used his impressions of the waterfalls of Lodore (**39–48**); while the lovely lines about the "troops of stars" visiting the dark mountain top (**30–32**) are based on a remark by little Hartley.

Despite all these local sources, Coleridge altered the setting to the grander and more fashionable Alps, as he explained in a letter of 10 September 1802 to William Sotheby: "I thought the Ideas etc. disproportionate to our humble mountains . . ." But he also incorporated, without acknowledgement, into his poem the actual text of a pious German lyric about the Vale of Chamouni by the Swiss poet Frederika Brun. The "Hymn" has thus been dismissed as one of Coleridge's most notorious "plagiarisms". But Brun's original is only twenty lines, while Coleridge's is eighty-five, and his sense of landscape remains recognizably his own. Some of the most striking effects in the poem are spatial and rhythmic: the soaring peaks, the plunging waterfalls, the suspended ice-flows. As Charles Lamb shrewdly pointed out, it is the thunderous and uncharacteristic repetition of God's name (**58–69**), which most betrays its teutonic source. Contrast with Shelley's godless sublime in "Mont Blanc" (1816).

First published in the *Morning Post* on 6 September 1802; collected in *Sibylline Leaves* 1817. Coleridge adapted this vivid account of his rambling through the wooded hills round Keswick from a German poem by Saloman Gessner, "Der Feste Vorsatz" ("The Fixed Resolution"). In particular he used Gessner's story of the woodland maiden, Isabel, who has left her artist's sketch – made on a piece of woodbark – outside her cottage for her lover to find (**152ff**). Isabel is evidently a projection of Asra, and the German original gave Coleridge a literary disguise for his own private feelings. The teutonic influence also shows in the mannered reference to Nymphs, Dryads, and Gnomes (**26–45**) who do not usually appear in Coleridge's landscapes at this date.

Despite the second-hand quality of much of the verse (which shows Coleridge losing confidence in the original Hill Walking form) there are several passages of moving confessional intensity, about his unhappiness (**17–25**) and his continuing sense of freedom when alone in the countryside (**46–58**). He quoted the former, as "lines descriptive of a gloomy solitude" which he had felt in the Lakes, years after in a letter of 27 May 1814 and again on 8 February 1826. The description of the lover's image reflected, and then suddenly dispersed, in the clear waters of the woodland pool (**91–104**), becomes a metaphor for the imaginative process itself. Coleridge later quoted it, to suggest the mysterious but unstable source of creative power, in the Preface to "Kubla Khan" (No. 74). The poem, which marks the end of the Hill Walking series, is perhaps best considered as a hybrid or transitional form: part open-air verse journal, part literary translation, part confessional meditation, and part philosophic notebook.

Notes to the Asra Poems

45. "THE KEEPSAKE"

First published in the *Morning Post* on 17 September 1802; collected in *Sibylline Leaves* 1817. Almost certainly the earliest of the Asra Poems, inspired by the memory of Coleridge's visit to the Hutchinson family farm at Sockburn, Durham, in late autumn 1799 when he first met the animated twenty-four-year-old Sara Hutchinson, and (as he later claimed) fell bewilderingly in love. The fine description of the northern farming landscape after the harvest, frames a decorative but recognizable picture of the "full bosom'd" and "auburn haired" Asra; while the phrase "the entrancement of that maiden kiss" (**36**) is based on a Notebook entry of November 1799 in which Coleridge reflects on the fatality of their encounter in the firelit parlour at Sockburn. The wild forget-me-not (**13, 30**), which Coleridge characteristically adopted from the German name *Vergissmein* *nicht*, in a learned botanical footnote, became one of their lovers' private symbols.

Nevertheless Coleridge disguised the love-poem for publication, by adding the fiction (or wish-fulfilment) of the future springtime marriage (**37–9**) on his return to the north, which was an impossibility; and by using the courtly name "Emmeline" (**14**) which Wordsworth also used for his future wife Mary Hutchinson, Asra's elder sister. These disguises and romantic displacements are typical of the Asra Poems, which frequently contain elements of subterfuge and sexual fantasy. Coleridge next met Sara Hutchinson over a year later in the Lake District.

46. "THE LANGUAGE OF BIRDS"

First published in the *Morning Post* on 16 October 1802; collected in *Sibylline Leaves* 1817. Originally with the subtitle, "Lines spoken extempore, to a little child, in early spring". Later retitled, "Answer to a Child's Question". The little child was Hartley aged seven; but the "Love" was Asra. Birds in traditional folklore declare their secret love on St Valentine's day (14 February), and Coleridge frequently used bird images to describe his feelings both in his poetry and his letters. The engaging swing of the verse brings it close to a nursery rhyme, which effectively disguises a more adult passion.

47. "A DAY-DREAM: MY EYES MAKE PICTURES"

First published in the *Bijou* magazine in 1828; collected in *Poetical Works* 1828. Composed shortly after Coleridge's clandestine three-week visit to the Hutchinson farm at Gallow Hill in Lancashire, in summer 1801, where the poem is set. The tender, erotic scenes under a willow by a fountain, and later in the firelit farmhouse kitchen, with both Asra and her sister Mary Hutchinson, the "two beloved women" (**36**), are later recalled in Coleridge's Notebooks of winter 1801–2, and recur in the "Letter to Sara Hutchinson" (No. 49) of the following spring. "Our sister and our friend" (**12**) are Dorothy and her brother Wordsworth, who was engaged to Mary at this time, and Coleridge seems to be continuing his fantasy of marrying Asra also. The plain but highly emotional language (there are fifteen exclamation marks in thirty-six lines) is skilfully contained within a tight lyric stanza, which floats away on a final feminine couplet. The traditional pastoral images – willow, fountain, moonlight, firelight, beehive – are all given a powerful sexual overtone, yet the effect is curiously innocent.

48. "THE DAY-DREAM: IF THOU WERT HERE"

First published in the *Morning Post*, 19 October 1852 (following "The Language of Birds", No. 46); collected in *Poetical Works* 1828. The original newspaper subtitle, "From an Emigrant to his Absent Wife", and the ambiguous reference to "Sara" (**22**), were both designed to disguise the true subject of the poem, which is Coleridge lying on his couch at Greta Hall having an erotic daydream about Asra in the firelit kitchen at Gallow Hill (**7–24**), until interrupted by little Hartley (**27–8**). In the Cornell MS. of the poem "Frederic" is explicitly called "Hartley". The theme is closely related to the previous poem (No. 47), with its similar title and stanzaic form; and contains tender images of firelight (**9**) and the warm breast of a nesting bird (**19–20**), which are carried over into the next poem (No. 49, "A Letter to Sara Hutchinson"). This erotic dream of Asra is also described in Coleridge's Notebook: "Prest to my bosom & felt there . . . I looked intensely towards her face – & sometimes I *saw it* – so vivid was the spectrum . . . sopha/lazy bed . . . the fits of Light & Dark from the Candle going out in the Socket . . . that last Image how lovely to me now." (CNB I, 985.) The intricate confusion of the dreamer's sexual identity (**12–18**) – is it the man, the woman, or the baby, who receives the kiss? – is characteristic of Coleridge's psychological subtlety, which in later work often seems to predict Jung's notions of the Anima.

49. "A LETTER TO SARA HUTCHINSON"

First published from MS. at Dove Cottage Library in 1947, and by Cornell University Press in 1988. The central poem of the Asra group, and the first version of the famous "Dejection" (see No. 50), its existence was unknown until the mid-twentieth century. Composed rapidly in April 1802, perhaps during the single, stormy night of Sunday, 4–5 April in Coleridge's upstairs study at Greta Hall, where the poem is set, it is over double the length of "Dejection" (340 against 139 lines) and retains the authentic, headlong out-pouring of a true love-letter, with much passion and much self-pity. It is not known if the original was actually sent to Asra. But one version was shown to Wordsworth within a fortnight (Dorothy, *Journal*, 21 April 1802); and chosen extracts to Coleridge's friends Poole, Sotheby, and Lord Beaumont.

The poem's twenty wild verse-paragraphs contain a clear, underlying structure of self-analysis: first Coleridge's remarkable description of mental depression, and the deadening of his feelings for natural beauty (**paras. 1–4**); a brief return to childhood hopes and longings which are unfulfilled (**para. 5**); then a series of reviving thoughts and erotic fantasies of Asra, inspired by a recent "guileless Letter" (**125**) she has sent him (**paras. 6–10**). Coleridge renounces hope of sharing an "Abiding Home" (**135**) with her, but gives a shrewd description of his marital unhappiness at Greta Hall, and guilty longings to leave his wife and be by Asra's bedside (**paras. 11–13**). The poem then moves dramatically back to the equinoctial storm, gathering outside Coleridge's study window at midnight (**216**), with images of violence and emotional release (**para. 14**). Coleridge then turns back to Asra, explaining his sense of lost youth (**para. 15**), the dulling of his creative powers in unhappy domesticity (**paras. 16–17**) and the frustrated love for his children (**paras. 18–19**). Finally in a passionate, almost operatic climax Coleridge breaks out into an assertion of renewed, inward spiritual powers – the Soul's "sweet and potent Voice of its own Birth" (**305**) – and wishes Asra unending joy in the living, natural world (**334**) which he will share as far as he can. For all its extravagance, the poem is one of the peaks of Romantic self-expression, containing a coherent philosophy of imagination, the "shaping Spirit" (**241**), an acute analysis of the creative personality, and a superb evocation of the Lake District in early spring. But it also remains a love-letter, and we will never know what Asra made of it.

50. "DEJECTION: AN ODE"

First version published in the *Morning Post* on 4 October 1802 (Wordsworth's wedding-day) addressed to "Edmund"; the version printed here collected in *Sibylline Leaves* 1817, addressed to an unidentified "Lady" viz. Asra. This is Coleridge's brilliantly rehandled, public version of the previous "Letter to Sara Hutchinson" (see No. 49). Compressing the text from 340 to 139 lines, he reconstructed it as an irregular Pindaric ode with eight verse stanzas of different lengths. The Pindaric form makes use of sudden short lines and tightened rhymes, to give emotional and lyric force to particular passages. The major alterations begin at stanza IV, editing in passages from much later in the "Letter", and centring the poem more impersonally on problems of imaginative feeling, emotional energy, and "joy" (the spiritual and psychological counter to depression). Coleridge reduced all explicit autobiographical material about his childhood, unhappy marriage and love affair to that contained in stanza VI.

From an intensely personal outpouring on Love – words for "love", "beloved", etc. appear twenty-one times in the "Letter", but only once ("loveless", **52**) in "Dejection" – Coleridge fashioned a high philosophical meditation on the loss and recovery of the Imagination. It forms an immediate dialogue with Wordsworth's contemporaneous "Ode: Intimations of Immortality in Early Childhood", and is later answered by Keats ("Ode on a Grecian Urn") and Shelley ("Ode to the West Wind"). Opening in a mood of "dull pain" and depression, "Dejection" questions the basis of human happiness, creativity and spiritual hope. Do the healing and renewing powers of Nature depend on human perception, the "fountains" within (stanza III)? Can the "shaping spirit of Imagination" itself be permanently destroyed by personal afflictions, and what Coleridge calls "abstruse research" – scholarship, philosophy itself (stanza VI)? (Some critics also gloss this as a disguised reference to opium addiction.) Or does the coming of the springtime equinoctial storms demonstrate that all natural energies, both in man and Nature, are renewed (stanza VII)? These profound, disabling doubts are not necessarily confirmed in the poem: they are given as the products of Coleridge's own "wan and heartless mood" (**25**), which he attempts to dismiss as "viper thoughts" at the psychological turning point of the poem (**94**), which ends with the same "blessing" of joy as the earlier "Letter".

The whole power and paradox of "Dejection" lies in this fact: that Coleridge can still write with unparalleled imaginative force about the threatened loss of the Imagination. The beautiful imagery of the rising wind, which commands the entire poem from the opening glimpse of the uneasy moon, is closely allied to the "spirit of Imagination" itself: the cleansing, fructifying late-winter wind (99–107), the Romantic *sturm*, which blasts through the terrible passivity of dejection to bring hope and rebirth. (Compare Shelley's "Destroyer and Preserver".) The immensely subtle and assured handling of this unifying wind-imagery is one of the technical achievements that distinguishes "Dejection" from the "Letter", together with its much greater stylistic and emotional control. All personal references are virtually suppressed, even such as that to Wordsworth and his poem or "lay" about "Lucy Gray" ("Letter", 210), altered to Thomas Otway, the young eighteenth-century playwright who died tragically young (120). But which is the more moving work of art – the spontaneous outpouring to Asra, or the profound meditation on imaginative renewal; the intimate letter or the formal ode?

51. "SEPARATION"

First published in *Poetical Works* 1834. Composed during the first year of Coleridge's absence in Malta, where it appeared in a Notebook draft of 1804–5. The last three stanzas are so closely based on a seventeenth-century love lyric by John Cotton, "Ode to Chlorinda", that it is clear that Coleridge's poem began with a plagiarism, and then expanded to describe his own circumstances. (Compare No. 43 and No. 62.) Coleridge's Malta Notebooks are full of dreams about Asra, and the fantasy of winning her heart by military prowess may not have been so strange in the wartime atmosphere of the garrison at Valletta, where astonishingly Coleridge became First Secretary to the Governor, Sir Alexander Ball, one of Nelson's toughest admirals. Note the echoes of "Kubla Khan" (No. 74) in lines 11–12.

52. "PHANTOM"

Composed, with a commentary, in Coleridge's Malta Notebook of 8 February 1805; first published *Poetical Works* 1834. Coleridge wrote: "Of Love in sleep, the seldomness of the feeling . . . a certain indistinctness, a sort of universal-in-particularness of form, seems necessary – *vide* my lines 'All look or likeness . . .' This abstract self is indeed in its nature a Universal personified – as Life, Soul, Spirit, etc." (CNB II. 2441.). The image of Asra as a figure on a tombstone may be drawn from Coleridge's memory of the Conyers tomb at Sockburn, where he first met her (see note to "Love", No. 35). But Asra is transfigured, rather than dead. The stone is "rifted" (5) – that is, split or sundered – implying some sort of resurrection: an escape from death, or time, or the material world. Her spirit shines (**8**) with the internal radiance that Coleridge always associated with transcendental energy. Such "emblems" of love and hope are frequent in Coleridge's later work.

53. "O SARA! NEVER RASHLY LET ME GO"

Composed in 1806–7, when it appears under the title "Nonsense", in a Notebook of the Coleorton period (CNB II. 2224 (48)) spent with Asra in Leicestershire after returning from Malta (see note to "To William Wordsworth" No.30). Coleridge often used this "Nonsense" heading, or "Metrical Exercise", for experimental verse in which he was exploring half-formed ideas, dream images, or even "forbidden" themes, without committing himself to the idea of a serious or finished poem. It was a method of getting round inhibitions, of making space for the creative unconscious, similar to his use of translations. This poem seems to be about his physical desire for Asra, which he cannot consciously accept: the image of pure "streams" (**3**) contrasted with "melted Metals" (**5**) has an evident sexual connotation. Coleridge may be drawing on his memories of a metal foundry which he visted at Portsmouth just before his departure for Malta, and vividly described in a letter of April 1804.

54. "AD VILMUM AXIOLOGUM"
(tr: "To William Wordsworth")

Original text in Latin hexameters, composed in a Notebook of 1807 while staying with Asra and the Wordsworths at Coleorton. (See note to No. 30.) Coleridge sometimes used Latin verse as an alternative way of expressing and ordering his feelings. The modern editor's translation, "Do you command me to endure Asra's neglect? . . ." is perhaps enough to give an idea of the "visceral" (**7**) strength of Coleridge's feeling for Asra, and his bitter resentment at the idea that Wordsworth was "forbidding" their love at Coleorton (**1–8**). Coleridge's Notebooks at this time record similar violent outbursts, confused masochistic fantasies and dreams, and even a terrible, jealous "vision" of Wordsworth in bed with Asra one Saturday morning – perhaps a result of Coleridge's heavy opium habit at this period. The decorous Latin should not hide the deliberate pathological note, as in Coleridge's reference to castration: "tear out my heart, and my eyes, or whatever is dearer. . . ." (**9–10**).

55. "YOU MOULD MY HOPES"

Text from a Coleorton MS. of about 1807; first published in *Poetical Works* 1912. Never titled by Coleridge, this lyric fragment may have been part of early drafts of a larger Asra poem (See also No.56). There is a characteristic, dreamlike movement between internal and external landscapes, dominated by shifting images of light and water. Here Coleridge's love seems completely unclouded by the doubts and jealousies described in No.54. These violent swings of mood add to the mystery of the whole relationship, even if they were exaggerated by opium.

56. "AN ANGEL VISITANT"

First published in *Literary Remains*, vol.I, 1836. Like the previous fragment, it is probably part of the Coleorton sequence of 1807, leading to "Recollections of Love" (No.57), with which it shares the rhyme-scheme but not quite the metre. The secret grove of holly-bushes (**1**), a magic lover's bower within which Coleridge imagines himself lying with Asra, may have existed on the Coleorton estate or may be part of the Quantocks landscape transfigured through memory as in the next poem. (Compare Wordsworth's poem, "This is the Spot".) Wild woodbine has a white, scented flower in the late spring.

57. "RECOLLECTIONS OF LOVE"

Composed at Nether Stowey, where Coleridge returned to stay with Tom Poole after eight years' absence (**6**) in the early summer of 1807; first published in *Sibylline Leaves* 1817. (Compare the earlier setting of "This Lime-Tree Bower My Prison", No. 25). Coleridge's long walks over the Quantock hills, in an attempt to bring his opium addiction under control, released the flood of memories which shape this beautiful lyric. The dreamlike transpositions of time and place across eight years (stanza III); the melting of child and adult identities (stanza IV); and the interlayering of Somerset and Lake District landscapes (stanza V) – the River Greta flowed behind his house at Keswick – show Coleridge trying to distance and idealize his predestined love for Asra. This love is now presented as an experience of metempsychosis: the airborne "spirit" of the beloved (**15**) transmigrating from a previous existence (**19**). This process of "neo-Platonizing" his feelings for Asra reaches its climax in "Constancy to an Ideal Object" (No. 58). The effect of various kinds of soft natural sound – breathing (**2**), bird-song (**10**), flowing water (**8, 28**), sighing (**13**), whispering (**27**) – is subtly deployed to produce the poem's "under-song" (**30**), an enchanted and musical quality almost like a lullaby.

58. "CONSTANCY TO AN IDEAL OBJECT"

First published in *Poetical Works* 1828. The last and perhaps the most mysterious of the Asra Poems. Coleridge probably added to it slowly over twenty years of composition between 1805 and 1825, as he reflected on the meaning of his love affair, which effectively ended when he left the Lake District in autumn 1810 and Asra remained with the Wordsworth household. The unobtrusive pentameter couplets contain a marked shift in style, from formal to intimate, as the subtle, reflective poem progresses. Beginning with an abstract, metaphysical enquiry (somewhat in the manner of Coleridge's favourite seventeenth-century poet, Fulke Greville) about the nature of Ideal Love in an inconstant universe (**1–10**), the poem moves surprisingly to more concrete and autobiographical images from Coleridge's own life associated with Asra: sheltering from a storm (**9**), seeking for a cottage home (**20**), being becalmed on the sea (**22**), and climbing a mountain track at dawn (**26**). But this is no longer a love poem, or even a retrospective one. It is more like an examination of philosophical conscience. Throughout Coleridge addresses the platonic Ideal of Love as "you" or "thou" (the "Yearning Thought", (**4**) or "Fond Thought" (**7**) in his imagination) rather than Asra herself who is only referred to anonymously in the third person as "she" (**12**). The striking emblem of the becalmed Helmsman, obviously recalling "The Rime of the Ancient Mariner" (No. 32), may also refer to the classical tale of Palinaurus, Odysseus's helmsman, lost overboard on the long return voyage to Ithaca (**22–24**). The haunting elusiveness of the poem, with its uneasy transitions (the cottage becomes a boat, the ocean becomes a mountainside) suggests obsessive reworkings of the text. Internal evidence might suggest it was begun while abroad in Malta (**16–24**); continued through the despairing period of 1810–14 (**7–10**); and finished in a more philosophic mood at Highgate in the 1820s. The image of the Brocken Spectre – "which the Author himself has experienced" – in the final lines (**25–32**) comes from a passage in the *Aids to Reflection* of 1825: "The beholder either recognises it as a projected form of his own Being, that moves before him with a Glory round its head, or recoils from it as a Spectre." (See also No. 39. The Brocken Spectre is a rare atmospheric phenomenon produced by the sun's rays throwing the viewer's shadow horizontally forward on to low cloud or mist, and encircling it with a rainbow spectrum generated by diffraction of the light through water droplets. It can occur on any mountain top, at dawn or dusk; and also be observed from aircraft.) This is the central issue of the poem, which asks if Love is the pursuit of a shadow (**32**), a self-created illusion (compare William Blake's "spectres"); or if it is a beautiful Platonic reality, a projected form of the "dear embodied Good" (**13**) which really exists in our own being, in others, and in Eternity. Coleridge does not answer, or turn back to the memory of Asra for reassurance; thus the sequence ends in a shimmer of haunting uncertainty.

Notes to the Confessional Poems

First published in the *Morning Post* on 7 October 1802; collected in *Sibylline Leaves* 1817. Composed during August 1802, during the unexpected but very welcome visit of Coleridge's friends from London, Charles and Mary Lamb (**41–2**), on a picturesque tour of the Lakes, when as so often on such occasions, it rained. The "very worthy, but not very pleasant "other guest at Greta Hall" who was *de trop* (**47**), was possibly Sir Charles Boughton, a brilliant bore. Coleridge wrote on 21 September: "We have been plagued to death with a swarm of Visitors – I thought of having a Board nailed up at my Door with the following Words painted on it – Visited Out, & removed to the Strand, opposite St Clement's Church, for the benefit of Retirement." This note of comic exasperation is cleverly sustained throughout the poem, but the light-verse treatment of that most English of subjects – bad weather – is deceptive. Each stanza hints at more serious, inner psychological troughs of low pressure. Coleridge is insomniac, and lying alone in the dark like "a blind man" (stanza I); he suffers from chronic illness, particularly arthritic pains and stomach disorders (brought on by opium) (stanza II); he promises to commit himself (humorously) to write one more unfinishable book (stanza III); he needs to discuss private "pain and grief" with the Lambs (stanza IV); he will promise anything to get rid of his "guest" and be left alone (stanza V). The rain is a symbol of depression (see "Dejection: An Ode", No. 50), and the flippant handling of it disguises the agonized feelings to be revealed in the following poem, "The Pains of Sleep" (No. 60)

First published in *Christabel; Kubla Khan; The Pains of Sleep* 1816. It was printed immediately after "Kubla Khan" (see No. 70), with this note by Coleridge: "As a contrast to this vision, I have annexed a fragment of a very different character, describing with equal fidelity the dream of pain and disease." Both poems are inspired by opium, but they are probably separated by four or five years, and by a gulf of experience. In style and subject, "The Pains of Sleep" clearly belongs to the later period of Confessional pieces, which began in the Lakes when Coleridge's opium addiction had become seriously disabling. The first known version was sent to Robert Southey on 11 September 1803; and a second to Tom Poole on 3 October. The subject is not opium-taking, but opium-withdrawal. The symptoms of withdrawal are now medically well-known: sweating, feverish shaking, muscular cramps, acute physical discomfort, diarrhoea and horrific nightmares. Both Coleridge's letters and Notebooks of this autumn vividly describe all these symptoms (without fully understanding their cause), especially the bad dreams from which Coleridge frequently awoke screaming (**37**) loud enough to wake the whole household at Greta Hall or Grasmere. In one letter of 1803 he wrote: "But with Sleep my Horrors commence; & they are such, three nights out of four, as literally to *stun* the intervening day, so that more often than otherwise I fall asleep, struggling to remain awake . . ." (*Letters*, 13 September 1803.) The poem is then an accurate transcription of Coleridge's sufferings, but remains curiously reticent about exactly *what* horrors the dreams actually contained (**18–32**). Scenes of humiliation, powerlessness, sexual perversion, fear, violence and shame, seem to be suggested. The verse, with its short, rapid lines and gasping couplets, brilliantly enacts the panting and mumbling of the tortured dreamer.

61. "TO TWO SISTERS"

First published in the *Courier* on 10 December 1807, under the pen-name "Siesti" (a disguise for his initials "STC"); reprinted with the entire central section removed (**8–44**) and falsely dated 1817 in *Poetical Works* 1834; not finally collected until 1880. This suggests Coleridge's sensitivity to the poem's personal revelations, about his desperate need for love and support during the crisis of his middle-life. The "two sisters" were Mary and Charlotte Brent, young women in their twenties then living in London with Mary's husband, John Morgan. Morgan was a businessman, who had been to Christ's Hospital, and made friends with Coleridge in Bristol; the Morgan household looked after Coleridge during the worst period of his opium addiction, 1810–1815, after his break with the Wordsworths, and became a substitute for the Grasmere household. Strange as it may seem, the poem clearly shows (**21–29**) that Coleridge was already consciously preparing Mary Morgan and Charlotte Brent for the emotional roles in his life once played by Mary Wordsworth and Sara Hutchinson (see the Asra Poems). There is some evidence from his letters that Coleridge made sexual advances to the younger and prettier Charlotte, during opium episodes (consider **12–15**). Indeed the whole poem is suffused with erotic imagery from the Asra sequence: the brooding mother dove (**4–5**), the sun melting the winter ice (**13**), the cosiness of the firelit room (**45**). In the final passage (**45–52**) Coleridge imagines all four women waiting for him in the same room, while he sits elsewhere in solitude, tenderly dreaming of them ("ah! dream and pine!"). As so often in these Confessional Poems, the informal, almost light-verse manner – here couplets which skilfully carry the impression of Coleridge's speaking voice – hide despairing undertones. Coleridge is also working on his personal mythology of middle-age: "disinheritance" by Nature, "guiltless" opium addiction, disappointed love, struggling solitary existence, and heroic spiritual exile.

First published in No.14 of *The Friend* on 23 November 1809; collected in *Sibylline Leaves* 1817. It is based on a translation from the seventeenth-century Italian poet Chiabrera whose famous collection of verse epitaphs (*Gli Epitaphi*) both Coleridge and Wordsworth were studying at this period. Wordsworth's version of this, the "Fifth Epitaph: for Ambrosio Salinero", is a literal rendering of twenty-three lines. Coleridge's is a greatly expanded one of forty lines, "imitated, though in the movements rather than the thoughts ... from Chiabrera". The long opening section (1-16) is expanded from only four lines of Chiabrera's; the conventional imagery of Parnassus is transformed into one of Coleridge's Cumberland hill-walks (21-28); and the final vision of the Philosopher's cave (28-37) appears nowhere in the original. So Coleridge has subtly transformed the Italian text into a new English poem and an imaginary epitaph for himself. The invented name "Idoloclastes Satyrane" (1), meaning literally "the Mocker of Idols or Illusions" in public affairs and fashionable opinions (see 8-12), is based on Spenser's knight-errant Sir Satyrane in *The Faerie Queene*. Coleridge used the pseudonym "Satyrane" in his travel letters from Germany (also printed in *The Friend*), and saw his own newspaper essay-writing at this period 1809-12 partly in this quixotic light: a return to "ancient truths" (5) as against party factions. There follows a mythically heroic, but recognizable, account of Coleridge's own "unconquered" struggles in these middle years with opium addiction and mental depression (14-19); his continuing delight in the "Muse" of poetry and the whole field of literature, "the Parnassian forest" (19-23); and his critical investigations into the nature of poetic inspiration and its psychological origins "traced upward to its source" (23-28). (In classical mythology "Hippocrene" (24) is the fount of poetry which was struck from the side of Mount Helicon by the hooves of the winged horse Pegasus.) The final movement of the poem (28-40) similarly reflects Coleridge's philosophical researches, using a remarkable "cavern" image reminiscent both of Plato's cave and those of Kubla Khan. The characterization of Salinero as "docile, childlike" (37) could only be applied to Coleridge with a degree of irony, as perhaps he intended. The skill of the whole adaptation can best be gauged by comparing it with Wordsworth's literal one:

> True it is that Ambrosio Salinero
> With an untoward fate was long involved
> In odious litigation; and full long,
> Fate harder still! had he to endure assaults
> Of racking malady. And true it is
> That not the less a frank courageous heart
> And buoyant spirit triumphed over pain;
> And he was strong to follow in the steps
> Of the fair Muses. Not a covert path

Leads to the dear Parnassian forest's shade,
That might from him be hidden; not a track
Mounts to pellucid Hippocrene, but he
Had traced its windings. – This Savona knows,
Yet no sepulchral honors to her Son
She paid, for in our age the heart is ruled
Only by gold. And now a simple stone
Inscribed with this memorial here is raised
By his bereft, his lonely, Chiabrera.

63. "THE PANG MORE SHARP THAN ALL"

First published in *Poetical Works* 1834. The date of composition is very
uncertain. Fragments of this poem exist in MS., apparently from the period
of Coleridge's crisis years in London, 1811–12; others are watermarked
1819, while the allegoric figures, and archaicisms ("guerdons" etc.) are
characteristic of the late 1820s. The style, vocabulary and stanzaic forms are
playful, mock-Spenserian. But all fragments contain the haunting central
vision of the "magic Child" who has been lost (stanza IV), and this gives
a mysterious bitterness to the poem, which Coleridge evidently re-wrote
over many years.

Who or what is this magic Child? Is it Hartley? He is "Hope's last and
dearest child, without a name" (stanza I); he is "the faery Boy that's lost
and gone" (stanza V). He is distinguished from his playmates, "twin-births
of his foster-dame" (**25**) who are a brother called "Esteem" and a sister
called "Kindness" (stanza III). He has gone for ever, but left his image in
Coleridge's "secret heart", like an image in Merlin's "crystal orb" (stanza
IV). (Merlin's ball of magic glass or crystal (**39–40**) comes from Spenser's
Faerie Queene, Book III, Canto 2: the magic glass contains through necro-
mancy all the lost dreams and unfulfilled desires of the world.) Coleridge
suffers grievously from his loss of the magic Child; but the "pang more
sharp" (**46**) comes when the sister Kindness dresses up in his "faded robe"
and "inly shrinking" pretends to be the Child, thus "counterfeiting absent
Love" (stanza V).

So one answer is that the magic Child is Love. In the allegory, Love
departs and is replaced by Kindness and Esteem, who together play the
cruel charade of "dressing up" in Love's clothes, as in a children's party
game. (Compare Rupert Brooke's poem, "When Love has changed to
Kindliness".) But a subtler reading, based on the central stanza IV, might
be more symbolic: the magic Child is Coleridge's inward image of his own
youth and creativity, "inisled" (**40**) in the glass of imagination, but now
powerless and languishing (**43**).

64. "HOPE AND TIME"

First published under the title "Time, Real and Imaginary", using only the second stanza, in *Sibylline Leaves* 1817. Coleridge's preface note of 1817 claims that it was "a schoolboy poem", and explains the title as follows: "By Imaginary Time, I meant the state of a schoolboy's mind when on his return to school he projects his being in his daydreams, and lives in his next holidays, six months hence; and this I contrasted with real Time."

But the early MS. of the complete poem (given here) in two stanzas dates from 1807–11, and here Coleridge explains the meaning rather differently: "The title of the poem . . . should be Time Real and Time Felt: in the sense of Time in active youth, or activity with Hope and fullness of aim in any period; and (Time) in despondent, objectless manhood. – Time objective and subjective."

The autobiographical picture of Coleridge's childhood in the "great City rear'd" of stanza I, is close to that in "A Letter to Sara Hutchinson" (No. 49, stanza V). While the allegoric figures of two children, a sister and a brother, also appear in "The Pang More Sharp Than All" (No. 63); and the image of dreamlike, effortless running recurs in "Youth and Age" (No. 69). The children run with outstretched arms, hoping to fly, like ostriches with their undeveloped wings (**17**): another of Coleridge's characteristic bird-images of poetic power. But the allegory is mysterious. The girl, Hope, runs looking ever anxiously *backwards* into the past (**21–22**) while the boy, Time, runs with the *blind*, dreamlike innocence of childhood, oblivious to all perils in the future (**23–25**). The force of the poem, "a sort of Emblem" (**14**), lies in its unexpected modulation from the playful, careless joy of childhood in the "elfish Place" (**16**), to a grief-stricken, adult awareness of blindness and vulnerability.

65. "THE SUICIDE'S ARGUMENT"

First published in *Poetical Works* 1828. A MS. draft dates from 1811, the period of Coleridge's quarrel with Wordsworth, and the start of his descent into the worst period of opium addiction, here described as "guilt, lethargy, despair" (**9**).

Coleridge's Notebooks and letters show that he seriously considered suicide during at least three periods of his life: in Italy 1806; in London 1811; in Bristol in 1813 – all closely connected to increased opium use and periods of enforced solitude. Stanza I echoes the grim Euripidian question: whether man was ever asked if he wanted to be born in the first place. Stanza II ("Nature's Answer") gives no Christian assurance whatever, but angrily threatens Coleridge with his culpable misuse of Nature's gifts. Coleridge here treats human life as a purely commercial contract between Man and Nature, in which the Suicide will be condemned if he returns damaged goods: "no worse for the wear? . . . Make out the inven'try" (**5, 10**). The reckless dactylic metre, which gradually collapses, suggests the running-down of mechanical energy. This is an early use of the question-and-answer form in the Confessional Poems, dramatizing two irreconcilable aspects of Coleridge's feelings; a Freudian reading might see it as an argument between the Ego and the Super-Ego.

66. "THE VISIONARY HOPE"

First published in *Sibylline Leaves* 1817, and probably composed in the deepest period of Coleridge's despair, either in London or Bristol 1811–12. Even the energy of "The Suicide's Argument" (No. 65) has gone from the verse, which creeps along in low, exhausted, alternating rhymes. Coleridge's depression is represented as a chronic illness (4), which has led him like a captive into a conqueror's "feast" (8). But the screams of his nightmares (11–14) have already been identified with opium in "The Pains of Sleep" (No. 60), and Coleridge recognizes his inability to deny himself the source of "pain" (16). The "one Hope" (27) which would save him is a return of Love, the "inward bliss and boast" (17) of his previous life; and Coleridge implies that this alone would make him strong enough to resist opium. The bleak emotional power of the poem derives from the recognition of "Hope" as a moral imperative, upon which the motive for all human actions must ultimately be based. Coleridge's Notebooks of this period begin to develop a metaphysics of "Hope" as fundamental to all activity in nature (see No. 19).

67. "HUMAN LIFE"

First published in *Sibylline Leaves* 1817, and probably composed towards the end of Coleridge's crisis period, while starting to work on the *Biographia Literaria* in 1815 at Calne in Wiltshire with the Morgan family (see No. 61 and note). This bitter meditative poem is constructed in the form of two sonnets, using a tight metaphysical style reminiscent of Fulke Greville and John Donne (see "On Donne's Poetry", No. 84). The possibility that man was a purely physical creature, without immortal soul or spiritual purpose (5–9), and a mere evolutionary "accident" of Nature (10–14), was never openly expressed by Coleridge in his published prose. But it recurs frequently in the later Confessional poetry. The implication for Coleridge, explored in the second stanza, is that not merely personal hopes and dreams (15–16) but even expressions of fellow feeling and sympathy for others, therefore become meaningless (19–24). Coleridge is left with a negation of the entire moral universe, so that human "being" is itself a contradiction in terms (29). The apparently abstract, fretful language frequently clarifies into vivid physical images: the beehive full of unproductive drones (9); the beautiful "vase" of Nature's conscious creation (11); the sinister mourner in the cowled hood (21). The poem refers to several of Coleridge's darker, metaphysical obsessions: the German philosopher Schelling's idea that man might be an "unconscious" creation of Nature, the product of a moment of distraction (**13–14**); and the almost mystical idea of man as an existential paradox, an echo of himself, a shadow of his own shadow, brought into being simply by his own fantasy of himself (**23**). Coleridge explored this terrible "negative" world further in "Limbo" (No. 68.)

68. "LIMBO"

First published in *Poetical Works* 1834. This disturbing poem suggests Coleridge's slow emergence from addiction and depression in his early forties, with a more daring exploration of the experiences he had survived. Looking back in a letter of 14 September 1828, Coleridge said it was the "pretended fragment" of a poet's soliloquy in a madhouse, and that it contained "some of the most forcible lines with the most original imagery that my niggard Muse ever made me a present of." A longer draft exists in a Notebook probably dating from 1811–15 (CNB III. 4073–4). Coleridge marked one of the rejected passages: "A specimen of the Sublime dashed to pieces by cutting too close with the fiery Four-in-Hand round the corner of Non-sense". In another MS. Coleridge unexpectedly compared "Limbo" with the much earlier "Phantom" (No. 52): "Another fragment, but in a very different style, from a Dream of Purgatory, alias Limbus." The comparison seems to be based on the conscious use of dream imagery in both poems.

Coleridge's "Purgatory" of the mind has two states, each with their corresponding physical settings. The first is the night-mare "Limbo" with which the poem opens and closes, a "crepuscular" or twilit (**4**) place of horror, where Time has become a ghastly impotent figure, so withered up that he cannot carry a scythe in his husk-like hands ("branny hands"). Here the spirit is jailed in a prison of non-being (**21–26**), and threatened with "positive Negation" (**28**). The second Limbo state is the moonlit garden, with its magical setting, which occupies the central section of the poem (**9–20**). Here Time has become a human figure: an Old Man standing outside at night, staring up at the moon (**13–19**). Like the Boy in "Hope and Time" (No. 64) the old man is blind (**12**). But with his "eyeless face all eye" (**16**) he can still somehow commune with the moon, and the joy he feels at this seems to promise some kind of salvation (**18**). These two contrasting states of Limbo reflect the polarities of Coleridge's mind at this stage in his career. The radiant moon, an emblem of the Imaginative vision since "Frost at Midnight", still offers the possibility of transcendence. But the final blankness of a "future state" also threatens Coleridge with the curiously mathematical, Newtonian horror of a positive negative (**28**).

69. "YOUTH AND AGE"

First published with two stanzas only (**1–38**) in the *Bijou* 1828; collected as three stanzas (**1–49**) in *Poetical Works* 1834. The shorter and more playful version appears in a MS. dated 10 September 1823, probably written while Coleridge was on his annual autumn holiday at Ramsgate (see "Fancy in Nubibus" No. 17 and "Aria Spontanea" No. 90). The final stanza (**39–49**), which considerably darkens the tone of the whole, is much later and originally appeared as part of "An Old Man's Sigh: A Sonnet" in *Blackwood's Magazine*, June 1832.

Coleridge had bitter feelings about his premature physical ageing, partly caused by his opium addiction, and sadly recalls his youthful hill-walking and sea-bathing (**9–12**). Many visitors to Highgate after 1819, such as Keats, Carlyle, and John Stuart Mill, noted his "drooping gait", heavy bulk and thick white hair (**34–35**). The "trim skiffs" (**12**) to which he compares his youthful self, were the early paddle-steamers which began to appear on the Thames and elsewhere after 1820. The psychologically acute imagery of old age as a form of charade, dressing-up, or grotesque fancy-dress party (**27–32**), is prepared for in "The Pang More Sharp Than All" (No. 63). The sonnet of 1832 also contains a familiar bird-image after line 41:

> That only serves to make us grieve,
> In our old age,
> Whose bruised wings quarrel with the bars
> Of the still narrowing cage.

Coleridge's mocking complaints against his ageing body begin as early as 1807 when he writes in his Notebook "O 'tis a crazy tenement, this Body, a ruinous Hovel, which the striving Tenant, tired out with the idle toil of patching it, deserts and leaves to the sap of the sure silent fire . . ." (CNB II. 3189). But this beautiful, quick, almost dance-like verse achieves a note of humorous pathos about the universal condition of ageing.

70. "THE GARDEN OF BOCCACCIO"

First published in the *Keepsake* 1829, with an engraved illustration by Stothard; collected in *Poetical Works* 1829. It was composed at Highgate in spring 1827, inspired by the gift of an exotically illustrated edition of *The Tales of Boccaccio*, given to Coleridge by Mrs Ann Gillman, his friend and confidante for the last eighteen years of his life (**11–16**). Mrs Gillmann was the young wife of Coleridge's landlord and doctor, the brilliant surgeon James Gillman, who finally brought Coleridge's opium addiction and depression more or less under control after 1816. Ann Gillman can be considered as the last of Coleridge's muse-figures, and her presence gives this relaxed, genial poem its playful, amorous undertone, and the atmosphere of magic calm and acceptance similar to the late "Byzantium" poems of W. B. Yeats.

The poem develops in three parts: an opening description of one of Coleridge's still-recurrent depressions, which threatens opium until distracted by the Boccaccio book (**1–24**); then an autobiographical account of Coleridge's search from boyhood for an ideal love which is revealed first as Poetry, and then as Philosophy (**25–56**); finally a joyful evocation of the pastoral, idealized Italian landscape of the illustrations, into which Coleridge physically enters – "I see no longer! I myself am there!" (**65**) – thereby curing his depression by imaginative (and also erotic) displacement into the world of art (**57–109**). The poem also reflects the fashionable cult of the Mediterranean South, "star-bright Italy" (**77**), championed by the younger Romantics like Shelley, Byron, Hunt and Keats, after 1818.

Coleridge also celebrates alongside Boccaccio, the other reading-worlds that had given him pleasure in earlier days: the Norse sagas, the Greek legends, the medieval European tales (**33–43**). "Skalds" (**35**) are the Scandinavian warrior gods. "Hertha" (**38**) is the goddess of Norse fertility. "Old Maeonides" (**98**) is Homer. "Ovid's Holy Book of Love" (**100**) is the *Ars Amoris*.

71. "PHANTOM OR FACT"

First published in *Poetical Works* 1834. There is no evidence as to the exact date of composition, but probably about 1830 at Highgate when Coleridge was in his late fifties. The poem concerns the disillusion of late middle-age, and the loss of the sense of youth, as in "The Pang More Sharp Than All" (No. 63), but seen at a greater distance and with a certain wistful irony. The dialogue form (compare "The Suicide's Argument", No. 65) now allows Coleridge to stand outside this retrospective vision of the "wild disastrous change" (**16**) which took place in the "Author's" life.

As The Friend suggests, the short "riddling" incident deliberately contains many puzzles. The visionary figure who appears at the "Author's" bedside seems to be his "own" youthful spirit. The "Author" can barely ("unnethe", **4**) control the implications of this idea, which suggest how far he has fallen from grace. Yet the beauty and tenderness of the figure (**1–3**) implies that she is actually a woman, who "woos" and loves him; and her sudden "shrinking back" and almost physical revulsion at what he has become (**9–10**), uncannily recalls Christabel's shrinking back from Geraldine. Perhaps the "lovely form" is really a Muse figure, half transposed (compare No. 72, lines **22–23**). In the final lines the "Author" suggests that what began as an imaginative contradiction in his art ("a fragment from the life of dreams") was eventually "matured" into an inescapable conflict ("the silent strife") in his actual life (**17–20**). This reversal of categories between art and life is frequent in the later poetry, and emphasizes Coleridge's sense of philosophic detachment and acceptance.

72. "LOVE'S APPARITION AND EVANISHMENT"

First published in an anthology, *Friendship's Offering*, 1834; collected in *Poetical Works* 1834. Coleridge dated the MS. August 1833, the last year of his life. This beautiful, melancholy vision is set in the back garden of the Gillmans' house at 3 The Grove, Highgate, where Coleridge had his "garden-bower" (11) overlooking Hampstead Heath and Caen Wood. The "ruined well" (3) symbolizes the springs of poetic inspiration run dry; but the "couch of camomile" (12) is a herb of refreshment and healing.

Many earlier poems are deliberately echoed. The "blind" Arab (1) recalls the similar poetic nomad in "The Blossoming of the Solitary Date Tree" (No. 77). Coleridge as the old man with the "eyeless face" (8) recalls the figure of Time in "Limbo" (No. 68). The "garden-bower" (11) brings back the garden of Nether Stowey in "This Lime-Tree Bower My Prison" (No. 26). "Hope" as Love's sister recalls the figures of "The Pang More Sharp Than All" (No. 63). "Life in Death" (27), a favourite conceit of Coleridge's in old age, reaches right back to the hallucinations of the Mariner.

The despairing tone of the poem is subtly modulated by its lyric grace, especially in the song-like lilt of the final eight lines, which promise conciliation. If Hope can die "anew" (28), it follows that she can also be "woken" again into life. From 1852 editors perversely added a wholly despairing four-line "Envoy" to the poem, which crushes out this delicate ambiguity. But it was written much earlier in 1824, and was deliberately omitted by Coleridge from the final text:

L'Envoy

In vain we supplicate the Powers above;
There is no resurrection for the Love
That, nursed in tenderest care, yet fades away
In the chill'd heart by gradual self-decay.

One might better cite a couplet from another fragment of 1829 ("Love, Hope and Patience"):

But Love is subtle, and doth proof derive
From her own life that Hope is yet alive.

73. "EPITAPH"

First published in *Poetical Works* 1834. The MS. is dated 9 November 1833, some eight months before Coleridge's death at Highgate.

Coleridge was fond of writing his own epitaph, and there are six MS. versions of this one, sent separately to friends including Tom Poole, J. H. Green, John Lockhart and Mrs Charles Aders. Mrs Aders was arranging, at Coleridge's request, a tomb-stone design by the artist Maria Denman. Maria Denman had added the voluptuous figure of a Muse, but Coleridge objected to this in a letter of November 1833: ". . . (these) homely, plain, churchyard Christian verses would not be in keeping with a Muse (tho' a lovelier I never wooed), nor with A Lyre, or Harp, or Laurel, or aught else Parnassian or allegorical . . . If any figure rather that of an elderly man – 'thoughtful, with quiet tears upon his cheek'". The quotation is from his own poem, "A Tombless Epitaph" of twenty years before (No. 62). In several of his letters, Coleridge explained the ambiguous penultimate line of the Epitaph – "Mercy for praise – to be forgiven for fame" (7) – as meaning "give me Mercy instead of praise, give me Forgiveness instead of fame". This replaces literary glory with Christian humility in a becoming manner. But the alternative meaning, characteristically proud and guilty, remains open: "have mercy on me for Praise received, forgive me for Fame achieved". Perhaps both readings are allowable. Coleridge once glossed the "Punic Greek" of his initials "STC" (4) as being a transliteration of ΕΣΤΗΣΕ – "he has stood", that is "kept faith". To Lockhart he glossed them in Latin: "*stetit: restat: resurget*". This could be rendered as: "he has stood; he now rests; he shall rise again."

Notes to the Visionary Fragments

74. "KUBLA KHAN"

First published in *Christabel; Kubla Khan, A Vision; The Pains of Sleep*, 1816. The date of composition, like much else about this celebrated "fragment" (including the fact of it *being* a fragment) is the subject of lively dispute among scholars. The original version almost certainly belongs to the late autumn of 1797, when Coleridge made several walking expeditions over the Quantocks to the coast; Dorothy refers to the poem's existence in 1798; and Coleridge was known to have recited it in London in 1799. But no MS. exists from this period.

A later draft, with slight textual variants ("twice six miles", 6; "Mount Amara", 41) was discovered in 1934 and probably belongs to about 1810. Known as the Crewe MS., it contains a circumstantial postscript by Coleridge: "This fragment with a good deal more, not recoverable, composed, in a sort of Reverie brought on by two grains of Opium, taken to check a dysentry, at a Farm House between Porlock & Lynton, a quarter of a mile from Culbone Church, in the fall of the year, 1797."

By 1816 Coleridge had expanded this account to form the preface, identifying his source in Samuel Purchas's *Pilgrimage* (1614, Book 4, Chapter 13), telling his famous story of the interruption by the "person on business from Porlock" (never subsequently identified); and using a passage from his own poem "The Picture" (No. 44) – "then all the charm is broken" – to introduce the informing analogy between water and inspiration. The preface thus became an integral part of the "Kubla Khan" fragment and, with its emphasis on the "psychology" of poetic creation, suggests that creative inspiration and its loss is itself the central subject.

In the poem Coleridge draws an extended analogy between the creation of an earthly paradise in the Orient, walled and domed, by the Tartar warlord Kubla Khan and the poet's creation of an imaginary paradise with its "sacred river" of inspiration (1–36). He then laments its loss, and hopes for the "revival" of his poetic powers (37–54), in imagery drawn from Plato's classical description of inspired poets in the *Ion*, who "like Bacchic maidens, draw milk and honey from the rivers when they are under the influence of Dionysus, but not when they are in their right minds". The paradisial landscape has strong local echoes of the Quantock region and its romantic folklore (12–16), while the spasmodic eruptions of the "mighty fountain" (17–24) obscurely suggest the "panting" effort of childbirth or even sexual orgasm, as a further analogy of poetic creation. There is a clear indication of a shift or pause after line 36, with the introduction of the black Muse figure with her symbolic "dulcimer" (compare Apollo's lyre), and a recapitulation of the "dome" and "cavern" themes (37–47). This might indicate a retrospective coda, or even a later addition.

Modern criticism, with its search for image-patterns and textual sources, has tended to overlook the hypnotic chant and exquisite dance-movement of the verse, which brilliantly enacts the trance-like state of inspiration itself. For Coleridge it was essentially a recitation piece, the signature-tune of his genius, and there are several accounts of his performing it. Charles Lamb wrote in April 1816: "Coleridge is printing Xtabel by Ld Byron's recommendation to Murray, with what he calls a vision, Kubla Khan – which said vision he repeats so enchantingly that it irradiates and brings heaven and Elysian bowers into my parlour while he sings or says it."

75. "THE WANDERINGS OF CAIN"

Various fragments of this unfinished epic in "three cantos" appeared in Coleridge's lifetime. The verses, "Encinctured with a twine of leaves", from "Canto I" were first published separately as a footnote to the conclusion of his *Aids to Reflection*, 1825; the prose "Canto II" was first published in the *Bijou* magazine, 1828; the whole fragment with its preface in *Poetical Works* 1828. The MS. of an alternative prose outline of the entire poem by Coleridge, was published in the *Athenaeum* magazine on 27 January 1894. No "Canto III" is known, or any contribution by Wordsworth.

The date of composition is problematic. Coleridge says the original belongs to his collaboration with Wordsworth of 1798; but he also adds in the preface that the verses belong to a later period, "years afterward", when friends suggested that he "commence anew", probably at Highgate after 1820; and this may also be true of parts of the prose "Canto II". The preface, with its psychologically acute account of the failed collaboration ("and the Ancient Mariner was written instead"); the fickleness of inspiration ("adverse gales") and the unreliability of artistic memory ("the palimpsest tablet" – i.e. a wax tablet over-written several times) has become a significant part of the fragment, as with "Kubla Khan".

Coleridge had considered writing an epic poem on "The Origins of Evil" as early as 1796. He always remained fascinated with the biblical figure of Cain, the first murderer and archetypal social outcast, together with his innocent little son Enos (the "lovely Boy" of the verse) who accompanied him in his exile. The verse fragment, with its haunting opening, is based on Coleridge's *Athenaeum* MS. of the poem's outline, which gives the following summary of "Canto I": "Child afeared by his father's ravings, goes out to pluck the fruits in the moonlight wildness. Cain's soliloquy. Child returns with a pitcher of water and a cake. Cain wonders what kind of beings dwell in that place – whether any created since man or whether this world had any beings rescued from the Chaos, wandering like shipwrecked beings from another world etc." The prose "Canto II" describes the wanderings of Cain and Enos: their rejection by Nature, their search for food in an inhospitable landscape of desolation, and their terrible meeting with the ghost of the murdered Abel. The stony landscape was based on Coleridge's memories of the "Valley of Rocks", with its bleak "steeples and battlements" of eroded stone, beyond Lynton on the north Somerset coastline. The main interest lies in the attempt to create the framework of a gothic epic out of biblical prose, and to imitate the effortless unfolding of dream narrative. "And Cain stood like one who struggles in his sleep because of the exceeding terribleness of a dream". It also indicates the huge body of work that could lie behind a single remaining verse fragment.

76. "THE MAD MONK"

First published in the *Morning Post*, 13 October 1800; first collected in *Poetical Works* 1880. The original title was: "The Voice from the Side of Etna; or the Mad Monk: an Ode in Mrs Ratcliffe's Manner." Anna Radcliffe (1764–1823) was the popular author of gothic-horror plays and novels, whose work Coleridge enjoyed but mocked in some early reviews. The element of gothic pastiche should not obscure Coleridge's own presence in the voice of the depressed, love-lorn "hermit or monk" (5), a familiar figure from the Asra Poems. Though the death of "Rosa" (33) is intended as a fragment of melodrama, the lover's guilt-ridden hallucination of the entire landscape suffused in her blood (29–45) contains an uneasy premonition of "Dejection: An Ode" (No. 50), and yields some startling images: "the sun torments me from his western bed" (42, compare "A Sunset", No 78).

The beautiful music of the verse evidently haunted Wordsworth, who used a close adaptation of the second stanza, "There was a time when earth, and sea, and sky . . ." (9–16) as the opening of one of his most famous poems, "Ode: Intimations of Immortality", begun eighteen months later in March 1802: "There was a time when meadow, grove and stream. . . ." (Indeed it is possible that Wordsworth first gave these lines to Coleridge before the "Ode" was conceived.)

A possible source for the grief-stricken hermit is Samuel Johnson's *Rasselas*, Chapter 21, "The Happiness of Solitude. The Hermit's History". This opens: "They came on the third day, by the direction of the peasants, to the hermit's cell: it was a cavern in the side of a mountain, over-shadowed with palm-trees . . . The Princess observed that he had not the countenance of a man that had found, or could teach, the way to happiness." Coleridge eventually visited Sicily (8) and climbed Etna for himself (twice), at a time of great unhappiness in 1804–5.

77. "THE BLOSSOMING OF THE SOLITARY DATE-TREE"

First published with Preface in *Poetical Works* 1828. Composed in Malta during the hot summer months of 1805, when Coleridge was Public Secretary to the British Governor, Sir Alexander Ball, and staying at his summer palace of San Antonio outside Valletta. The botanical gardens of San Antonio are still famous, and Coleridge kept extensive notes of his botanical reading (including Linnaeus) and nature studies and observations there. The phenomenon of the "fruitless" (because unpollinated) date-tree can be found in many other species such as the rowan. For Coleridge it is another image of unfulfilled creativity: "blossom" being something showy and ephemeral (like talk), while "fruit" is nourishing and lasting (like poetry). Coleridge's preface again explores the question of fragmentary work (suggesting that some "congenial spirit" might versify the prose for him!). The declared theme of "the yearning of a human soul for its counterpart", and the solitary being who cannot bear "fruit" until inspired by a predestined other, is similar to Goethe's idea of "elective affinities", and closely related to the Asra Poems. The beautiful third stanza can be read as Coleridge's personal credo, with the central idea of the poet keeping the "buoyant child" (21) creatively alive in the adult (compare "The Pang More Sharp Than All", No. 63). Coleridge also explores the idea that "incompleteness" like his own is really part of Nature's generosity, "her largeness, and her overflow" (26). Many other images, such as the "blind Arab" (30), recur in the later Confessional Poems.

78. "A SUNSET"

First published in J. D. Campbell's edition, *Poetical Works* 1893; Campbell also supplied the title. Composed in Malta 1804–5, with a commentary by Coleridge in a Notebook dated 16 August 1805. "These lines I wrote as nonsense verses merely to try a metre; but they are by no means contemptible; at least in reading them over I am surprised to find them so good.

Now will it be a more English music if the first and fourth [*lines*] are double rhymes and the fifth and sixth single rhymes? or all single, or the second and third double? Try." (CNB II. 2224(29)) Though Coleridge's primary concern seems to be the "music" of the verse, the visionary landscape of mountains, "ancient" woods, caves and fountains has a Delphic quality – viz. prophetic – reminiscent of "Kubla Khan" (No. 74), though its meaning remains obscure. "Cone or mow of fire" (5): an image drawn from a corn-stook ("mow") at harvest-time, drawn into a cone-shaped bundle before being carted away, as the splayed shafts of sunlight are gathered together in a single "stook" of fire before descending below the horizon. The sun's symbolic departure from the earth, "submitting" (5) his great power to moon-like uncertainty and change, suggests some premonition of natural disaster in the world, at which the leaves tremble and the fountain mutters uneasily (12–13). This disaster may be the loss of Life, or Love or Hope; or there may be some suggestion, after the manner of the German poet Jean Paul Richter (1763–1825), of the retirement of God from His creation.

79. "A DARK SKY" [COELI ENARRANT]

First published in E. H. Coleridge's edition of *Poetical Works* 1912, with the editor's curious title – "Coeli Enarrant", "Heaven's Witness" – inexplicably in Latin. Composed at Nether Stowey in 1807 while Coleridge was revisiting his old Quantock haunts, with this note: "I wrote these lines in imitation of Du Bartas as translated by our Sylvester." (CNB II. 3107).

The French sixteenth-century religious poet Du Bartas wrote an epic account of the Seven Days of the Creation, which was translated first by Sir Philip Sydney, and then by Joshua Sylvester in *Divine Weekes and Works*, 1608. Using Du Bartas's images, Coleridge reverses the traditional and consoling religious trope of the night sky as God's alphabet book (6), in which men may read His design and learn His benevolence. (Compare "Invisible Powers", No. 96): ". . . For all that meets the bodily sense I deem / Symbolical, one mighty alphabet . . .") Instead, Coleridge now presents a vision of terror and religious doubt, in which the stars have become rebellious "spies" (2–3), and the Heavenly "book" has become a grim "Black Letter" Bible (7) wielded by a cruel schoolmaster (8). The Black Letter was the Old English or German Bible, printed in the heavy, black gothic typeface of the seventeenth-century printers, and still often used in schools. Coleridge was perhaps recalling the violence of his old headmaster James Bowyer, overseeing his schoolboy "task" or prep (9) at Christ's Hospital, where Bowyer was reputed once to have knocked out a boy's teeth with one of these Bibles. The cry of schoolboy fear and submission (10), is also the mouthed shape of "O" – zero, nothing, an empty universe to which a "groaning" world must submit. So loss of religious faith reduces Coleridge to the condition of a terrified child – hunted and spied on by the stars, bullied and beaten by a "darkened" (2) Heaven.

80. "THE TROPIC TREE"

First published in E. H. Coleridge's edition of *Poetical Works* 1912. A draft appears in Coleridge's Notebooks of 1807 and may possibly have been written at Coleorton where Coleridge was staying with the Wordsworths and Asra (CNB II. 3004). This puzzling but vivid fragment describes a huge and isolated tree, growing on the banks of a tropical river (1–6). A grotesque tribal totem or carved idol is mounted in the fork of its branches for pagan worship (7–8). Beneath the tree sits a tribal priest or "Faquir" (9). Above, in the spreading branches of the tree, some unidentified "Horror" broods (10–11). In the MS. draft Coleridge also describes the idol as "the nail-boss'd Santon": viz., a wooden Hindu idol with nails hammered into it to denote ritual worship. But the repetition of the words "horror" and "horrid" suggest human sacrifice or even cannibalism. The poem has the form of an unfinished sonnet (requiring a third rhyme-line, and a closing couplet), and is clearly emblematic or symbolic, but no critic has interpreted it successfully. An earlier fragment of 1804 describes a similar scene: a huge alder tree, with "vast hollow Trunk", hanging above a river, its sinister branches with "elk-like head/And pomp of antlers". Both poems present images of monstrous power. Coleridge's Notebooks of this period record extensive reading of anthropological studies of African and Caribbean superstitions; and also of Coleridge's growing jealousy of Wordsworth's poetic self-confidence and emotional domination of the women in the Coleorton household, and their "idolatry" of him. These two ideas may be unconsciously fused in the fragment. Nine years later, in Chapter 22 of the *Biographia Literaria*, Coleridge compared Wordsworth's imagination "by a fantastic analogue and similitude" to a rocky African landscape producing a few huge trees, "the gigantic Black Oak, Magnolia Magniflora . . . and a few stately Tulip Trees".

81. "PSYCHE"

First published in the *Biographia Literaria* 1817; collected in the *Literary Remains* 1836. Coleridge's original prefatory note reads: "the fact that in Greek 'Psyche' is the common name for the soul, and the butterfly, is thus alluded to in the following stanzas from an unpublished poem of the Author." No further stanzas are known. Another MS. note reads: "in some instances the Symbolic and the Onomastic are united as in Psyche = Anima et papilio." The fragment was composed about 1808, and draws on extensive botanical notes on the life-cycle of the caterpillar, and the "great agony" of their physiological metamorphosis into "the winged state", taken from a scientific textbook in spring 1803. The fragment is in the "emblematic" (2) style of the seventeenth-century religious poets like George Herbert and Francis Quarles, in which natural objects are presented for spiritual meditation. But Coleridge swiftly directs attention away from the immortal aspect of the butterfly-soul (3–4), and concentrates instead on its earthly aspect as caterpillar-soul, the "reptile's lot" (5). The caterpillar "psyche" is condemned to futile and painful wriggling, as it eats and destroys the green leaves which nourish it (5–7); just as human beings destroy the tender substances (love, trust, hope) which nourish them. (William Blake's "Sick Rose" achieves a similar vision, though in an utterly different style.)

82. "THE SEA MEW"

First published in E. H. Coleridge's edition, *Poetical Works* 1912. Originally composed in a Notebook of 1795–6, when Coleridge probably observed the sea-bird flying over the Bristol Channel. But Coleridge's fascination with the symbolism of bird-flight and bird-song developed steadily, and closely connects this with the next fragment (No. 83). In both cases, the bird is the emblem of the poet at work, seen in different moods. (The analogy between birds and poetry – flying, singing, trapped or caged – is so frequent in Coleridge's letters and notebooks that it deserves a separate study.) Here the unbroken, sliding, blank-verse sentence suggests the creative "drifting" of the poet's imagination, "posting" forward through the air and then "yielding" freely to the cross-currents of ideas. (Later Coleridge described similar analogies with the movement of water-beetles, in Chapter 7 of the *Biographia Literaria*.)

83. "THE YELLOW HAMMER"

First published in *Poetical Works* 1912. Composed in a Notebook of 1807–8, perhaps when Coleridge had returned to the Quantocks. See previous note. Here the tight, end-stopped lines and laborious metre of the couplets, together with the image of metal-working with a file, suggests the patient, meticulous, craftsmanlike skill of the poet polishing and refining his work. Both birds present characteristic aspects of Coleridge's poetry.

84. "ON DONNE'S POETRY"

First published in the *Literary Remains* 1836. Written in the fly-leaf of a copy of *Chalmers's Poets*, which Coleridge was reading at Highgate in 1816–18. Coleridge was one of the first modern critics to re-direct attention to the seventeenth-century metaphysical poets. He wrote in Chapter 1 of the *Biographia Literaria*: ". . . From Donne to Cowley, we find the most fantastic out-of-the-way thoughts, but in the most pure and genuine mother English . . . Our faulty elder poets sacrificed the passion and passionate flow of poetry, to the subtleties of intellect, and to the starts of wit." The verse

fragment compresses and enacts these critical observations, with an affec-
tionate mimicry (rather than a parody) of Donne's style, with its tortuous
phrasing and almost ludicrously ingenious metaphors – dromedary riding,
iron forging, print (or cider?) pressing. "Fancy's maze and clue" (3): the
original meaning of "clue" was a ball of yarn, and hence a direction-guide
to unroll through a maze (as Theseus did through the Minotaur's labyrinth).
"Meaning's press and screw" (4): the image is drawn from the old hand-
operated printing presses, or fruit presses, both of which used a pressure-
plate operated by a helical screw. Coleridge had used a cider press in the
Quantocks, and a printing press in the Lake District.

85. "THE KNIGHT'S TOMB"

First published in *Poetical Works* 1834. James Gillman said he heard Cole-
ridge reciting these lines "as an experiment in metre", in the early days at
Highgate 1816–19. The form suggests that it is the fragment of an unwritten
ballad, possibly even the unknown Part III of "Christabel", with the Lake
District setting (3), the medieval figure of the knight, and the haunting
sense of seasons passing. The last three lines were also overheard at Highgate
by a friend of Sir Walter Scott's (probably his son-in-law and future biogra-
pher, Lockhart), who repeated them to the novelist the following day.
They subsequently appeared as an unauthorized epigraph to Chapter 8
of Scott's *Ivanhoe* 1819; and later, complete and acknowledged, in *Castle
Dangerous* 1834. Scott was known to be a great admirer, and even imitator,
of "Christabel". One reading of the fragment is that it represents Coleridge's
farewell to the ballad, an inspired poetic landscape to which he cannot
return; or more generally to the Lake District where he can never recapture
his happy life with the Wordsworths. Coleridge is himself the dead knight,
buried in his favourite spot on Helvellyn, among his unfinished creation.

86. "FOUR METRICAL EXPERIMENTS"

First published in E. H. Coleridge's edition, *Poetical Works* 1912. They are
collected from a vast number of MS. sources dating between 1801–1820.
One Malta Notebook of 1805 contains no less than forty-eight numbered
specimens of different metres and stanzaic schemes, many from German
and Italian sources. Coleridge frequently illustrated his discoveries with
rough verse-sketches dismissively entitled "Nonsense Verse", "Experiment
in Metre", or the technical name of a metre, or simply of the mood or
feeling evoked by it. But many of them seem rather more than "nonsense",
and like the four selected here, are of striking beauty and haunting musical
power.

First published in Act III, Scene 1, of Coleridge's Spanish melodrama *Remorse* 1813; collected in *Poetical Works* 1828. The play was originally written in 1797 as *Osorio*, and sent to Sheridan at Drury Lane, but was refused. Coleridge recovered the MS. from Godwin (who had the only remaining copy) in 1812, rewrote it, and had it produced with brilliant success at Drury Lane in January 1813, where it ran for twenty nights, an outstanding run for a "literary" verse drama at that period. The text, issued simultaneously, also ran to three editions; and the play was revived in 1817. Commercially, *Remorse* was the greatest single success of Coleridge's career, earning three years' income (£400 plus copyright) in three weeks. It is set in Spain during "the reign of Philip II, just at the close of the Civil Wars against the Moors", and concerns the rivalry between two aristocratic brothers, Don Alvar (1797: Albert) and Don Ordonio (1797: Osorio), who have both fallen in love with a beautiful "orphan Heiress", Dona Teresa (1797: Maria). Act III, Scene I, takes place in the "Hall of Armory" of their fifteenth-century castle on the coast of Granada, with a musical instrument "of Glass or Steel" playing behind the arras. Alvar, who is thought by his villainous younger brother Ordonio to have been assassinated (on Ordonio's own orders), has disguised himself "in a Sorcerer's robe" and pretends to summon up his own departed spirit with this "Song" of invocation to the dead: "Soul of Alvar!/Hear the mild spell, and tempt no blacker charm ... /Pass visible before our mortal sense!". The "Song" is based on the medieval Christian rites of Intercession for the Dead (**5–10**) with its repeated Latin chant "Have Mercy, O Lord". But it is also intended by Alvar to threaten Ordonio with the prospect of a vengeful ghost; and by Coleridge as a fragment of pure verbal witchery and incantatory magic.

88. "SONG FROM *ZAPOLYA*"

First published in Act II, Scene 1, of Coleridge's *Zapolya*, 1817; collected in *Poetical Works* 1834. Coleridge composed *Zapolya* at Calne, Wiltshire, in 1814–15 as a cabinet play, describing it as "a Christmas Tale ... in humble imitation of the Winter's Tale of Shakespeare". It was rejected by Drury Lane in 1816. The play is a chivalric romance, set in the mountains of "Illyria", where Zapolya the Illyrian Queen is deposed during a civil war, and finally restored with her son, Prince Andreas. Among her faithful supporters is the passionate Glycine, the orphan daughter of one of the mountain chiefs, splendidly described as a "sword that leap'dst forth from a bed of roses" (Act IV, scene 1). The "Song" is sung by Glycine as she climbs among the mountain crags, armed to the teeth, and looking for her lover (who will turn out to be none other than Prince Andreas, future King of Illyria). The "Song" is overheard by Queen Zapolya, hiding in a cave, and is the first glimmer of hope that her freedom-loving mountain subjects may yet support her. So the bird "so bold" in the shaft of sunlight (3), is not merely a symbol of love but also of political hope and inspiration for the future. (The bird is evidently a skylark (5), and Coleridge's use of this romantic symbol may be compared to Shelley's "To A Skylark", 1819. Compare also Nos. 82 and 83.) Again, Coleridge catches this mood of urgency and enchantment by a deliberate fragment of pure verbal magic, ending in an almost abstract musical repetition of one rhyme-sound (11–16).

89. "ARS POETICA"

First published in chapter 15 of the *Biographia Literaria* 1817; collected in J. D. Campbell's edition *Poetical Works* 1893. The quoted line in the prefatory note comes from Coleridge's own poem, "France: An Ode" (No. 95), and prepares the reader for the dynamic "coastal" imagery of the two illustrative fragments. This is one of Coleridge's most compact and lucid demonstrations of his psychological theory of the Imagination. It seems possible to prefer the plain, rather Wordsworthian first version, to the "poetic" inversions and exclamations of the second version, with its blatant reliance on the pathetic fallacy of the pine trees' "streaming" tresses of hair. However, Coleridge's "transference" of imaginative spirit has genuinely, and rather mysteriously, taken place: in the first version the pines are stoic, masculine, monk-like ("shorn and bowed"); in the second they have become terrified, "wild" and feminine. Rhythm, mood, and sexual atmosphere have all been "modified" and intensified to produce a quite different perception of the same physical landscape.

90. "ARIA SPONTANEA"

First published as a note to "Youth and Age" (No. 69) in J. D. Campbell's edition *Poetical Works* 1893. In this MS., Coleridge amusingly describes how the opening verse or musical "air" of his poem "Youth and Age" came to him in a flash of inspiration one morning in September 1823. He then compares this to a much earlier memory, in 1807 or perhaps even 1797, when he was walking over the Quantock hills and met a speeding bumble-bee with its "sharp and burry" sound, and then a skylark with its "Song-Fountain" of music climbing far above the horizon. These sudden, delightful dawn encounters with bee and bird are both analogies of creative inspiration, in which the "music" of a verse is unexpectedly presented like a gift of Nature's. The comic bravura of Coleridge's descriptions – the bee is compared to a dandified gentleman in a snuff-coloured waistcoat ("Rappee Spenser") with scarlet stripes – while the skylark's song is compared to a decorated Gothic column – catches him in one of the childlike moods of wonder and extravagance that never quite left him.

First published in E. H. Coleridge's edition *Poetical Works* 1912. Composed on 25 February 1825 at Highgate. The prefatory letter is addressed to Coleridge's confidante Mrs Ann Gillman (see "The Garden of Boccaccio", No. 70) and continues with a draft of the sonnet "Work Without Hope" (No. 19) which has been omitted here. The physical advances or encroachments of old age are compared to the sinister, and even repulsive, cocoon of webbing which the spider spins to form its "windowless" room, with "viscuous masonry of films and thread". Light is closed off, and the senses progressively muffled and paralysed. Eventually the "dusky chamber" with its horrible "tent-like Hangings", becomes a premonition of the tomb and funeral shroud. This comparison, as with the poem "Psyche" (No. 81) is based on close botanical observation, which Coleridge uses in the emblematic style of George Herbert to describe a claustrophobic sense of spiritual solitude. The only relief is represented by a mirror or looking-glass within the room, a "Sister Mirror", which is the emblem of true friendship or "elective affinity", showing Coleridge his true self. Ann Gillman was that Sister Mirror for Coleridge – "the Alone Most Dear" (**14**) – but in a moment of depression he believed that her friendship was "broken". (She afterwards wrote on the MS. that Coleridge was mistaken, and it was only his "fancy".) Coleridge later published the sonnet, but abandoned the Spider poem as a fragment too obsessive and horrible to retain. Part of its power comes from the domestic neatness of the creature in its "lurking parlour or withdrawing room", which is really a relentless and implacable monster.

First published in E. H. Coleridge's edition *Poetical Works* 1912. Composed in summer 1828 during a nostalgic tour through the Rhineland and Holland, which Coleridge undertook with Wordsworth accompanied by his beautiful twenty-four-year-old daughter Dora Wordsworth (whom Wordsworth adored and Coleridge greatly admired). This was partly a celebrity tour – they met Schlegel and other Continental worthies – and partly a journey of reconciliation for the two old friends, facilitated by Dora's soothing presence. Coleridge made many fine Notebook entries on the Dutch and German countryside, and many rude remarks about the towns. This fragment of Dutch landscape is an almost perfect imagist poem, in a single brushstroke of observation. The MS. contains two more lines, which appear to be the false start of a second stanza, "Water, wide water, greeness and green banks . . ." The suspended, magical, innocent state of vision, in which a newborn world seems about to float off or dissolve in mist, seems as much part of Coleridge's mood as his geographic location.

Notes to the Political, Ideological and Topical Poems

93. "AN ODE ON THE DESTRUCTION OF THE BASTILLE"

First published *Poetical Works* 1834. Composed by the sixteen-year-old Coleridge at Christ's Hospital, after the fall of the Bastille on 14 July 1789. News of the storming of the notorious Paris prison by a crowd of citizens and militia soon spread right across Europe as a universal symbol of Liberty (stanza I). This is young Coleridge's gleeful schoolboy response, echoing a hundred similar Odes and Effusions published in newspapers and pamphlets of the time. Stanzas II and III are missing from the MS. Stanza IV imagines the sufferings of the Bastille prisoners (in fact there were only seven incarcerated at the time, but previous guests had included Voltaire and de Sade). Stanza V sees Liberty spreading down to the humblest of farm-labourers, and to new freedoms of speech and the press. Stanza VI traces the spread of Liberty in national independence movements across northern Europe, but ends on a proper note of British patriotism. It is interesting that, at this date, Coleridge expresses no expectation of an English revolution and no feeling that Britain was anything but "the freest of the free" (40). His political radicalism only began at Cambridge (see No. 8 and No. 94). The style is similarly conventional, a sub-Miltonic verse of lofty circumlocutions and personifications, which carries little but its own (rather engaging) enthusiasm.

94. "TO A YOUNG ASS"

First published in the *Morning Chronicle* on 30 December 1794; collected in *Poems* 1796. Composed during Coleridge's last term at Jesus College, Cambridge, and one of the first public statements of his radicalism. Inspired by the sight of an actual donkey and foal, tethered on college grounds known as Jesus Piece, the poem is a witty political protest against poverty, cleverly combining the ideas of animal philanthropy (1–4), Jacobin fraternity (19–20) and Christian brotherhood (26). The mixture of pathos and humour, in treating the foal as a fellow-member of an "oppresséd race" (1), and a "meek Child of Misery" (10) given to quoting Hamlet's soliloquy on suicide (12) moves between the touching and the absurd. A private version, sent in a letter of 17 December 1794 to Southey, is more openly subversive, referring both to their Pantisocratic scheme (see No. 8) and to King George III in terms that amount to "seditious libel" (then an imprisonable offence). These alterations read: "Of high-soul'd Pantisocracy to dwell" (28); and rather wittily to end the poem (33–6):

> Yea! and more musically sweet to me
> Thy dissonant harsh bray of joy would be,

Than Handel's softest airs that soothe to rest
The tumult of a scoundrel Monarch's breast.

As a result of the poem (especially **26**), Coleridge was later brilliantly ridiculed in a donkey cartoon, published by the conservative *Anti-Jacobin Magazine* (1799), and mocked by Byron as "Laureate of the long-ear'd kind". But the idea of man's essential fellowship with the animals appears frequently in Coleridge's letters of this period ("I call even my Cat sister in the Fraternity of universal Nature"), and is central to "The Rime of the Ancient Mariner" (No. 32). Is this the first Animal Rights poem?

95. "THE PRESENT STATE OF SOCIETY"
    [EXTRACT FROM "RELIGIOUS MUSINGS"]

First published as here, with the title "The Present State of Society", in Coleridge's journal, the *Watchman*, 9 March 1796. Coleridge later expanded it to form a 419-line "desultory Poem written on the Christmas Eve of 1794" (when it was probably begun but certainly not finished), loosely entitled "Religious Musings". This was published in *Poems* 1796 and then collected in *Poetical Works* 1828.

This was the work that Coleridge disowned as "Elaborate and swelling" in his early Conversation poem to Charles Lamb (see No. 22). Bombastic, compassionate, and almost unbearable to read, it gives a clear impression of Coleridge's apocalyptic radicalism at this period, with its mixture of kindly philanthropy and millennial rant. The footnotes, ranging from Bruce's *Travels* to the *Book of Revelations*, are suggestive of later work. The final paragraph given here, which Coleridge added in the expanded text, enumerates his intellectual heroes at this date: John Milton, republican and epic poet; David Hartley, philosopher and physiologist; and Joseph Priestley, Unitarian radical and physicist (who gave an example to the Pantisocrats by emigrating to the Susquehanna region in America, when a royalist mob burnt down his house in Birmingham). Wordsworth, who had recently come back from the actual Revolution in Paris, said he particularly admired the passage describing the "massy gates of Paradise" glimpsed by "the favoured good man in his lonely walk" (**86–97**).

96. "INVISIBLE POWERS"
    [EXTRACT FROM "THE DESTINY OF NATIONS"]

First published as the opening section of a long political poem, "The Destiny of Nations", in *Sibylline Leaves* 1817. The extract given here (with the editor's title) was originally composed as a separate fragment during the course of 1795–6, but not published at that time. Much later, Coleridge combined it with materials called "The Vision of the Maid of Orleans" (which he had originally contributed to Southey's verse drama *Joan of Arc* in 1796), with which it has virtually no connection. Together these elements form the chaotic 470-line poem, or ragbag of political descriptions and metaphysical speculations, entitled "The Destiny of Nations". Significant further material (**100–109**) was added as late as 1834.

"Invisible Powers" forms a relatively coherent section within the political framework. It presents various metaphysical, theological, scientific, and anthropological speculations about the sources of power and meaning in the natural universe. A sublime Platonic version of reality (compare No. 79), is contrasted with a materialist's reductionist world, a Pantheist view, one of Newtonian atoms, or Leibnitz's monads. Coleridge insists on some kind of transcendental view of power, however primitive, which avoids total materialism or the "gloom" of nihilism and "trains up to God" (**48–51**). He turns to the folklore of Lapland and Greenland, and their symbolic mythologies. His descriptions of "the Giant Bird Vuokho" (**81–5**), and the "Good Spirit Torngarsuck" with its "malignant" underwater double (**86–100**, and footnote) are remarkable premonitions of the world of the "Ancient Mariner".

97. "FIRE, FAMINE, AND SLAUGHTER"

First published in the *Morning Post*, 8 January 1798; collected in *Sibylline Leaves* 1817. Composed 1796–7 when the savage crushing of the Vendée rebellion in the north-west of France exposed the cruelty of the Revolutionary government in Paris. Coleridge compares this with the equally violent suppression of the United Irishmen's rebellion by the British government under William Pitt (**46f**). Pitt's name is never actually printed (**63**, "Letters four do form his name") which might have opened Coleridge to a charge of seditious libel. The poem is one of violent political protest, using the allegoric form of a nightmare dialogue between three Sisters (Fire, Famine and Slaughter) who are obviously inspired by the three witches in *Macbeth*. Ideologically, the poem served to establish Coleridge's liberal "left of centre" position, which is characteristic of all his journalism between 1798 and 1804, opposed to the French Revolutionary regime, but not identified with the British wartime government whose measures he regarded as repressive and reactionary. (His famous and damning newspaper profile of William Pitt was published two years later in the *Morning Post* on 19 March 1800.) In *Sibylline Leaves* 1817 Coleridge republished the War Eclogue, with a long and ingenious "Apologetic Preface", arguing that the poem had no subversive or propaganda intent against the government; that the "grotesque union of epigrammatic wit with allegoric personification" had a purely imaginative impact on the reader; and that (like Lytton Strachey in 1914) he had been prepared "to interpose his own body" to defend "Mr Pitt's person" from physical assault at that time.

First published in the *Morning Post* on 16 April 1798; re-issued in a quarto pamphlet (J. Johnson, 1798, with "Frost at Midnight" No. 27, and "Fears in Solitude", No. 28); re-published with No. 28 in the *Morning Post* on 14 October 1802; republished in the *Poetical Register* 1812; collected in *Sibylline Leaves* 1817.

The extensive publication history of this Ode indicates its significance as a public statement of Coleridge's shift from a radical, pro-French Revolutionary, Jacobin position to that of a liberal defender of "Freedom" (**64**) and "Liberty" (**105**). The original title of 1798 was "The Recantation: An Ode"; and the "Argument" was written by Coleridge for his newspaper readers in 1802. Such public "recantations" appeared all over Europe at this time, as the warlike and imperialist intentions of the French became evident with the invasion of Switzerland (in March 1798): in Germany, celebrated ones were published by Goethe, Klopstock, Schiller, Wieland and Kotzebu. It is interesting to compare Coleridge's exclamatory and rhetorical public style here (**95**, "Priestcraft's harpy minions"), with his more intimate treatment of the same theme in the contemporaneous "Fears in Solitude" (No. 28). Yet the poem has powerful passages (such as stanza IV); and some of Coleridge's gigantesque imagery, such as the description of the awaking figure of France (**22–25**), has been compared to Goya's allegorical paintings of the period.

99. "THE DEVIL'S THOUGHTS"

First published with fourteen stanzas in the *Morning Post*, 6 September 1799; collected as ten stanzas in *Poetical Works* 1828; enlarged to seventeen stanzas (as here) in *Poetical Works* 1834. This brilliant squib, in the manner of the popular "broadsheet ballads" of the mid-eighteenth century (often obscene), was originally written with Southey when Coleridge returned from Germany in autumn 1799. The first three stanzas were improvised by Southey "as he hummed in front of his shaving-mirror", and the remainder were dashed off by Coleridge over breakfast. The poem caused a sensation when it first appeared in the newspaper (unsigned), probably because it was infinitely extendable, and everyone could add their own stanzas. The humour has broadened from political to social satire: the Devil's creatures are all unpopular "rich" professions, who are exploiting the poor, the underprivileged and the credulous at a time of wartime poverty and uncertainty. They include the standard figures of the Lawyer, the Apothecary, the Bookseller (special pleading here, perhaps), the Prison Governor, the Preacher, the Politician. The Devil is finally scared back to Hell by a scarlet-faced General, in one of Coleridge's most excruciating puns (**70**).

The anonymous ballad soon became public property, and many subsequent versions and updatings appeared, including one by Shelley ("The Devil's Walk", 1812), another by Byron ("The Devil's Drive", 1813), and a third purporting to come from Coleridge's old Professor of Greek at Cambridge, the drunken Richard Porson (1830). Eventually Southey thoroughly overdid the joke by expanding it to fifty-seven stanzas. The best image in the ballad, Coleridge's stanza V, directly inspired Shelley's great protest poem, "The Mask of Anarchy", 1819.

100. "A CHARACTER"

First published in *Poetical Works* 1834. Probably composed in 1825–6 at Highgate, after some reflection on Hazlitt's bitter attack on his political "apostasy" (27–30) in his essay "Mr Coleridge" in *The Spirit of the Age*. (Compare Coleridge's immediate reaction in "Work Without Hope", No. 19.)

The image of himself as some kind of "bird" (1) runs right through Coleridge's letters, and many of the poems, and would perhaps reward special study. Here he is an innocent, liberal tom-tit (18) set upon by vicious, Jacobin or radical "bats" (4) who were once, like Hazlitt, his "nest-mates" and now accuse him of apostasy and money-making and wanting a knighthood (31–36). It should not be forgotten at this time that Southey was Poet Laureate, Wordsworth had a valuable government sinecure as Distributor of Stamps, while Coleridge was dependent on scattered literary fees and charity from the Royal Society of Authors, and reduced to living in a two-room apartment in James Gillman's house (77–89).

The humorous treatment of this deadly, personal theme contains some sly rejoinders, such as the disguised attack on Wordsworth, for whom he "plough'd and sow'd, while others reapt" (42–6); and Hazlitt's radical chic journalism and flaunting with "doctrines Jacobinical" (47–52). Yet the nimble, bouncy wit does not entirely disguise Coleridge's special pleading for himself, as the honourable, penniless, "poor Bird . . . poor Bard" who had followed his conscience in a world of cowards, bloodsuckers, and cynics. "Phoebus" (16), like Apollo, is the sun god of the poets. "Sir Joseph Jay" (36) is a composite name referring to various knighthoods distributed among his successful contemporaries, like Joseph Banks, James Mackintosh, and Humphry Davy. "Pitt been Fox" (56): they had been respectively Prime Minister and Leader of the Opposition. "Goose and Goody" (64) are the foolish Prince Regent and his Prime Minister, Lord Grey. "Punic Greek" (72–3, see note to "Epitaph", No. 23).

101. "THE DELINQUENT TRAVELLERS"

First published by E. H. Coleridge in *Poetical Works* 1912. This delightful and unexpected late *jeu d'esprit* of the ageing Coleridge was probably started during one of his autumn holidays with the Gillmans at Ramsgate (82), which took place regularly beween 1820 and 1830. An undated draft exists in a MS. given to his last amanuensis and literary executor, the surgeon J. H. Green. The reference to Captain Lyon's *Private Journal* (1824) of his voyage with the polar explorer Sir William Parry (**3**), suggests a date around 1824–5; while the descriptions of Boulogne and its exiles (**92–9**) suggests a much later date, after Coleridge and Wordsworth had made their own last voyage to the Continent in summer 1828 (see "The Netherlands", No. 92).

Coleridge's wry evocations of the modern mania for travel by every possible means of transport, including steamship and gas-balloon (**16–21**), makes a surprising, humorous coda to the great, strange voyage of "The Rime of the Ancient Mariner". Coleridge identifies not with the comfortable fashionable tourists, but with the "delinquent" travellers – bankrupts, criminals, cashiered soldiers, smugglers, exiles, emigrants, all "who go because they cannot stay" (**65–77**). Coleridge finally sees himself as embarking on yet one last fantasy voyage southwards: to Australia, the land of the "black swan and kangeroo", where he will found a new dynasty of pineapples and pantisocrats (**102–19**). "Pegasus" (**63**) is the mythological winged horse, symbol both of travel and artistic inspiration (see note to "A Tombless Epitaph", No. 62)

INDEX OF TITLES AND FIRST LINES

A bird, who for his other sins   287
A blessed lot hath he, who having passed   40
A Character   287
A Dark Sky   245
A Day-Dream: My Eyes Make Pictures   166
Ad Vilmum Axiologum   187
A green and silent spot, amid the hills   49
Ah! far removed from all that glads the sense   269
A Letter to Sara Hutchinson   169
Alice Du Clos   127
All look and likeness caught from earth   185
All Nature seems at work. Slugs leave their lair   25
All thoughts, all passions, all delights   123
A lovely form there sate beside my bed   220
A mount, not wearisome and bare and steep   140
An Angel Visitant   189
And this reft house is that the which he built   19
An Ode on the Destruction of the Bastille   265
An Ode to the Rain   199
Are there two things, of all which men possess   20
Aria Spontanea   257
Ars Poetica   256
As late I journey'd o'er the extensive plain   8
As late on Skiddaw's mount I lay supine   147
As some vast Tropic tree, itself a wood   246
A Stranger Minstrel   147
A sunny shaft did I behold   255
A Sunset   244
A sworded man whose trade is blood   184
A Thought Suggested by a View of Saddleback in Cumberland   145
A Tombless Epitaph   206

Beneath yon birch with silver bark   121

Charles! my slow heart was only sad, when first 18
Christabel 101
Composed on a Journey Homeward 17
Constancy to an Ideal Object 192

Dear native Brook! wild streamlet of the West! 11
Dejection: An Ode 179
Do you ask what the birds say? The Sparrow, the Dove 165
Duty Surviving Self-Love 26

Encinctured with a twine of leaves 233
Epitaph 222
Ere on my bed my limbs I lay 202
Ere the birth of my life, if I wished it or no 211

Fancy in Nubibus 23
Farewell parental scenes! A sad farewell! 10
Farewell, sweet Love! yet blame you not my truth 22
Farewell to Love 22
Fears in Solitude 49
Fire, Famine, and Slaughter 277
Flowers are lovely, Love is flower-like 257
For what is Freedom, but the unfettered use 273
Four Metrical Experiments 252
France: An Ode 280
Friend of the wise! and Teacher of the Good! 59
From his brimstone bed at break of day 284
Frost at Midnight 46

Go little Pipe! for ever I must leave thee 252

Hast thou a charm to stay the morning-star 149
Heard'st thou yon universal cry 265
Hear, sweet Spirit, hear the spell 254
He too has flitted from his secret nest 208
Hope and Time 210
How warm this woodland wild Recess! 190
Human Life 213
Hymn before Sun-Rise, in the Vale of Chamouni 149

If dead, we cease to be; if total gloom 213
If thou were here, these tears were tears of light! 168

I heard a voice from Etna's side   239
I know it is dark; and though I have lain   199
Imagination; honourable aims   242
Inscription for a Fountain on a Heath   146
In the great City rear'd, my fancy rude   210
In Xanadu did Kubla Khan   230
I speak in figures, inward thoughts and woes   259
I stood on Brocken's sovran height, and saw   143
It is an ancient Mariner   81
It may indeed be phantasy, when I   24

Kayser, to whom, as to a second self   27
Kubla Khan   229

Lady, to Death we're Doom'd   21
Lady, to Death we're doom'd, our crime the same!   21
Life   2
Like a lone Arab, old and blind   221
Limbo   214
Lines Composed while Climbing the Left Ascent of Brockley Coomb 139
Lines Written in the Album at Elbingerode, in the Hartz Forest   143
Love   123
Love's Apparition and Evanishment   221
Low was our pretty Cot: our tallest Rose   38

Me n'Asræ perferre jubes oblivia? et Asræ   187
Mild Splendour of the various-vested Night!   7
My eyes make pictures, when they are shut   166
My heart has thank'd thee, Bowles! for those soft strains   13
My pensive Sara! thy soft cheek reclined   13

No cloud, no relique of the sunken day   56
No cold shall thee benumb   252
No more my visionary soul shall dwell   14

Of late, in one of those most weary hours   217
Oft o'er my brain does that strange fancy roll   17
O! it is pleasant, with a heart at ease   23
On a Ruined House in a Romantic Country   19
Once again, sweet Willow, wave thee!   253
On Donne's Poetry   250

On Quitting School for College   10
On Receiving an Account that his Only Sister's Death was Inevitable   9
On stern Blencartha's perilous height   145
On the tenth day of September   257
O Sara! never rashly let me go   186
O Sara! Never Rashly Let Me Go   186

Pantisocracy   14
Phantom   185
Phantom or Fact   220
Pity   15
Poor little Foal of an oppreséd race!   267
Psyche   247

Recollections of Love   190
Reflections on Having Left a Place of Retirement   38

Sad lot, to have no Hope! Though lowly kneeling   212
Schiller! that hour I would have wish'd to die   12
Sea-ward, white gleaming thro' the busy scud   248
Separation   184
Since all that beat about in Nature's range   192
Sisters! sisters! who sent you here?   277
Some are home sick—some two or three   290
Song from Remorse   254
Song from Zapolya   255
Stop, Christian passer-by!—Stop, child of God   222
Sweet Mercy! how my very heart has bled   15

The Ballad of the Dark Ladié   121
The Blossoming of the Solitary Date-Tree   241
The butterfly the ancient Grecians made   247
The Day-Dream: If Thou Wert Here   168
The Delinquent Travellers   290
The Devil's Thoughts   284
The Eolian Harp   36
The Frost performs its secret ministry   46
The Garden of Boccaccio   217
The grapes upon the vicar's wall   71
The Keepsake   163
The Knight's Tomb   251

The Language of Birds	165
The Mad Monk	239
The Netherlands	260
The Nightingale	56
The Pains of Sleep	202
The Pang More Sharp Than All	208
The Picture, or The Lover's Resolution	152
The Present State of Society	269
The Rime of the Ancient Mariner	81
The Sea Mew	248
The spruce and limber yellow-hammer	249
The stars that wont to start, as on a chase	245
The Suicide's Argument	211
The sun is not yet risen	127
The tear which mourn'd a brother's fate scarce dry	9
The tedded hay, the first fruits of the soil	163
The Three Graves	69
The Tropic Tree	246
The Visionary Hope	212
The Wanderings of Cain	232
The World That Spidery Witch	258
The Yellow Hammer	249
This Lime-Tree Bower My Prison	43
This Sycamore, oft musical with bees	146
Through weeds and thorns, and matted underwood	152
Thus far my scanty brain hath built the rhyme	35
Thus she said, and, all around	252
'Tis a strange place, this Limbo! —not a Place	214
'Tis the middle of the night by the castle clock	102
'Tis true, Idoloclastes Satyrane!	206
To a Friend (Charles Lamb)	35
To A Friend who Asked, How I Felt	18
To Asra	20
To a Young Ass	267
To a Young Friend on his Proposing to Domesticate with the Author	140
To know, to esteem, to love, —and then to part	204
To Nature	24
To the Author of The Robbers	12
To the Autumnal Moon	7
To the Rev. W. L. Bowles	13
To the River Otter	11

To the Young Artist   27
To Two Sisters   204
To William Wordsworth   59

Unchanged within, to see all changed without   26
Upon the mountain's edge with light touch resting   244

Verse, a breeze mid blossoms straying   215

Water and windmills, greenness, Islets green   260
Well! if the Bard was weather-wise who made (*A Letter . . .*)   169
Well! If the Bard was weather-wise, who made (*Dejection*)   179
Well, they are gone, and here must I remain   43
When they did greet me father, sudden awe   16
Where is the grave of Sir Arthur O'Kellyn?   251
With Donne, whose muse on dromedary trots   250
Within these circling hollies woodbine-clad   189
With many a pause and oft reverted eye   139
Work Without Hope   25

Ye clouds! that far above me float and pause   280
You mould my Hopes you fashion me within   188
You Mould My Hopes   188
Youth and Age   215

READ MORE IN PENGUIN

In every corner of the world, on every subject under the sun, Penguin represents quality and variety – the very best in publishing today.

For complete information about books available from Penguin – including Puffins, Penguin Classics and Arkana – and how to order them, write to us at the appropriate address below. Please note that for copyright reasons the selection of books varies from country to country.

In the United Kingdom: Please write to *Dept. EP, Penguin Books Ltd, Bath Road, Harmondsworth, West Drayton, Middlesex UB7 ODA*

In the United States: Please write to *Consumer Sales, Penguin USA, P.O. Box 999, Dept. 17109, Bergenfield, New Jersey 07621-0120*. VISA and MasterCard holders call 1-800-253-6476 to order Penguin titles

In Canada: Please write to *Penguin Books Canada Ltd, 10 Alcorn Avenue, Suite 300, Toronto, Ontario M4V 3B2*

In Australia: Please write to *Penguin Books Australia Ltd, P.O. Box 257, Ringwood, Victoria 3134*

In New Zealand: Please write to *Penguin Books (NZ) Ltd, Private Bag 102902, North Shore Mail Centre, Auckland 10*

In India: Please write to *Penguin Books India Pvt Ltd, 706 Eros Apartments, 56 Nehru Place, New Delhi 110 019*

In the Netherlands: Please write to *Penguin Books Netherlands bv, Postbus 3507, NL-1001 AH Amsterdam*

In Germany: Please write to *Penguin Books Deutschland GmbH, Metzlerstrasse 26, 60594 Frankfurt am Main*

In Spain: Please write to *Penguin Books S. A., Bravo Murillo 19, 1° B, 28015 Madrid*

In Italy: Please write to *Penguin Italia s.r.l., Via Felice Casati 20, I-20124 Milano*

In France: Please write to *Penguin France S. A., 17 rue Lejeune, F-31000 Toulouse*

In Japan: Please write to *Penguin Books Japan, Ishikiribashi Building, 2-5-4, Suido, Bunkyo-ku, Tokyo 112*

In South Africa: Please write to *Longman Penguin Southern Africa (Pty) Ltd, Private Bag X08, Bertsham 2013*

READ MORE IN PENGUIN

POETRY LIBRARY

Blake	Selected by W. H. Stevenson
Browning	Selected by Daniel Karlin
Burns	Selected by Angus Calder and William Donnelly
Byron	Selected by A. S. B. Glover
Clare	Selected by Geoffrey Summerfield
Coleridge	Selected by Richard Holmes
Donne	Selected by John Hayward
Dryden	Selected by Douglas Grant
Hardy	Selected by David Wright
Housman	Introduced by John Sparrow
Keats	Selected by John Barnard
Kipling	Selected by Craig Raine
Lawrence	Selected by Keith Sagar
Milton	Selected by Laurence D. Lerner
Pope	Selected by Douglas Grant
Rubáiyát of Omar Khayyám	Translated by Edward FitzGerald
Shelley	Selected by Isabel Quigly
Tennyson	Selected by W. E. Williams
Wordsworth	Selected by Nicholas Roe
Yeats	Selected by Timothy Webb

READ MORE IN PENGUIN

Coleridge: Early Visions   Richard Holmes

'Beautifully written and sympathetic . . . Holmes's book adds to our sense of Coleridge's greatness . . . It is informed by love and humour as well as research; and it rises to a climax of narrative writing in the last chapters, in which you feel he has reached into the soul of his subject as every biographer hopes to, but few actually do' – Claire Tomalin in the *Observer*

'A deeply moving life of a troubled genius. From a great mountain of research, Holmes has fashioned a compelling narrative which inspires considerable affection and respect for Coleridge. This stimulating book is one of the most enjoyable biographies I have read' – Michael Sheldon in the *Daily Telegraph*

Selected Poetry and Prose   Samuel Taylor Coleridge
Selected by Kathleen Raine

As well as Coleridge's finest poems, this Penguin edition contains selections from his letters and his main critical writings, including extracts from *Biographia Literaria* and several of his revolutionary essays on Shakespeare. 'His genius,' wrote William Hazlitt, 'had angelic wings and fed on manna. He talked on for ever; and you wished him to talk on for ever . . .'